The Struggle for Peace in Central America

The
Struggle
for
Peace
in Central America

Dario Moreno

University Press of Florida
Gainesville / Tallahassee / Tampa / Boca Raton
Pensacola / Orlando / Miami / Jacksonville

Copyright 1994 by the Board of Regents of the State of Florida
Printed in the United States of America on acid-free paper ∞
All rights reserved

99 98 97 96 95 94   6   5   4   3   2   1

Library of Congress Cataloging-in-Publication Data

Moreno, Dario.
   The struggle for peace in Central America / Dario Moreno.
      p.   cm.
   Includes bibliographical references and index.
   ISBN 0-8130-1274-0.—ISBN 0-8130-1275-9 (pbk.)
      1. Central America—Politics and government—1979–   2. Central
   America—Foreign relations—1979–   3. Negotiation.   I. Title.
   F1439.5.M67   1994
   327.728—dc20   93-36885
                  CIP

The University Press of Florida is the scholarly publishing agency for the
State University System of Florida, comprised of Florida A & M University,
Florida Atlantic University, Florida International University, Florida State
University, University of Central Florida, University of Florida, University of
North Florida, University of South Florida, and University of West Florida.

University Press of Florida
15 Northwest 15th Street
Gainesville, FL 32611

To my best friend and nephew, Shane Michael Connally

Contents

PREFACE / ix

1. The Limits of Sovereignty / 1

2. The Central American Crisis / 23

3. The Failure of Intervention / 49

4. The Arias Peace Plan / 78

5. The Peace Process / 106

6. Peace in the Isthmus / 130

APPENDIXES / 147

1. Report on the Contadora Communiqué / 149

2. Document of Objectives, September 1983 / 152

3. Contadora Act on Peace and Co-operation in Central America / 156

4. Peace Plan by Oscar Arias, 15 February 1987 / 184

5. Esquipulas II / 191

6. Sapoa Cease-fire Agreements / 199

7. Tesoro Beach Accord / 202

8. The Tela Agreements / 206

NOTES / 209

BIBLIOGRAPHY / 229

INDEX / 245

Preface

Central America has disappeared from the daily headlines. The Central American crisis, which obsessed U.S. policymakers for a decade, is now over. The passion that characterized the endless debate over how to resolve the economic, political, and social turmoil in the region has subsided. The removal of the Central American conflict from the global agenda is silent testimony to the success of the Central American peace process. The Central American Peace Accord was unique because it achieved peace in the isthmus by recognizing the complicated web of domestic and international actors involved in the Central American crisis.

In recounting the story of the Central American peace process, this book attempts to answer the question that James N. Rosenau asked of his graduate students: "What is this an instance of?" In other words, what does the struggle for peace in Central America tell us about Central American politics and inter-American relations at the end of the cold war? The book's central thesis is that the Central American peace plan succeeded because it acknowledged the fundamental link between domestic and foreign politics in Central America. The plan's chief architect, President Oscar Arias of Costa Rica, appreciated how the region's mounting interdependence required the democratization of the region if peace were to be achieved. The plan rested on two pillars: all the Central American states were to accept the legitimacy of each of the existing governments, despite their sharp ideological differences, and each of the regimes was to commit itself to the progressive democratization of the region. The accord was unique because not only did it attempt to regulate the external behavior of the Central American states, but its most important provisions were those requiring each of the regimes to open up its internal political system.

To analyze the complex web of interdependency that made the peace process possible, we need a fresh approach that goes beyond the traditional state-centric method. This book adopts a bifurcated approach in which the state-centric world coexists and interacts with a diffuse multicentric region consisting of diverse nonstate actors. The "Arias plan" succeeded because it was the only one of the international efforts to resolve the conflict that linked domestic and foreign politics. The plan recognized that a unique state system has been created in Central America by U.S. imperialism and by the region's heritage of unity and intervention and its economic dependency on the world economy. These three factors have formulated a regional state system in which no meaningful distinction can be drawn between internal and domestic affairs. Events that have traditionally been considered domestic have an immediate and direct impact on the foreign policy of all the isthmian states. Similarly, events that have traditionally been viewed as international have an immediate and direct impact on the domestic politics of all the Central American states.

The history of the Central American peace plan also points to the changing nature of inter-American relations and the decline of U.S. hegemony. Although the plan succeeded only after a change in U.S. administration and only after the Bush administration publicly endorsed it, the process also illustrates the autonomy of the Central American states from the United States. Despite their small size and their weak economies, the Central American states were able on several occasions to frustrate U.S. policy toward Central America. The peace accord, which was signed and implemented despite U.S. opposition, was called by former Salvadoran president Napoleon Duarte "Central America's second declaration of independence." President Arias, taking advantage of the Iran-Contra scandal, pushed through his peace plan despite the serious reservations of the Reagan administration. The Sandinista regime survived ten years despite extensive economic, political, and military pressure from the United States. Moreover, the Sandinistas remained the largest political party in Nicaragua and consolidated many of the revolution's social and political changes, despite their defeat in the February 1990 election. Similarly, both the FMLN and the rightists in El Salvador thwarted U.S. designs, and even Honduras had a couple of maneuvers not to the liking of the United States.

In writing this book I have incurred many scholarly and professional debts. I acknowledge the Council for International Exchange of Scholars, which made possible my research in Costa Rica. In particular, I am grateful to the Escuela de Relaciones Internacionales at the Universidad Nacional de Costa Rica for providing a base while I conducted my research. The director of the school, Mayrand Rios-Barboza, was especially useful as a source of information and contacts for my interviews in Costa Rica. I also recognize both the Latin America Studies Association and the Hemisphere Initiative for giving me the opportunity to serve on different commissions on compliance with the Central American Peace Accord, which awakened my interest in the Esquipulas process. Without such financial and institutional help, this book could not have been completed.

In this context, I thank especially friends and colleagues at Florida International University who helped with institutional or financial arrangements. Art Herriott, dean of the College of Arts and Sciences, and Joel Gottlieb, chair of the Political Science Department, were especially useful in providing release time and financial support for the project. Mark Rosenberg, director of the Latin American and Caribbean Center, funded numerous trips to Central America and provided useful insights. John Stack, of the Political Science Department, offered invaluable assistance at every stage of the project and was instrumental in the writing and publication of this book. Dario Perez, my teaching assistant, was also essential in its publication, relieving me from my teaching duties and doing useful research work in the final stages of the writing.

This book also benefited from friends outside of Florida International University whose views were important in shaping it. My teachers Abraham F. Lowenthal and James N. Rosenau are still influencing my thinking about international and inter-American relations. David Dent, Kenneth Mijeski, and Frederick S. Weaver spent hours of their valuable time critiquing the entire manuscript and making extensive suggestions for revision. Finally I thank my graduate students, who spent part of a semester critiquing the manuscript: Carlos Maceo, Alex Quevedo, Larry Sharer, Raymond Hatfield, and Carol Chambers.

1 *The Limits of Sovereignty*

Central America was besieged by a crisis that claimed more than two hundred thousand lives and displaced more than two million refugees between 1978 and 1991.[1] Recommendations abounded about what might be done to end the political, economic, and social turmoil in the region. North, South, and Central American politicians proposed and negotiated various solutions to the crisis: the Enders mission, the Kissinger report, Contadora, and the Manzanillo talks are some of the best-known efforts. None of these initiatives, however, succeeded in bringing peace to Central America. Not until President Oscar Arias of Costa Rica proposed his now-famous plan was meaningful progress made toward peace and stability.

The "Arias plan" succeeded because it was the only one of the international initiatives to link domestic and foreign politics. The Central American Peace Accord of August 7, 1987, which Arias proposed, rested on two pillars: all Central American states accepted the legitimacy of each of the existing governments, and each regime committed itself to the progressive democratization of the region. The accord was unique not only because it attempted to regulate the external behavior of the Central American states but because its most important provisions required each regime to open up its internal political systems.

The accord limited the sovereignty of the states of the isthmus because it assumed that the conflict was due in part to the closed nature of the Central American regimes. Arias reasoned that the cause of regionwide violence would disappear if each state went through a process of national reconciliation and dialogue, held "free and fair" elections, declared an amnesty, and took other measures toward democratization.

The Arias plan recognized that the region's mounting interdependence intensified the interaction between domestic and foreign affairs. To implement the agreement, the Central American republics agreed to subject their political systems to international scrutiny. For example, in order to assure that the Nicaraguan elections of February 25, 1990, were "free and fair" as required by the accord, the Sandinista regime invited more than two thousand foreign observers to monitor them.[2] The plan forced each republic to submit to international standards of political freedom and to surrender a basic principle of the doctrine of sovereignty: the right to judge its own controversies.

Central Americans accepted this level of foreign intervention in their affairs because the distinction between domestic and international politics has never made much sense in the region. Three factors have contributed to the strong interaction between external and internal political behavior: a tradition of Central American unity, U.S. imperialism, and regional economic interdependency. These factors all served to internationalize Central American politics.

The Central American Heritage

The five states of the region once formed a single nation (1824–38), a heritage that continues to blur the distinction between domestic and regional issues and also creates certain problems. Central American leaders have always shared an interest in the ideological makeup of their neighbors. For 150 years the states of the region have tried, but failed, to unite, federate, or confederate under various forms of government.

In November 1824, three years after securing independence from Spain, the five provinces of Central America promulgated a constitution and set into operation the Federal Republic of Central America. This attempt at union had clearly failed by 1838, and the individual states seceded and went their separate ways. From 1842 until the present, however, the idea of reestablishing the federal republic has never completely disappeared. On at least twenty-five different occasions, formal and official steps were taken to reconstitute the states into a single form of government. No attempt lasted more than a few months or included all five of the nations.[3]

A side effect of this desire for unity is the so-called Central American disease, the chronic interference of the Central American states in one another's affairs. The ideology of unity and claims of regional loyalty have frequently justified the attempts of Central American dictators to extend the horizon of their personal power. The *caudillos* of Central America have attempted to increase their power and influence by arming exiles from neighboring countries and even by direct intervention. This legacy of interprovince-interstate meddling began during the colonial era and continued after the breakup of the Federal Republic of Central America. Rafael Carrera, who ruthlessly ruled Guatemala, was one of the first kingmakers of Central America. From 1842 until his death in 1865, Carrera made and then unmade the presidents of El Salvador, Honduras, and Nicaragua. He reasoned that by aiding fellow conservatives in neighboring republics and preventing liberals from obtaining power he could secure his own rule at home.

Carrera's liberal successor, Justo Rufino Barrios, continued this practice of intervening in the affairs of his neighbors. In the name of re-creating the Central American union under his own leadership, Barrios maneuvered into positions of power like-minded liberals in El Salvador and Honduras, and he resorted to arms when diplomacy failed to obtain the support of Nicaragua and Costa Rica for the new union. He formed a thirteen-thousand-member Guatemalan army to force the Central Americans to accept his leadership. His plan for military conquest failed when his former friend and ally, President Rafael Zaldivar of El Salvador, betrayed him by siding with the two intransigent states. The death of Barrios at the battle of Chalchuapa on April 2, 1885, laid to rest once again the hope of reunification.[4] After his death the mantle of regional leadership fell to José Santos Zelaya, leader of Nicaragua from 1893 to 1909.

Zelaya's ambitions were similar to those of Barrios: to unite all Central America under his own leadership by overturning governments in the neighboring states and putting in his puppets.[5] Mainly through his efforts the three interior nations of El Salvador, Honduras, and Nicaragua joined together to form the República Mayor, a shaky and somewhat limited confederation that lasted from 1895 to 1898.[6] This experiment was brought to an end by a Salvadoran barracks revolt, but Zelaya was soon active again in promoting Central American unity. In 1902 he was able to arrange a conference in which the principle of arbitration of disputes was established through the Central American Tribunal. But Zelaya's ambitions soon aroused the concern of Guatemalan dictator Manuel Estrada-Cabrera, who became Zelaya's main rival for power and influence.

As a result of this rivalry, for the next several years Central America experienced an incredible assortment of political intrigues and counter-plots. The regional struggle for power was complicated by outside forces. Fearing a strong Guatemala and recognizing that Zelaya was hostile to Washington's influence in the region (the U.S.-backed Estrada-Cabrera), Mexico's political leadership allied itself with the Nicaraguan strongman.[7] The situation exploded in mid-1906 when Guatemalan exiles based in each of the other four Central American nations tried to overthrow Estrada-Cabrera. Bad feelings generated by this unsuccessful action continued well into 1907, when Zelaya invaded Honduras in order to remove Manuel Bonilla, who had allied himself with Guatemala. At the battle of Namasigue, Nicaraguan troops toppled the Bonilla government and Zelaya selected Miguel Davila to head the new regime.

The Honduran invasion created fears of Nicaraguan expansion, and a general Central American conflagration seemed imminent. Estrada-Cabrera mobilized his forces in reaction to the threat. The Salvadoran government, under Fernández Figueroa who only a year before had fought the Guatemalans, now joined Estrada-Cabrera to combat a Nicaraguan invasion. Faced with a Guatemalan-Salvadoran alliance, Zelaya realized he had overextended himself. To avoid a disastrous war, the Nicaraguan leader agreed to a proposal for a general Central American peace conference to be cosponsored by the United States and Mexico.

At the Washington Peace Conference (1907) the leaders of Central America attempted to address the problem of fratricidal chaos. The key was to establish an accord under which the incessant intervention in each other's affairs would cease. The Central Americans realized that an international structure needed to be developed that would prevent such interference. The Washington treaties attempted to create such a system by establishing a Central American Court of Justice empowered to adjudicate all cases brought before it pertaining to peace in Central America. The perennial problem of the Central American political exile was made the responsibility of the individual Central American nations. Honduras was neutralized.

The treaties attempted to prevent unconstitutional regimes from coming to power by adopting the Tobar doctrine.[8] Devised by Ecuadorian statesman Carlos Tobar, it argued that the American republics should refuse to extend diplomatic recognition to any hemispheric governments resulting from revolutionary movements directed against legitimate constitutional authority.[9] Article 1 of the General Treaty of Peace and Amity declared that "the high contracting parties shall not recognize any other government which comes into power in any of the five republics as a consequence of a coup d'état, or of a revolution against the recognized Government."[10] Article 2 called on the isthmian states to abstain from intervening in each other's internal conflicts. It declared that "no government of Central America shall in the case of civil war intervene in favor of or against the Government of the country where the struggle takes place."[11]

The Washington treaties were an important watershed in the history of the Central American republics. The signatories recognized that to achieve lasting peace and security in the isthmus they must accept each other, despite sharp political differences. More importantly, the treaties reflected their understanding that stability in the region required them to accept constraints on their own domestic and international behavior.

If the Central American delegates in Washington felt the treaties would render their home governments less vulnerable to domestic political instability, they were sadly mistaken. In the years following the Washington conference, unrest continued to plague the region. At the 1922–23 Washington conference the Central Americans tried to foster stability by strengthening the recognition provision of the 1907 treaty. The delegates hoped that by refusing recognition to governments that came to power through illegal means deviations from democratic norms could be prevented.[12]

However, Central Americans soon soured on the nonrecognition policy as it became a pretense for U.S. intervention in the region. The 1924 Honduran crisis, the 1925–26 Nicaraguan recognition dilemma, the Guatemalan crisis of 1930, and the Salvadoran affair of the early 1930s all illustrated how the Tobar doctrine had become an instrument of U.S. foreign policy. For example, in 1926–27 the United States justified an intervention in Nicaragua in terms of protecting the constitutional government of Adolfo Díaz.[13] Latin dissatisfaction with the pretext that the policy provided for U.S. imperialism came to a head when Gen. Maximiliano Hernández Martínez overthrew the civilian-elected government in El Salvador.[14] The new regime's authority and control was absolute and undisputed, though not constitutional. The anti-interventionist mood on the isthmus led Costa Rica and the other Central American republics to depart from the Tobar principles and recognize the new government.

The demise of the Tobar doctrine ushered in a new era of dictatorship in Central America: Martínez in El Salvador, Jorge Ubico in Guatemala, Tiburcio Carías in Honduras, and Anastasio Somoza in Nicaragua. The four dictators resorted to interfering in each other's domestic affairs, and their fear of the influence of neighboring democratic regimes led them to plot to destroy democracy throughout the isthmus. For example, during the Costa Rican crisis of 1948, Somoza was disposed to send troops from Nicaragua to pacify the country and prevent the anticommunist democrat and social reformer José Figueres from taking power. Somoza feared that, once in power, Figueres would allow Somoza's enemies the use of Costa Rican territory as a base for their activities.[15]

Similarly, both Nicaragua and Honduras allowed the United States to use their territories for Eisenhower's intervention against the elected leftist government in Guatemala. Somoza was angered when Guatemalan president Juan José Arévalo severed relations with Nicaragua. Arévalo embarrassed the dictator when he told the inter-American conference meeting at Chapúltepec, Mexico, "While we should not meddle in the internal affairs of countries . . . we cannot be forced to maintain friendship with governments that have transformed republican practices into those of monarchy."[16] When Somoza sensed Washington's displeasure with the agrarian reform programs of Arévalo's more radical successor, Jacobo Arbenz, he decided to even the score. Meeting with State Department officials during a 1952 trip to Washington, the Nicaraguan dictator boasted that if the United States would supply him with sufficient arms, "I'll clean up Guatemala for you in no time."[17]

Two years later Somoza welcomed the establishment of CIA bases in his country principally for the purpose of training Guatemalan exiles to overthrow the Arbenz regime. In fact, one of the training camps was established at the dictator's own plantation, El Tamarindo, and was used to instruct about 150 men in sabotage and demolition. Another 150 exiles and mercenaries went to the volcanic island of Momotombito in Lake Managua for weapons training. Finally, the CIA assigned about a dozen pilots to an airstrip at Puerto Cabezas on the Atlantic coast (the same airstrip used for the Bay of Pigs invasion of Cuba seven years later).[18] Honduras, pressured by U.S. ambassador Whiting Willauer, also joined in the plot against Guatemala by setting up a clandestine radio transmitter on Swan Island, off its Atlantic coast.[19]

After the U.S.-sponsored coup in Guatemala, the stability that characterized Central American politics led to a revival of the dream of unity. Central American leaders, concerned over lagging economic development, decided to follow the European model and create a common market to promote trade within the isthmus. Trade among the Central American states accounted for a mere 3 percent of the region's total. Manufacturing scarcely made a mark on finance ministers' charts. Directed by the United Nation's Economic Commission for Latin America, a common market was proposed. The first stage included a number of bilateral and multilateral treaties to improve regional trade, but the keystone of the new approach was a 1960 agreement among Guatemala, Honduras, and El Salvador, the Treaty of Economic Association. The major provision of this treaty was that free trade privileges would be granted on all goods originating in the three states. The agreement pushed the remaining states into the common market through the Treaty of Managua, which was implemented in 1961 by all the nations of the region except Costa Rica. Costa Rica ratified the document in 1963.[20]

The Central American Common Market was an instant success. As early as 1965 more than 95 percent of all items in Central American trade passed freely from one state to another. Growth was astonishing: between 1960 and 1968 intrazone trade increased on an average of 28.2 percent annually, nearly three times the average increase of the region's extraregional trade. In the years since, the rate has declined to about 12 percent a year, still a rewarding figure. Intraregional trade for 1973 amounted to more than $388 million, compared with $40 million in 1962, the last year before the commercial treaty went into effect. Perhaps more to the point, regional trade in 1975 accounted for nearly 25 percent of the total Central American trade with the world, three times the 1960 rate.[21]

The very success of the common market, however, proved to be its downfall. Guatemala and El Salvador were consistently the chief exporters, and Costa Rica and Nicaragua just as consistently ran trade deficits, which on occasion prompted unilateral, retaliatory action. The position of Honduras was worse.[22] As a consumer but not an exporter of manufactured consumer goods, Honduras quickly developed trade imbalances with the other Central American nations, particularly with neighboring rival El Salvador.

The trade deficit, as well as the three hundred thousand Salvadoran peasants who had migrated to sparsely populated Honduras, created tensions between the two states. Of Honduras's banana workers, 30 percent were Salvadorans. Needing a scapegoat for the trade deficit and other economic problems, Honduras announced it was deporting all Salvadorans. The ensuing hundred-hour war was ridiculed by the foreign press as the "soccer war" because of the rivalry between the two nations' sports teams.[23]

The Salvadoran air force bombed the Honduran capital on July 14, 1969. El Salvador retaliated with an invasion that claimed huge chunks of Honduran territory before an OAS peacekeeping team rushed to the scene to oversee a truce. The war put an end to the common market and sealed the Honduran border to landless and jobless Salvadorans. Although Honduras broke diplomatic and commercial relations with El Salvador and blocked Salvadoran exports in transit to the southern republics, Honduras did not at first leave the common market. This decision was taken only in December 1970, after the other states (excluding El Salvador) failed to reach agreement on a reform package proposed by Honduras.[24]

The Central American practice of interference in each other's domestic affairs was resurrected during the Sandinista revolution of the 1970s. Costa Ricans, who had a deep distaste for the Somoza dictatorship, allowed the Sandinista insurgents to operate freely in their territory.[25] Northern Costa Rica became the rear guard base for the Sandinistas' southern front.[26] Virtually all Costa Ricans adopted the Sandinista cause as their own,[27] and numerous young Costa Ricans, including former president Figueres's son Mauricio, volunteered for service with the rebels in Nicaragua. Costa Rica also led the diplomatic campaign against Somoza and, according to some accounts, convinced Mexico to break ties with Managua just nine days before the guerrillas launched their final offensive from Costa Rican territory.[28]

Central America's conflicted heritage of unity and intervention has blurred the distinction between domestic and international issues. During the last 150 years regional leaders have feared ideological contamination from their neighbors and thus have taken a keen interest in one another's domestic politics. For Nicaraguans to wish to influence events in El Salvador (and vice versa) and for Nicaraguan exiles to organize in Honduras to change the government in Nicaragua (and vice versa) are not new phenomena.[29] This legacy of affinity and interference would play an important role in the internationalization of the Central American crisis in the 1980s. Civil wars in Nicaragua and El Salvador created a crisis for the other Central American republics, all of which had a stake in the outcome of these internal conflicts.

Imperialism

The second factor that strengthened the link between domestic and foreign affairs was the hegemony of the United States. The United States has often defended its perceived interests in Central America by interfering in the region's affairs. In fact, the U.S. presence is so pervasive that Washington's support is often considered essential by local politicians seeking power in the region. Direct military intervention has also been employed when more subtle methods failed to achieve U.S. objectives.

U.S. interest in the isthmus evolved slowly. In the earliest years, physical hardships and the inconveniences of travel made diplomatic contact between the United States and the Central American republics extremely difficult. Of the eleven U.S. diplomats accredited to the isthmus before 1849, three died en route; another succumbed before he started on his mission; one was dismissed before he embarked; another contrived to draw his salary for more than a year without going near Central America; and another traveled the length of his assigned country, unable to find a government to receive him. The remaining four reached their destinations and were formally received, but only one stayed beyond a few months, and he committed suicide soon after his return to the United States.[30]

U.S. influence in Central America began in earnest after the Mexican War. The establishment of a continental United States caused Washington to focus its attention on Central America and the Caribbean. The fastest transit route between the east coast of the United States and the newly conquered territories on the Pacific was through the Isthmus of Panama. Expansionist officials argued that the United States could not allow a foreign power to control the main transit route between the two ocean coasts of the nation. By the late 1840s reports of British adventurism in the Caribbean and Central America had become numerous enough to concern the State Department. The decision to oppose British imperialism in the isthmus sparked an intense Anglo-American competition that very nearly resulted in war.

Conflict was averted in 1854 when the protagonists signed the Clayton-Bulwer treaty, an agreement that ignored the interests of the Central Americans and addressed only the security interests of the two great powers. The treaty guaranteed Britain and the United States access to any future isthmian canal and ensured that transit tolls or charges would be equal for the citizens of both countries. Each power also agreed not to fortify the canal or its vicinity, nor to colonize or assume any domain over Central America. The Clayton-Bulwer Treaty and the U.S. Civil War temporarily ended official U.S. interest in building an isthmian canal or in territorial aggrandizement in Central America.[31]

Interest in a transisthmian canal was not rekindled until the end of the nineteenth century. By then U.S. sea power had supplanted British dominance in the Caribbean Basin, and industrialization in the United States encouraged businessmen to expand trade with Latin America. This shift in the balance of power enabled American military leaders to ponder a different role for the United States in Central America. The most prominent of these leaders was Alfred Thayer Mahan, president of the Naval War College. Mahan concluded that U.S. security required a two-ocean navy to protect the continental territory from invasion and to defend the nation's expanding commercial interests. Furthermore, Mahan reasoned, to ensure the sea lanes of communications between the two fleets, the United States had to control the territory separating the Atlantic and the Pacific. Fundamental to Mahan's strategy was U.S. hegemony over the Caribbean basin, U.S. control over the proposed canal, and exclusion of all foreign bases from the Caribbean.[32]

The strategic doctrine articulated by Mahan led to U.S. intervention in Panama in 1903. Once canal construction and operation were under way, the United States used troops in Panama and Nicaragua to ensure a canal monopoly and protect the canal itself. The desire to establish and control the Panama Canal was used to justify U.S. military intervention in Central America during the next thirty years

(1902–32). The rationale for these interventions was commonly expressed in terms of safeguarding U.S. control over the approaches to the Panama canal.

The United States further protected its interests by ensuring that only pro-American regimes came to power throughout Central America. Whenever revolutionary violence erupted on the isthmus, the U.S. invariably took vigorous action to ensure the survival of governments and factions that were supportive of North American interests. This policy was first implemented in Nicaragua, where U.S. interests were being threatened by the anti-American president José Santos Zelaya, who was moving to expropriate the mining properties of the Pittsburgh-based U.S.-Nicaragua concession. The relations between the two countries were further complicated by rumors that Zelaya was planning to grant the Japanese rights to build a canal across Nicaragua.[33] In retaliation, U.S. investors encouraged and supported a revolt against Zelaya by the governor of Bluefields, Juan Estrada. Direct U.S. military intervention followed Zelaya's execution of two U.S. citizens who were serving in the rebel army. As a result, Zelaya was overthrown and replaced by a pro-American president.

The intervention entangled the United States in a feud between Nicaraguan Liberals and Conservatives for the next two decades. The United States intervened again in Nicaragua in August 1912, when the conservative regime of Adolfo Díaz came under attack from Liberal forces. After the defeat of the revolutionaries, the United States withdrew the bulk of its forces, leaving behind in Managua a one-hundred-man legation guard to provide a visible token of official U.S. support for the Díaz government and subsequent conservative regimes. The United States also took advantage of its dominant position in the country to secure its long-postponed objective of obtaining rights to a canal route through the San Juan River and Lake Nicaragua. A willing Nicaraguan minister, General Emiliano Chamorro, helped draft the agreement that came to be known as the Chamorro-Bryan Treaty, whereby Nicaragua, in exchange for $3 million in gold, granted to the United States in perpetuity exclusive rights to such land as was deemed necessary for a transisthmian canal, a renewable ninety-nine-year lease on Corn Island, and the right to establish a naval base in the Gulf of Fonseca.

Chamorro was elected president in 1917, a reward for his surrender of Nicaragua sovereignty. During his four-year term the country acquired all the trappings of a U.S. protectorate. A High Commission consisting of two Americans and the Nicaraguan Finance Minister was established in Managua to oversee the country's revenue. Chamorro was conceded a sum just under ninety-six thousand dollars to cover the expenses of his administration; the rest was apportioned to Nicaragua's foreign creditors. New York wags soon began to call Nicaragua the "Brown Brother Republic," a reference to the fact that most of the loans granted to Nicaragua had been subscribed by the banking house of Brown Brothers and Seligman.[34]

This overt alliance between the United States and Nicaraguan Conservatives prompted Nicaraguan Liberals to seek outside support for their own drive for political power. As early as 1916 prominent Nicaraguan Liberals sought Mexican support for their struggle with the United States and its Conservative clients. Liberals were outraged in October 1925 when Emiliano Chamorro launched a coup d'état against a coalition government headed by the Conservative Carlos Solorzano and the Liberal Juan Sacasa. In May 1926 Mexican-backed revolutionaries headed by the banished Liberal vice-president Sacasa landed on Nicaragua's Atlantic coast. Anticipating that their action would inspire an anti-Chamorro uprising throughout the country, the Liberals had planned to set up a rival government on the Atlantic side of the country at Puerto Cabezas. The byzantine nature of Nicaraguan politics led once again to bloody conflict between Liberals and Conservatives.

The crisis escalated in December 1926 when U.S. marines landed on Nicaragua's Atlantic coast. When the Liberal army moved into Chinandega, U.S. air support helped government troops drive them out. "Neutral" zones manned by U.S. troops were created in the key Pacific port of Corinto and in the cities of Chinandega and León, along the railway line to the capital. Another was set up in the city of Matagalpa, in the mountainous center of the country. The detachment stationed at Bluefields was reinforced, and the Liberal strongholds on the Caribbean coast were occupied. Sacasa's "capital" at Puerto Cabezas was taken; local Liberal troops were disarmed and their weapons and ammunition were cast into the sea. In a matter of weeks the United States built up its forces in Nicaragua to more than two thousand.[35]

The United States justified its intervention by citing Mexican meddling in Nicaraguan affairs, insisting that Mexican military aid sustained Sacasa's Liberal forces. In the estimation of President Calvin Coolidge, Mexico, "a foreign power," was promoting anarchy in Nicaragua, thereby endangering U.S. interests in the nation, and by extension, throughout the isthmus.[36] By April 1927 the United States felt that conditions were appropriate for a negotiated settlement to the Nicaraguan conflict. Coolidge sent Henry Stimson to seek an accord among the warring Nicaraguans so that the United States might begin to extricate itself from the conflict. Stimson's peace proposal contained two key elements: the U.S. would supervise free elections in 1928, and it would help the Nicaraguan government organize a nonpartisan guard to exercise police and military functions. On May 12, 1927, the Liberals agreed to the U.S. proposal and signed what was known as the Pact of Espino Negro. Washington and the Nicaraguan Liberal Party had finally resolved their long-standing conflict. The newly formed, U.S.-trained national guard would permit U.S. forces to withdraw and would serve, in theory, as the impartial guarantor of public order and electoral probity.[37] All the Liberal leaders except Augusto Sandino accepted the U.S. proposal.

Sandino, who viewed the U.S.-imposed settlement as a betrayal of Nicaraguan independence, declared himself head of the "army of national sovereignty" (Ejército del Defenso de la Soberanía Nacional de Nicaragua) and started an anti-interventionist war against U.S. occupation. Sandino pursued a low-level guerilla campaign against U.S. forces and the national guard for six years (1927–33), successfully resisting U.S. efforts to capture him. The war was a standoff, and because of anti-interventionist sentiment in the United States, the marines were withdrawn in 1933.

The departure of U.S. forces marked the start of a new era of imperialism in Central America. The Sandino war convinced the United States that promoting stability was the best way to protect its security interests in the region. The Roosevelt administration abandoned U.S. adherence to the Tobar doctrine, the refusal to extend diplomatic recognition to unconstitutional governments. Instead, under the Good Neighbor Policy, the United States adopted a policy of nonintervention in the internal affairs of Central American states. To promote security in the isthmus the United States began to endorse Central American strongmen.

In Guatemala the United States used subtle political pressure to maneuver Gen. Jorge Ubico into power.[38] It also dropped its objections to a coup d'état sponsored by Gen. Maximiliano Hernández Martínez in El Salvador when he demonstrated he could preserve stability in the country. The United States was impressed by the efficiency of Martínez's repression of a communist uprising in El Salvador in 1932.[39] The *matanza*, where an estimated ten thousand peasants were killed, established the Salvadoran general's reputation as the champion of anticommunism.[40] Finally, the United States turned a blind eye to General Somoza's seizure of power in Nicaragua.

This age of Central American dictatorship ushered in a new age of stability in the isthmus. Martínez of El Salvador, Ubico of Guatemala, and Carías of Honduras all remained in power until the Guatemalan revolution of 1944 and the Costa Rican crisis of 1948. U.S. reaction to these events was shaped by the fear that Soviet-style communism might establish a beachhead in the Americas.

Fear of communism led the United States to support the Social Democratic revolution of José Figueres. Figueres was able to convince many Costa Ricans and some U.S. policymakers that his political opponents were communists.[41] The United States' support for this short and bloody revolution was decisive in Figueres's victory.[42]

U.S. intervention in Guatemala also clearly reflected the cold war mentality of U.S. policymakers. The Guatemalan government of Jacobo Arbenz moved forward with aggressive land reforms started by the previous government. The main target was the United Fruit Company. In a sequence of expropriations beginning in December 1952 and ending in 1954, the government seized more than 4 million acres of United Fruit's holdings, equivalent to approximately one-seventh of all the arable land in Guatemala.[43] The main concern of U.S. policymakers, however, was not the land reform measures but the appointment of communists to high-level positions in the Guatemalan government. Early in 1952 communists were invited to help form a National Democratic Front, which became the majority party in congress. Communists were appointed to important positions in the police, the department of agrarian reform, and the trade union movement.

The administration of President Dwight D. Eisenhower interpreted these developments as cold war threats to U.S. security; its response to the Guatemalan situation seemed based on security considerations, not on concerns about private U.S. investments.[44] Consequently, the United States covertly sponsored a military invasion of Guatemala, which overthrew the Arbenz government and replaced it with a pro-U.S. regime.

After the Guatemalan counterrevolution, U.S. Central American policy was characterized by support for right wing regimes. Decision makers reasoned that governments based on an alliance between the military and the oligarchy provided stability and the best defense against communist subversion in the isthmus. Throughout the 1960s and the 1970s the United States turned a blind eye to human rights abuses in the region. Anastasio Somoza was the United States' principal ally in Central America during this period, in a relationship based on the dictator's anticommunist ideology, his maintenance of social stability, and his willingness to provide logistical assistance for U.S. interventions in Guatemala and Cuba. The extent of the "special relationship" between Washington and Somoza was illustrated when the portrait of Nixon's ambassador to Managua, Turner Shelton, was placed on Nicaragua's twenty-*córdoba* note.[45] Thus it was not surprising that the U.S. State Department raised no objections when the dictator declared a state of siege on December 28, 1974.

U.S. policy changed dramatically with the advent of the Carter administration. President Carter's policy was based on the assumption that Central America's existing political institutions had failed to respond to changing social and economic realities and that new interest groups were being excluded from the political process, thereby creating a dangerous situation.[46] Carter feared that a leftist movement would capture the imagination and loyalty of these disaffected groups. Moreover, as a result of increased social tension, Central American regimes were becoming even more repressive.[47] This was leading otherwise moderate reformist movements, deprived of an opportunity to enter a meaningful political process, to turn to extreme measures. Carter hoped that by promoting human rights and pressuring exclusivist regimes to broaden the political process, a social explosion could be averted. His Central American policy was based on the belief that social tension could be reduced if change could be produced through open government channels.[48] To convince the traditional regimes of the region to open up their political system, Carter tied U.S. economic and military aid to human rights performance. Nicaragua became the test case for Carter's new foreign policy, as the United States attempted to persuade Somoza to improve the human rights situation in Nicaragua.

Carter's policy, however, was unable to prevent a social explosion in Nicaragua. The victory of the Sandinistas in the Nicaraguan revolution led to a different U.S. approach to stability in Central America. To avoid revolutions in the rest of Central America, the United States adopted a policy of "controlled evolution" based on the belief that the best way to protect U.S. interests in the region would be through actions aimed at managing inevitable social and economic change. The Carter administration formulated an evolutionary strategy designed to identify with and promote the process of basic change within the region. While discarding traditional methods, the policy sought to maintain U.S. influence in the region and ensure that none of the Central American republics became dependent on nations hostile to the United States. To manage this process of regional change, Carter sought to revive the political center composed of moderate and reformist democrats, while opposing both the traditional right and the radical left.[49]

This policy of attempting to manage change in Central America led the Carter and Reagan administrations to support new internal political arrangements within each Central American state. The United States supported a new alliance between the military and conservative elements within the middle class (excluding the oligarchy) in order to maintain regional stability in the wake of the Nicaraguan revolution. The strategy of these conservative-reformist regimes (Duarte, Suazo, Cerezo) combined social and economic reform to co-opt the democratic left, with repression of the revolutionary left to assuage the right's fear of reform.

The United States' policy of supporting pro-American regimes in Central America continued through the 1980s. In the Reagan years the political crisis infecting the region was perceived by the U.S. government as another battleground in the cold war. The Reagan administration interfered in the internal politics of the Central American republics, supporting the Christian Democratic junta in El Salvador and the anti-Sandinista forces in Nicaragua, just as from 1910 to 1920 the United States had supported Nicaraguan conservatives. U.S. intervention on behalf of its local clients in the region served to severely limit the autonomy of the Central American republics.

Dependency

Central America's economic dependency is another factor that links internal and external politics in the region. The integration of Central America into the world economy resulted in foreign penetration of the local economies. Central American economies are linked to the world capitalist economy through foreign investments (especially in the banana industry) and dependency on external trade for economic growth. Consequently, Central American regimes are constrained by economic pressures that outside forces may impose on their country, for example, the U.S. trade embargo against the Sandinista regime in Nicaragua. Thus the evolution of export-oriented economies in the region made the states of the region vulnerable to external pressure.

Beginning in the late 1870s the Central American republics transformed their economies to export-oriented ones. This export-led model of economic growth was based on the belief that Central America's competitive advantage lay in producing primary commodities for the world market in exchange for manufactured goods.[50] The fifty years following the adoption of this model was a period of steady if not unbroken economic progress, based on the solid foundation of two export crops (coffee and bananas) that appeared to be well suited to climatic conditions in Central America and were easily absorbed by the world market. To facilitate the establishment of coffee and banana production, almost no sacrifice was considered too great. The liberal revolutions of the 1870s were followed by a series of reforms and concessions involving considerable political and social upheaval.[51]

Coffee and banana exports led to the integration of the region into the world capitalist economy. The region became open to foreign investment as the states strived to develop the export sector. The banana industry was completely foreign controlled. By the 1930s a single company, United Fruit Company of Boston, exported almost one-third of all the bananas that traveled from Latin America to the United States and Europe, and it was the leading banana grower in every Central American and Caribbean country. It produced four times the volume of its closest competitor, Standard Fruit Company.

Coffee was also closely linked to the international economic system, although production was controlled by Central American nationals. Not only was almost all the coffee sold to the external market but it created a powerful new cosmopolitan upper class. The descendants of the powerful coffee families tended to marry foreigners; they were educated abroad; and in time they became a new breed, differing from the rest of the nation not only in social mores and prejudices, but even in physical appearance.[52] Coffee created a new elite who more closely resembled the European and North American bourgeoisie than their fellow Central Americans.

The Central American economies became dependent on these export crops for economic growth. These products quickly dominated investment, credit, and imports; the latter heavily influenced commerce and many branches of industry, while foreign trade determined government revenues.[53] Consequently, the Central American economies became vulnerable to adverse shocks in the commodities market. The susceptibility of coffee and bananas to world prices was illustrated by the shock of the Great Depression.

After the depression the Central American republics began to diversify their exports. Trade expanded to include five products: coffee, bananas, cotton, sugar, and beef. Reduction in commodity concentration lowered the vulnerability of the economy to adverse shocks in one market, while increasing the susceptibility to adverse shocks in all commodities markets.[54] The new export products were also mainly in national hands, so that the extent of foreign control of exports was reduced. Also, with the creation of the Central American Common Market, each republic sought to reduce its dependency on the world market by emphasizing regional trade, and a vibrant regional trade in manufactured exports was begun.

The demise of the common market following the Honduran-Salvadoran War led private sector interest groups to advocate a return to the policy of encouraging export to the global market. The Central American bourgeoisie, with its close ties to the international economic system, argued that the export-led model was the best method for achieving self-sustained growth. They argued that, under favorable circumstances, the nonexport economy might grow so rapidly under the stimulus of the export-led model that the openness of the economy would decline, making it less vulnerable to adverse external shocks. The stimulus to the nonexport economy would come from the demand for intermediate goods and for the supply of raw materials, as well as other indirect stimuli based on the complementary nature of many branches of the nonexport economy, such as internal transport, financial institutions, and the provision of taxation for the expansion of government services.[55]

The evolution of the Central American economies reflects the region's dependency on the international economic system. The political and economic crises of the 1980s illustrate the vulnerability of the region to external pressures. In addition, the failure of the Sandinista regime to break away from dependency testifies to the powerful constraints imposed by global economics on the Central American economies. The export-led model of economic growth that Central America adopted in the 1870s put the region at the mercy of the international economic system.

The Central American State System

A unique state system was created in Central America by the region's mixed heritage of unity and intervention, U.S. imperialism, and dependence on the world economy. The central characteristic of this regional system is the blurring of the distinction between domestic and international politics. The strong link between the internal and external system is illustrated by the strong historical and cultural bonds between the five Central American republics. As a result, regional leaders have often taken a keen interest in the domestic politics and ideological orientations of their neighbors. The sovereignty of the Central American states was limited by the desire of each state to influence events in the other states of the region. The so-called Central American disease, the chronic interference of the isthmian states in each other's affairs, served to weaken the independence and autonomy of the regional states.

The region's sovereignty was also diluted by the long history of U.S. intervention. Central America's role in the traditional definition of U.S. security interests has led the United States to interfere in the internal affairs of the republics to assure that pro-American regimes were maintained in power. Direct U.S. military intervention was often used when more subtle methods failed to remove unfriendly regimes. Finally, Central American sovereignty was compromised by its export-led economic model, which made it dependent on the global economic system.

These three factors formulated a regional state system in which no meaningful distinction can be drawn between internal and international affairs. Events traditionally seen as domestic matters—the election of a Christian Democrat in Guatemala, the appointment of a right wing general as chief of staff in Honduras, or a socialist revolution in Nicaragua—had an immediate and direct impact on the foreign policies of all the isthmian states. Similarly, events traditionally viewed as international—a joint military exercise between the United States and Honduras or a trade pact between Nicaragua and the Socialist bloc— had an immediate and direct impact on the domestic politics of all the Central American states.

This phenomenon of linkage between internal and external politics, while more extreme in Central America, is found throughout the international system. Political scientists postulate that in an age of interdependency the traditional distinction between comparative and international politics is no longer applicable. The complicated nature of the linkage between international and domestic politics is due to two historic processes that have shaped today's world. They consist of those dynamics that are conducive on one hand to integration (e.g., the Central Common Market, Contadora, Group of Eight) and on the other to disintegration (Salvadoran civil war, contra terrorism, etc.). One observer called the twin processes, formed by the disintegration of long-standing authority relations and the advent of complex interdependence, "cascading interdependence."[56] The process is described in these terms: "Today, precisely because scarcities are greater, subgroups stronger, and governments weaker, these tensions can spread and interlock with comparable tensions in other systems, thereby producing changes which cascade endlessly upon each other across the global system."[57]

The linkage between internal and external politics in Central America led to the immediate internationalization of the crisis. The Nicaraguan revolution, as shown in chapter 2, led to a regional chain reaction that transformed all the political systems in the region. The Sandinista victory was immediately followed by a military coup d'état in El Salvador, political reforms in Honduras (leading to the first free election in a decade), and a new wave of violent political repression in Guatemala.

The Sandinista revolution also ushered in a period of foreign intervention in Central America. As chapter 3 illustrates, Ronald Reagan reacted to the establishment of an anti-American regime in the region by using U.S. political, military, and economic power in an all-out effort to overthrow the Sandinistas. U.S. policy served to internationalize the crisis, as the Reagan administration justified its policy by linking the Central American conflict to the Soviet-American struggle. The fear of direct U.S. military intervention in Central America led other Latin American nations to find a peaceful solution to the crisis. Contadora was Latin America's attempt to diminish regional tension by legitimizing the Sandinista regime and reducing armaments and foreign interference. The Contadora process also epitomized the effort of Latin nations (especially Mexico and Venezuela) to increase their influence in Central America. The Iran-Contra scandal, which forced the Reagan administration to cease military aid to the contras, and the collapse of the Contadora peace effort demonstrated the failure of foreign intervention in the isthmus.

This failure created a diplomatic opportunity for Central Americans. As chapter 4 explains, Costa Rican president Oscar Arias took advantage of this opening to present his vision for peace. Arias's proposal rested on two principles. First, all the Central American states were to accept the legitimacy of the existing governments, despite their sharp ideological differences. This meant that all the republics pledged not to interfere in each other's internal affairs. Second, each of the regimes committed itself to the progressive democratization of the region. The accord was unique because not only did it attempt to regulate the external behavior of the Central American states but its most important provisions required each regime to open up its internal political systems. The Arias peace plan acknowledged the limits of sovereignty in Central America and recognized the strong linkage between domestic and international politics in the region.

The peace plan was well received by the other Central American presidents, who adopted it on August 7, 1987, in Guatemala City. The accord, as chapter 5 shows, began a long process of negotiations as the Central American states attempted to comply with the agreement. The difficulties associated in working out an arrangement that would democratize Nicaragua in exchange for ending the contra war led to a series of presidential summits where disputes over implementation and compliance were worked out. The defeat of the Sandinistas in the

Nicaraguan election and the disarming of the contras signified the success of the Arias plan. Chapter 6 looks at the aftermath of the Nicaraguan elections and whether the Central American peace process will usher in a new era of regional integration and cooperation.

The Arias peace plan succeeded because it acknowledged the fundamental link between domestic and foreign politics in Central America. The Costa Rican president succeeded where others failed because he understood the linkages between internal, regional, and international actors. The plan also recognized how the region's mounting interdependence intensified this interaction. To analyze the peace process we must take an approach that goes beyond the state-centric method. To understand the success of the Arias plan, this book adopts a dual approach in which the state-centric world coexists and interacts with a diffused multicentric region consisting of regional and international entities, bureaucracies, and nonstate actors.[58]

2 *The Central American Crisis*

The Sandinista victory of June 1979 revolutionized Central America. The Nicaraguan Revolution created a chain reaction that transformed the political systems of the region. The Central American crisis referred to the challenges the isthmian states faced in the wake of the rapid political, economic, and social change that followed the Sandinistas' triumph. Somoza's fall was immediately followed by a reformist coup d'état in El Salvador, the end of military rule in Honduras, and a new wave of political repression in Guatemala. Concurrently with political instability, Central America confronted a period of economic depression in the 1980s resulting in the most severe crisis in the history of the region.

The challenges and risks that the Central American republics faced after the Nicaraguan Revolution were due in large part to the strong links between domestic, regional, and international politics. The interdependency of Central America meant that revolutionary change in Nicaragua spilled over to the other states. This process of "cascading interdependency," where change in one political system provokes change in another system, explains the internationalization of the crisis. The strong connections between domestic and regional political systems, which characterize the Central American state system, meant that the revolutionary triumph in Nicaragua had profound domestic implications for the other isthmian states.

The revolution exposed the deep contradictions and inherent instability of the old political order. The traditional alliances between military and oligarchic forces that had dominated Central America were shown to be hopelessly obsolete. The Sandinista triumph illustrated how right wing authoritarian regimes failed to respond to changing realities and the demands of new social groups for a role in the political process. The success of a revolutionary movement in Nicaragua and

23

incipient civil wars in El Salvador and Guatemala underscored the fact that political repression caused otherwise centrist political movements to ally themselves with extremists.

The Central American elites, in order to forestall violent revolution, adopted a new political formula designed to give reformist elements a voice in governance. The centerpiece of this new arrangement was the replacement of the old military-oligarchy alliance with a new partnership between the military and conservative elements in the middle class. This new political composition hoped to prevent the revolutionary option in the region through a two-track approach: social and economic reform to co-opt and placate moderate reformist elements, and repression of the radical left to destroy the guerrillas and assuage the right's fear of reform. This new political arrangement was legitimized through the electoral process in El Salvador (1982, 1984, 1985, 1988, 1989), Honduras (1981, 1985, 1989), and Guatemala (1985, 1990).[1]

The military-cum-reform strategy was encouraged by the United States. Both the Carter and the Reagan administrations supported the two-track strategy as the best method to avert the extremism of either a right wing coup d'état or a guerrilla military victory. The United States feared that unless meaningful political, social, and economic reforms were carried out, it would be faced with a regionwide revolution. Thus both administrations adopted policies that attempted to manage and control the inevitable social and political transformation of Central America.

U.S. pressure on traditional Central American regimes to reform illustrated how the interlocking relationship between domestic and regional politics resulted in the penetration of all the regional polities by international forces. The crisis also witnessed a whole array of nonstate actors challenging the sovereignty of the Central American republics, by making alliances, waging wars, and conducting campaigns across national borders. For example, the Sandinista regime in Nicaragua confronted not only U.S.-sponsored guerrillas based in Honduras but also an internal nonviolent opposition with close links to Washington. Similarly, the Christian-Democratic military junta in El Salvador was opposed not only by guerrillas with close ties to Cuba and Nicaragua, but also by a nonviolent opposition with close ties to Mexico and France, and by pressure from the United States Congress to improve human rights conditions.

The web of alliances, relationships, and competitions that characterized Central America in the 1980s created a crisis that was beyond the
power of individual states to address within their own political systems. For example, in order for Nicaragua to resolve its internal conflicts it needed to negotiate not only with its internal opposition but
also with the United States and Honduras. To understand the internationalization of the Central American crisis, it will be useful to explore
the level of foreign penetration that has occurred in each of the Central
American states.

Nicaragua

Nicaragua is a prime example of how foreign penetration
forced the Central American states to search for an international solution to the crisis. The Sandinista regime was confronted by a series of
challenges rooted in the international system, over which Nicaragua
had no control. These external forces, whose aim was to destabilize the
regime, were able to penetrate Nicaraguan society to such an extent
that peace and prosperity became dependent on forces outside the
country. International pressure against the Sandinistas became so extensive that Nicaragua was forced to negotiate a peace settlement that
surrendered a significant portion of the nation's sovereignty.

The Sandinistas realized that although they might survive and deal
blows to their enemies, they could not make economic or societal
progress. The regime could survive, but it could do little else. International forces were able to pressure the Sandinistas because the society
was heavily dependent on the international system. Nicaragua's dependency made it vulnerable to the economic, political, diplomatic, and
military pressure generated by the United States.

The most important area of foreign penetration was the economy.
The Reagan administration's hostility toward the Sandinistas contributed to the deterioration of the Nicaraguan economy. The FSLN engaged in what President Daniel Ortega described as a "life-and-death"
struggle against U.S. power—and lost, as the war, the U.S. trade
embargo, and loss of Western credit created an economic nightmare.
The most damaging effect of this policy was hyperinflation, which the
Sandinista government blamed on military spending made necessary
by the country's eight-year war against U.S.-financed guerrillas. Infla-

tion stood at 747 percent in 1986, 1,800 percent in 1987, 30,000 percent in 1988, and 1,500 percent in 1989.[2] Moreover, according to Ricardo Chavarría, vice-minister of the Nicaraguan Institute of Social Security and Social Welfare (INSSBI), the war killed some forty-three thousand Nicaraguans on both sides, displaced more than three hundred thousand civilians, and cost the government more than $12 billion.[3]

The U.S. trade embargo and the war also resulted in a deterioration of export levels. At the time of the Sandinista victory, Nicaragua exported about $600 million a year; since 1979, this has declined steadily. In 1986 and 1987, partly because of the continuation of the war and U.S. economic pressure, Nicaraguan exports declined to just above $200 million.[4] In 1989 Nicaragua exported $253 million.[5] The crisis in production was reflected in the decline of Gross Domestic Product (GDP). It was estimated that when adjusted for inflation, the Nicaraguan economy was one-third smaller in 1989 than it was at the time of the revolution. GDP has declined in all but three years since the revolutionary triumph. Meanwhile, inflation devastated the real wages of average Nicaraguans, with average monthly wages being deflated by more than 92 percent since 1981.[6] By 1990 the minimum wage for a state farm worker was seventy cents a day, and a teacher made thirteen dollars a month. The state of the Nicaraguan economy was described by Domingo Sánchez-Salgado, a socialist member of the National Assembly, in these terms: "If you compare Nicaragua's economy to a human body it is close to death."[7]

Nicaragua's plight was worsened by conflict between the government and the private sector. Continued low productivity was due partly to the failure of the private sector and the government to achieve a mutually acceptable accommodation. The private sector, especially the large producers, allied with foreign forces against the Sandinistas. The government accused its enemies in the private sector, especially members of the conservative Consejo Superior de la Empresa Privada (COSEP, or Superior Council of Private Enterprise), of sabotaging the economy to aid the United States in destabilizing the regime. The mistrust between the FSLN and large producers led to continuous conflict between the regime and the most productive sector of the economy, which lowered public confidence in the economy. Daniel Ortega exemplified the tension between the government and the private sector when he declared, "We have tried to avoid confrontation [with COSEP], but if they want class struggle, we will give them class struggle."[8]

The second method that external forces used to penetrate the Nicaraguan polity was the contra war. Contra refers to the Nicaraguan counterrevolution that was formed by the remnants of Somoza's National Guard, Somocista politicians, and conservative anti-Somocistas who broke with the Nicaraguan revolution. It included men like Alfonso Robelo, Arturo Cruz, Alfredo César, and Edén Pastora, who parted company with the Sandinistas after having held important posts in the revolutionary government. They generally accused the FSLN of subverting the revolution and breaking promises made before the triumph.[9] The contras were aided in their effort to overthrow the Sandinista regime by external forces. The Guatemalan, Honduran, and Argentine military immediately started to organize the armed anti-Sandinista guerrillas.[10] By August 1981 the most important guerrilla front, the Nicaraguan Democratic Force (FDN), was formed. Based in Honduras, the FDN was trained by the Argentines and funded by the United States.[11]

The principal foreign sponsor of the contras was the Reagan administration. At the end of 1981 the United States allocated monies to the Central Intelligence Agency (CIA) for covert operations against the Sandinistas.[12] The CIA proposed building "popular support in Central America and Nicaragua for an opposition front that would be nationalistic, anti-Cuban and anti-Soviet."[13] Initially, this involved five hundred men and $19.95 million. On December 18, 1981, President Reagan signed National Security Directive 17, which endorsed the program.

Counterrevolutionary activity commenced that same month. The operation, code-named Red Christmas, involved guerrilla attacks along Nicaragua's remote northeastern border. Attacks on the country's only refinery and cement plant were also reported. The war escalated throughout 1982. In the one-hundred-day period from March 14 through June 21, at least 106 insurgent incidents occurred within Nicaragua.[14] Contra operations during this period included the burning of crops, sabotage of highway bridges, attempted destruction of fuel tanks, sniper fire, and forays against small military patrols, attacks by small guerrilla bands on individual Sandinista soldiers, the assassination of minor government officials as well as Cuban advisers, and the burning of a customs warehouse and several buildings belonging to the Ministry of Construction.[15]

The contra war reached its zenith between 1983 and 1985. By early 1983 the CIA's original five-hundred-person force had increased eight-fold to four thousand troops. By mid-1984 CIA officials claimed that the contra army numbered sixteen thousand. In December 1982 and again in March, April, and October 1983 contra troops mounted coordinated raids on northern Nicaragua in an effort to establish a liberated zone. The CIA also launched a series of attacks on Nicaraguan port facilities. On September 8, 1983, agency speedboats attacked Port Sandino. Five weeks later frogmen returned to the Pacific port city and sabotaged an underwater oil pipeline. Another major attack took place at Corinto, Nicaragua's largest port. CIA-trained commandos fired mortars and grenades at five huge oil and gasoline storage tanks, igniting 3.4 million gallons of fuel. More than a hundred people were injured in the raid and twenty-five thousand inhabitants of the city had to be evacuated while the fire raged out of control for two days.[16]

Contra activities increased dramatically in 1984. On March 7 and again on March 30 petroleum storage facilities at San Juan del Sur and Puerto Sandino were attacked. Contra forces also seized the oceanside village of San Juan del Norte for forty-eight hours on April 9. But by far the biggest military operation against Nicaragua was the mining of the harbors in the spring of 1984.[17] By the first week of April, ten commercial vessels had struck the mines, six of them non-Nicaraguan. Ships registered to Japan, the Netherlands, Liberia, and Panama, as well as the Soviet oil tanker *Lagansk,* sustained damage; five Russian seamen were among fifteen sailors injured by the exploding underwater charges.[18]

The escalation of the war led the Sandinistas to implement a draft and to deploy Soviet-built helicopters. This quickly turned the tide of battle. By the end of 1984 the rebels' southern front had been demolished, and in the following year contra forces in the northern and eastern region were defeated. In 1986 contra activity was reduced to economic sabotage and terrorism against civilians.[19]

Despite these setbacks for the contras, the Sandinistas felt constant pressure from the armed resistance until the eve of the 1990 elections. In August 1989 more than two thousand rebels infiltrated Nicaragua from Honduras and Costa Rica. In October 1989 they launched two especially bloody attacks, which led the Nicaraguan government to claim that the guerrillas were engaged in a remobilization. On October 8 six army reservists were killed while protecting a voter registration center in the central department of Chontales, and thirteen days later the contra killed nineteen peasants in Río Blanco. The FSLN, frustrated by the escalation in the war, suspended the cease-fire with the contras in November 1989. Ortega announced, "We can no longer go on with our hands tied. All Nicaraguan troops will be mobilized and ready for action."[20] To make matters worse, the Bush administration, while making it clear that the contras were no longer a military option, refused to abandon the rebels completely. The administration kept the rebels intact but idle while political and diplomatic negotiations took place. Bush requested and obtained $50 million in humanitarian aid for the contras and pressured the Honduran government to allow the rebels to remain in their territory in order to keep pressure on the Nicaraguans.

External forces also interfered in Nicaraguan politics by openly financing and backing the nonviolent opposition. The United States, for example, played a key role in the 1984 election, within and outside Nicaragua. Senior U.S. officials and Nicaraguan opposition politicians, including Arturo Cruz, acknowledged that the United States sought to persuade, through pressure and finances, prominent individuals and parties (or factions within parties) to withdraw from or not enter the election.[21] Outside Nicaragua, Reagan officials dismissed the 1984 election as a "Soviet-style sham" before, during, and after the campaign had officially begun.

After the 1984 election the United States maintained its ties with the nonviolent opposition by helping fund both the opposition newspaper *La Prensa* and the private sector business group COSEP. In fact, close association of *La Prensa* with the United States led the government to suspend publication of the newspaper during the height of the contra war. The Sandinistas' concern over U.S. influence on the Nicaraguan opposition increased during preparations for the 1990 presidential campaign. On July 10, 1988, the Sandinistas arrested thirty-eight critics of the revolutionary government who participated in an antigovernment rally in Nandaime, temporarily closed down *La Prensa*, silenced Radio Católica, confiscated the San Antonio Sugar Mill (the single largest private enterprise in the country), and expelled Ambassador Melton and eight other U.S. diplomats.

The regime claimed that the expelled diplomats, including Ambassador Melton, encouraged and pressured opposition groups to provoke physical confrontations with the government. The Sandinistas also mounted a major publicity campaign to denounce U.S. efforts to aid the opposition.[22] The Nicaraguan government claimed that the U.S. embassy played a key role in the organization of the main opposition group, the United Nicaraguan Opposition (UNO). These fears were exacerbated by press reports that the Bush administration was behind efforts at finding a charismatic opposition candidate for the 1990 presidential elections.[23] Violeta Barrios de Chamorro, widow of the slain national hero Pedro Joaquín Chamorro, was the candidate in this strategy to end FSLN political control.

Bush vigorously pursued a policy of interfering in the 1990 Nicaraguan election by openly financing and backing Chamorro. The president justified U.S. assistance to the Nicaraguan opposition by claiming that it guaranteed a free and fair election. U.S. aid to the Nicaraguan opposition for the 1990 election was conducted openly through the National Endowment for Democracy (NED). The U.S. Congress approved a special aid package of $9 million for the February election. Specifically earmarked for the UNO "party infrastructure" was $1.5 million for sixty-two vehicles and gasoline, $1.4 million in cash, $815,000 for party members' salaries and expenses, $600,000 to pay twenty thousand poll watchers, $300,000 for office equipment, and $50,000 for trips abroad by UNO members.[24] Of the remaining $4 million, $1.05 million was committed for three international election-monitoring teams; the rest was designated as "flexible funds" used to support the electoral process. The State Department also gave $2 million to the Nicaraguan Supreme Electoral Council in compliance with the 50 percent rule on foreign donations, leaving $950,000 of flexible funds to be disbursed by the State Department.[25]

U.S. pressure against Nicaragua forced the Sandinistas to surrender a significant portion of their country's sovereignty. The regime entered into the Central American peace process because it was the only mechanism available to counter foreign penetration of their society. Nicaragua was willing to accept Arias's definition of democracy and free elections in exchange for ending the contra war and U.S. economic sanctions. The Sandinistas realized that they might survive, but they could do little else. Economic recovery and peace depended on the

FSLN's arriving at a settlement with its internal and external opponents that would not only recognize the legitimacy of the revolutionary order in Nicaragua but also establish the framework in which power could be fairly contested in the future. The Esquipulas agreement was viewed as the first step toward this arrangement and as the only way out for the beleaguered regime.

El Salvador

El Salvador also proved incapable of resolving its own bitter political conflicts within the context of the national polity. Civil war remained the central political reality of Salvadoran society after ten years of reforms, elections, and violence. El Salvador was forced to the bargaining table by the failure of the Christian Democratic reforms, which were designed to complement the counterinsurgency campaign by gaining popular support for the regime. The key to this effort was land reform, but by the mid-1980s the program, after some initial success, had stagnated. The military-cum-reform strategy also failed to defeat the rebels on the battlefield, despite more than $3 billion in U.S. military aid. The polarization of Salvadoran society forced political leaders to search for national reconciliation through international negotiations.

The deep divisions within Salvadoran society were rooted in the political formula that had allowed the country's coffee oligarchy and military to dominate the country's political, economic, and social life. Each time a military ruler was overthrown between the years of 1932 and 1979, and there was even a distant possibility of democratization, the oligarchy and conservative military officers were able to revive the formula of political domination and restore the system to its usual mode of operation.[26]

The root of the Salvadoran crisis lay in what was required to maintain this system of control. In order to remain competitive, achieve maximum profits, and survive periods of low export prices, the Salvadoran oligarchy relied on low agricultural wages. Furthermore, as Enrique Baloyra pointed out, the oligarchy "was adamantly opposed to any attempt to change a very unequal system of land tenure, which enabled it to monopolize the profits of the export trade and to use these to control the financial sector as well."[27]

As the population density of this agricultural nation increased, and as the middle class became more prominent, pressure for basic economic and social reform mounted. The crisis became acute when the military used massive fraud and repression to deny the moderate Christian Democrats victory in the 1972 election. The Christian Democrats had become the largest political party in the country by advocating a program of wide-ranging agrarian and social reforms. The powerful "fourteen families" that made up the core of the Salvadoran oligarchy were unwilling to give up their privileged position. They urged the military to use violence against advocates of change. The privileged elites organized paramilitary death squads, made up of off-duty army and police officers, to repress and frustrate the efforts of civilians to change political and economic conditions.[28] These squads killed and terrorized anyone who opposed or criticized the political order, including peasant and labor unions, Christian Democrats, and even socially active religious workers. One motto of the death squads was "Be a patriot, kill a Jesuit." By the time of the Nicaraguan revolution this traditional political system was incapable of adapting to the profound social changes that were transforming Central America.

The triumph of the Sandinista revolution in June 1979 focused international attention on El Salvador. The deteriorating political situation in that country led many Latin American experts to conclude that El Salvador was destined to be "another Nicaragua." Viron Vaky, Carter's assistant secretary of state for inter-American affairs, told Congress that El Salvador was near insurrection, a view that was shared by a representative group of Salvadoran intellectuals.[29]

Given the revolutionary situation in El Salvador, it was not surprising that there was widespread relief when a group of progressive military officers overthrew the right wing regime of Gen. Humberto Romero on October 15, 1979. The young officers moved to replace the old political and economic order, fearing that unless fundamental reforms were initiated the Salvadoran military would be swept away by the same revolutionary forces that destroyed the Nicaraguan National Guard. The removal of Romero was viewed as the last opportunity to avoid civil war.

The United States reacted enthusiastically to the reformist military coup. The day after the coup, State Department spokesman Hodding Carter III gave an optimistic account of the coup, telling reporters that "the new leadership had appealed to both the left and the right to end violence, and had promised moderate and nonviolent solutions to the country's problems, including social and economic reforms and free elections."[30] The State Department concluded that the direction of the new government was "encouraging." El Salvador became a test case of the Carter administration's policy of supporting moderates while simultaneously opposing both the traditional right and the radical left.[31] This strategy of supporting the implementation of reforms while aiding the military's effort to crush the leftist guerrillas was further refined by the Reagan administration.

This military-cum-reform strategy ended in stalemate. After ten years and $3.6 billion in U.S. aid, the entire reform project in El Salvador remained in doubt. Politically, El Salvador was more polarized in 1987 than at any time since 1980; politically motivated violence was up sharply.[32] Economically, El Salvador was more dependent on U.S. aid than any sovereign nation had been since South Vietnam.[33] Militarily, the ten-year war against the Marxist guerrillas showed no sign of abating; an optimistic estimate by U.S. officials was that the conflict would drag on at least until 1994.[34] The intense political-military struggle was the motivating factor for the country's participation in the Arias peace plan. Salvadorans realized that the country's problems could only be resolved through an international solution.

The failure of the military–Christian Democratic alliance to end the civil war was the principal factor that led to Salvadoran participation in the Central American peace process. Although the Salvadoran armed forces had taken the "tactical initiative," the conflict had remained locked in stalemate since 1985. A report prepared by four U.S. army officers concluded that "the Farabundo Martí National Liberation Front (FMLN) is tough, competent, highly motivated, and can sustain its current strategy indefinitely. The Salvadorans have yet to devise a persuasive strategy for winning the war."[35] Despite claims that the Salvadoran government was winning, "the war has settled into a fixed pattern."[36] Rebel attempts to seize power were frustrated, but government attempts to take the offensive had also failed. The continuing vitality of the Salvadoran rebels after ten years of war was demonstrated on November 11, 1989, when forces of the FMLN launched their largest offensive in the decade-long war, striking in the country's principal cities: San Salvador, Santa Anna, Usulatán, and Zacatecoluca.[37] The rebels also hit several important "psychological targets," including President Alfredo Cristiani's residence and the headquarters of the capital's elite First Brigade barracks. The rebel offensive, although failing to bring down the regime or igniting a popular uprising, illustrated that the Salvadoran civil war was no closer to termination than when hostilities began.

The armed forces also contributed to the polarization of Salvadoran society by refusing to surrender their central role in the country's governing apparatus. Although the Salvadoran military had failed to defeat the insurgency, they did manage to strengthen their institution with arms, money, and a high political profile. In fact, the military was the primary beneficiary of U.S. aid, which permitted it to expand from ten thousand troops in 1979 to sixty thousand in 1990. The army purchased sophisticated fighter aircraft, helicopters, and state-of-the-art weaponry, making it one of the richest and best-armed military forces in Central America.[38] Given their privileged position, the military proved unwilling to negotiate with those calling for radical reform. Instead, many Salvadoran military officers called for a "Guatemalan solution"—that is, an all-out war against the FMLN and its civilian supporters.

At the same time, the FMLN and its moderate supporters in the Democratic Revolutionary Front (FDR) were unlikely to give up armed struggle unless the structure of the military was radically transformed.[39] This point was made clear in the series of negotiations conducted by the guerrillas and Duarte. At the first meeting at La Palma, Duarte argued that the conditions were now ripe for the guerrillas to lay down their arms and compete for power as a political party. A month later at Ayagualo the guerrillas ridiculed Duarte's pretensions to democratic rule and demanded participation in a provisional government that would arrange new elections and reorganize the military. The talks broke down. In 1987 the two sides met again in San Salvador; their positions had changed little. The guerrillas demanded the expulsion of U.S. advisers, a territorial cease-fire, government reorganization to include rebel leaders, and new elections.[40]

Notwithstanding their intransigence, the guerrillas, who numbered ten or twelve thousand by 1983 and enjoyed considerable civilian support, were unable to seize power. The combined factors of U.S. aid and the military–middle class alliance had created a situation that proved exceptionally resistant to guerrilla insurgencies, even those with thousands of combatants.[41] Despite their failure to win the war, the FMLN still claimed to represent the vast majority of Salvadorans. Guerrilla leader Joaquín Villalobos wrote, "No doubt the FMLN is the political actor most in touch with the people, since its entire strategy has been deployed from the masses and toward the masses, with different degrees of quality and breadth."[42] Yet during the November offensive, the guerrillas failed to create a widespread insurrectionary response. According to one observer, by centering the more conventional military confrontation in the barrios, the FMLN left residents with only two options as the battle escalated, flee or fight. Given the level of bombardment, fighting would have required incredible heroism. The more varied, irregular, and limited kinds of collaboration available in the early days—building barricades, providing food and intelligence, using homemade weaponry—were no longer effective, and most residents chose to flee.[43]

External forces contributed to the military and political stalemate in El Salvador. U.S. aid to the Salvadoran military allowed the armed forces to resist serious negotiations with rebels.[44] To a lesser extent, foreign military aid to the rebels helped sustain the FMLN. Nicaraguan president Daniel Ortega admitted in 1987 that some arms for the FMLN were still passing through his country.[45] In November 1989 a Nicaraguan plane carrying antiaircraft missiles to the rebels crashed in El Salvador, creating a diplomatic crisis between the two states. U.S. intelligence reports indicated that Cuba supplied cash, explosives, and specialized training in sabotage and military organization. In fact, a former senior Sandinista official contended that the Rolex watch worn by FMLN leader Villalobos was a present from Fidel Castro.[46] Nonetheless, U.S. officials conceded that outside aid to the FMLN had declined. In its place the rebels developed an extensive cottage industry producing increasing quantities of not-so-primitive weapons.[47]

El Salvador, like Nicaragua, was forced to the bargaining table by economic disaster. The civil war forced the government to develop a war economy that functioned just above total collapse. Gross Domestic Product (GDP) fell 17 percent between 1979 and 1986, largely as a result of the sabotage of crops and economic installations, military expenditures to finance the war, and an overall decrease in investments. Total agricultural production dropped 18 percent from 1980 to 1987, and total manufacturing declined by 8 percent during the same period. Per capita income declined 38 percent compared to 1980 levels, and underemployment and unemployment climbed to 60 percent.[48] Only a regular infusion of U.S. aid enabled the Salvadoran economy to survive. The aid reached immense proportions by 1987 when, for the first time, the $608 million provided by the United States exceeded El Salvador's own national budget, coming to 105 percent of the $582 million budget.[49]

Given the polarization of Salvadoran society, the military and political stalemate, and the sharp economic downturn, the civil war clearly remained the central political, economic, and social reality in the country. Both the guerrillas and the military could avoid losing the war, but neither could win it. But the obstinacy of the right and the extremism of the FMLN prevented a quick settlement of the dispute. Complicating the situation was the outside aid received by both sides, which allowed them to resupply and maintain their intransigent positions. To resolve its internal conflict the Salvadoran leadership was forced to resort to international negotiations. The Central American peace process offered the only viable option for national reconciliation.

Honduras

The violation of Honduran sovereignty symbolized throughout the 1980s by the Nicaraguan contras' occupation of large sections of the southern half of the country led Honduras to the negotiating table. Thoughtful Hondurans worried that their country had become nothing more than an "unsinkable aircraft carrier" for North American interests, and they feared that their military had sold the national interest in exchange for U.S. military assistance.[50] Others feared that the country's international reputation was damaged by its close association with Reagan's foreign policy and the contras.[51] Honduras participated in the Central American peace plan as the most practical way to regain national sovereignty and dignity.

Honduran foreign policy can only be understood in the context of the interaction between the interests of the Honduran armed forces and U.S. objectives in Central America. The central objective of U.S. policy in Honduras was to establish a base of operation for the Nicaraguan contras. The contras needed a safe haven from which to launch their attacks against the Sandinistas, and Honduras was willing to serve as such a base for a price. The armed forces under Gen. Alvarez Martínez were willing to give the contras control of large tracts of national territory in exchange for U.S. security assistance. In fact, General Alvarez played a crucial role in selling the Reagan administration on the viability of the contra project.[52] The Honduran military used the Nicaraguan conflict to establish a "special relationship" with the Reagan administration. This arrangement assured that the military received the lion's share of the benefits accrued as a result of the country's cooperation with U.S. Central American policy.

The de facto alliance between the Reagan administration and the Honduran military would have serious consequences for both nations. The Iran-Contra scandal originated from these secret operations, but the repercussions for Honduras of becoming a pawn of U.S. policy in Central America were far more serious. The "special relationship" between the Honduran armed forces and the United States tilted the balance of power within the country in favor of the military at the very moment when Honduras was making the delicate transition toward democracy. General Alvarez, as architect of this policy, achieved unrivaled political power in a country where the military had always held a privileged position. This concentration of power endangered the process of democratization begun in 1981.

The Nicaraguan revolution set the stage for reform in Honduras.[53] By 1978–79 the situation in Central America had begun to deteriorate. Honduras looked as if it could be an "island of stability" in a sea of turmoil.[54] U.S. policymakers sought to encourage mild reforms and elections to create alternatives to insurgency, but at the same time they wanted to strengthen Honduran military forces with aid and advisers to ensure that order would be maintained.[55] Honduras appeared to be a country where Carter's military-cum-reform strategy might work. Honduras, heretofore virtually ignored by Washington, began to acquire geographic significance among top-level policymakers.[56] Carter used diplomatic pressure and U.S. largesse to encourage those who backed elections, and the election timetable was maintained after the Reagan administration took office.[57] In 1980–81 relatively free and open elections (by Central American standards) were held, first to elect a constituent assembly and then to elect a new government.

But Honduras, despite its claims of being an "oasis of peace and tranquillity," was quickly drawn into the Central American quagmire.

Honduras's central geographic location on the isthmus made it a key player in regional politics. Never before in its contemporary history had its foreign policy and the perception of its national security acquired the importance that it did during the height of the Central American conflict. The United States realized that this small country bordering on both the Salvadoran and Nicaraguan civil wars was a vital strategic asset. Thus the United States quickly moved into Honduras to secure a base against both the leftist regime in Nicaragua and the Marxist guerrillas in El Salvador. By 1981 U.S. military and economic assistance began to arrive, bases were established, U.S. experts and advisers arrived by the planeload in Tegucigalpa, and the U.S. ambassador to Honduras became a virtual proconsul, openly interfering in the most delicate affairs of Honduran internal politics.

The United States found willing allies in Honduras because General Alvarez's interests dovetailed nicely not only with U.S. policy but also with the personal ambitions of President Suazo. Eager to defeat the National Party, which had been symbiotically close to the military, Suazo allied himself with then-Colonel Alvarez, head of the national police. Alvarez was an ambitious and important, but younger and lesser-known, figure in the military hierarchy. Alvarez's conditions for supporting Suazo were no post hoc investigations of military corruption, a veto over all cabinet appointments, dominance in foreign policy-making, and absolute autonomy over all matters pertaining to the military itself.[58] The alliance was a brilliant stroke in terms of breaking the traditional Nationalist-military alliance, but it would force Suazo to exchange the mildly antimilitary reformist traditions of the Liberal Party for the continued support of Alvarez and his military colleagues. Suazo may have manipulated Alvarez at first, but the deal eventually became the undoing of Suazo and the liberals. When Suazo took office in January 1982, as the country's first civilian president in a decade, he enjoyed immense popularity and legitimacy. But rather than promote the national interest with his electoral mandate, Suazo preferred to diminish and weaken democratic forces and organizations (including his own liberal party) for the apparent purpose of promoting his political monopoly.[59]

Suazo, Alvarez, and U.S. ambassador John Negroponte formed a troika that ruled Honduras during the next two years, guided by the personal ambitions of the two Hondurans and Reagan's Central American policy. Using and abusing the power of the presidency, Suazo ably protected U.S. interests in a neat quid pro quo. Honduran national security policy would be dominated by pro-United States concerns; in exchange, there would be little U.S. interference in the country's internal affairs.[60] With this arrangement Alvarez assured the total autonomy of the Honduran military and received substantial levels of U.S. military assistance. Many Hondurans believe that Alvarez's goal was to achieve the same level of U.S. military support as El Salvador had. During the general's official visit to Washington in June 1983, he made it known that the military needed "at least $400 million over a period no greater than three years."[61]

The special relationship between U.S. and Honduran security services that General Alvarez established caused great concern in civilian sectors. Many Hondurans worried that the relationship would jeopardize their country's traditional internal tranquility, endanger its security, compromise its sovereignty, and destroy Honduran democracy. Concern over these issues contributed to the downfall of Alvarez in March 1984 and eventually led Honduras to participate in the Central American peace process. Honduran civilian politicians used the peace process to regain control over security and foreign policy matters that Suazo had surrendered in his agreement with Alvarez.

First, the bases established in Honduras by the Nicaraguan contras caused a great deal of apprehension among civilians who saw the potential for a major internal security threat. Estimates vary, but the contras consisted of a fighting force with about twelve thousand soldiers, most of whom were based in Honduras throughout the conflict. Leading Hondurans became preoccupied with the domestic impact of the armed Nicaraguan resistance.[62] Many openly feared that the military would not be capable of controlling the contras.[63] The presence of the contras also invited Nicaraguan raids into Honduras. In March 1986 and again in March 1989 Sandinista troops crossed the border in hot pursuit of the contras. Thoughtful Hondurans feared that these raids might escalate into a Nicaraguan-Honduran war. At the highest level Hondurans maintained, especially after 1986 when the war started to go badly for the contras, that the United States should play a role in relocating the Nicaraguan resistance. Honduran anxiety increased during the waning days of the Reagan administration when Morris Busby, the president's special envoy, stated in Honduras that the contras were a "Honduran problem."[64]

The second matter for concern was the contras' occupation of large sections of Honduran territory. The contras established what was virtually a state within a state, with their own government, law, schools, hospitals, and military. Small Honduran coffee growers were driven out to make way for the contra infrastructure. Adding to the foreign presence was the evolution of a semipermanent U.S. military presence in Honduran territory. During the Reagan administration the United States moved aggressively to establish Honduras as a forward base of military operations in Central America. The establishment of an air base at Palmerola as well as other bases throughout the country gave the United States a unique staging ability, as well as alternatives to installations in Panama. The occupation of national territory by foreign forces was viewed by many Hondurans as an affront to national dignity. The internal frustration with the foreign military presence was reflected in a celebrated editorial in the opposition newspaper *Tiempo* titled "Everything, including honor, has been lost." In it the author lashed out against the regime's position of open submission to foreign exploitation in the country.

Civilians also worried that the relationship of the Honduran armed forces with the U.S. embassy might endanger democracy. There was widespread concern among politicians that the militarization of the country and the presence of foreign troops on Honduran territory greatly weakened the power of the civilian sector. Many feared that Honduras would became a national security state.[65] Critics of Honduran security policies pointed out that emphasis by the U.S. and Suazo administrations on security and the contras diminished the chances for democratization. U.S. policy emboldened the military in all aspects of its institutional life.[66] Nowhere was this better illustrated than in the issues of human rights.

Human rights activists charged that the Honduran military, with the "copious aid of the United States," conducted a "dirty war" against its opponents.[67] The military campaign against subversives was designed to prevent the upsurge of a strong revolutionary movement; its targets were those the security forces considered "potentially subversive." In particular, the repression aimed to break up the support networks that Salvadoran revolutionaries had successfully organized in Honduras.[68] Some 130 Hondurans "disappeared" as a result, and the government achieved the distinction of being the defendant in the first case brought before the Inter-American Court of Human Rights of the Organization of American States.[69] Although human rights violations decreased after the removal of General Alvarez, his successors failed to dismantle the security apparatus. Instead, repressive units such as Battalion 3/16 simply lowered their profile. International human rights groups still charged that "a steady succession of human right abuses indicated deepening political violence in Honduras and an erosion in respect for fundamental human rights."[70]

Third, many nationalists were outraged when Honduras signed a treaty of alliance with its traditional enemy, El Salvador. In 1969 the two nations fought a brief but bitter war over immigration and border disputes. The outbreak of the Salvadoran civil war and pressure from the United States caused the Honduran military to reevaluate its military doctrine. El Salvador was no longer the enemy, they maintained; the new danger to Honduran security was leftist revolutionary movements in Central America. A general peace treaty was signed between the two countries in 1980.

The General Peace and Limits Treaty was viewed as an informal alliance between the two neighbors to quell the Salvadoran insurgents.[71] The Honduran military began cooperating with the Salvadoran military in a counterinsurgency campaign along the common border. Honduras also became an important staging area for U.S. surveillance of guerrillas in El Salvador.[72] But the most controversial aspect of the Honduran-Salvadoran alliance was the training of Salvadoran troops in Honduras. The insecurity in El Salvador, and the high cost of training in the United States, led the United States to train Salvadorans at the Regional Center for Military Training (CREM).

Many Hondurans saw the training of those they still considered their enemies as a betrayal of Honduran national interest for the sake of U.S. policy. As one critic sarcastically pointed out, "The army that invaded Honduras in 1969 returned to our country this time as the guest of General Alvarez and Suazo Córdoba."[73] Although Salvadoran officers were banned from CREM after the fall of Alvarez, the two neighbors continued to cooperate in the war against the Salvadoran rebels. Gen. Paul Gorman, former chief of staff of the United States Southern Command, observed: "Honduras has been induced to show extraordinary generosity toward its old enemy, El Salvador, training Salvadoran troops in Honduras and patrolling its border areas where Salvadoran insurgents have their sanctuaries."[74]

Meanwhile, the anticipated "shower of dollars" did not come. The fear that Honduran national interest was sold to U.S. security interests in the region was enhanced by growing Honduran frustration over the United States' reluctance to provide higher levels of military and economic aid.[75] The progovernment Honduran Confederation of Workers (CTH) complained before the Kissinger Commission that "Honduras shows signs of true friendship, and in response we only receive from the United States a cool indifference towards our economic and social problems."[76]

President Suazo Córdoba practically demanded that the Reagan administration donate approximately $400 million to help with the country's urgent economic problems, emphasizing the political risks that Honduras had assumed in helping to implement U.S. strategy at a "minimal cost to the United States."[77]

The Central American peace process was viewed by many Hondurans as the best method for solving the perplexing array of problems caused by the crisis. The Arias plan offered a face-saving formula to dispose of the contra problem while reducing the threat to the Honduran social order presented by the Sandinistas and the Salvadoran guerrillas. The peace process also offered a convenient mechanism to reduce the influence of U.S. and Honduran security forces in the nation's decision-making process.

Guatemala

The Central American crisis also spilled over into the Guatemalan polity. After the Sandinista victory in Nicaragua and the outbreak of civil war in El Salvador, Guatemala erupted into what many observers described as the "dirtiest war" in Central America.[78] The well-trained Guatemalan army embarked in the summer of 1982 on an infamous counterinsurgency campaign that culminated in extensive massacres, scorched-earth programs, and population displacement, all designed to prevent the Mayan Indians of Guatemala from rebelling.

By the end of 1982 the bloody campaign had succeeded in preventing the Indian population from joining the guerrillas, but in the process the country had become an international pariah.[79] Pressure from the United States and Western Europe forced the Guatemalan military to relinquish power in 1986, as the country initiated a new experiment in democracy. Guatemalan participation in the peace process was viewed by the civilian government as the best method for strengthening the nation's democratic institutions. Civilians hoped that implementation of the peace plan would break the military's lock on power. The military accepted the peace plan as a necessary ploy for ending Guatemala's international isolation. At the same time the army made sure that the peace process did not affect the balance of power between the armed forces and the civilian sector within the Guatemalan society.

Guatemala's foreign policy can only be understood in the context of the hegemony of the armed forces. The Guatemalan military, which has ruled the country directly or indirectly since the fall of Jacobo Arbenz in 1954, responded to the Central American crisis with a program of massive repression. This counterinsurgency campaign was directed by Gen. Efraín Ríos-Montt, who came to power through a coup d'état on March 23, 1982. The military coup that brought Ríos-Montt to power was the culmination of simmering discontent across a broad spectrum of Guatemalan society. The ruling elite felt that the corrupt dictatorship of Romero Lucas-García was incapable of rising to the challenge posed by the Nicaraguan revolution and the Salvadoran civil war. Lucas-García unleashed the death squads against the advocates of reforms in Guatemala, but he lacked a long-term strategy for dealing with the incipient revolution. Military officers felt a stronger hand was needed.[80]

Ríos-Montt, a self-proclaimed born-again Christian, advocated a doctrine of total war against subversion. According to this doctrine, when the security situation had slipped so badly that the army could no longer see a distinction between the guerrillas and their supporters, then both combatants and civilians were to be treated the same. Consequently, the Guatemalan army began a campaign to wipe out not only the rebels but their Indian supporters as well.[81] When asked about army killings of unarmed civilians, Ríos-Montt replied, "Look, the problem of the war is not just a question of who is shooting. For each one shooting there are ten working behind him."[82] Ríos-Montt clarified his position further: "We have no scorched-earth policy," he said. "We have a policy of scorched communists."[83] Ríos-Montt's press secretary, Francisco Bianchi, justified the repression in the following terms: "The guerrillas won over many Indian collaborators, so therefore the Indians were subversives. And how do you fight subversion? Clearly, you have to kill the Indians, because they were collaborating with subversion. People would say, 'You are massacring innocent people,' but they weren't innocent. They had sold out to subversion."[84]

Towns and villages believed to be sympathetic to the revolution were erased from the map. More than 440 villages were burned to the ground; 100,000 to 150,000 civilians, mainly highland Indians, were killed or "disappeared," leading to charges of genocide.[85] The human rights report *Americas Watch* gave this description of the horrors of the Guatemalan war: "The Army does not waste bullets on women and children. We were repeatedly told of women being raped before being killed, and of children being picked up by the feet and having their heads smashed against the wall, choked to death or killed with machetes and bayonets."[86]

The violence of Plan Victoria 82, as the counterinsurgency campaign was called, was due partly to the fact that the Guatemalan military was not constrained by U.S. assistance and could, therefore, act with impunity. In 1977 the Carter administration attempted to pressure Guatemala to improve human rights conditions by threatening to cut off military aid. The Guatemalan armed forces reacted angrily to Washington's demand. They renounced "for the sake of national dignity" all military assistance from the United States, claiming that U.S. criticism of human rights was an infringement on Guatemala's sovereignty.[87] This freed the Guatemalan military from the U.S.-imposed constraints that forced the Salvadoran military to run a "clean" counterinsurgency program in which civilians were no longer systematically eliminated. In sharp contrast to El Salvador, the Guatemalan military was able to attack not only the guerrillas but their support network within the country.

Plan Victoria 82 was a big success. The unprecedented violence almost completely destroyed the Guatemalan guerrillas, but more importantly the use of state terror dissuaded the Mayans from aiding the rebels. The destruction of the guerrillas' social base guaranteed the end of large-scale revolutionary activity in Guatemala. However, the level of violence shocked the world, and the Reagan administration, while supporting the Ríos-Montt regime, was prevented from providing aid by congressional concerns over human rights abuses. Guatemala found itself almost completely isolated by the beginning of 1983.

At the same time, the country desperately needed economic aid.

Until the late 1970s Guatemala had a stable and growing economy. In 1970 the gross national product was $4.2 billion; by the end of 1979, it had grown 67 percent to $7 billion. Per capita income was $356 in 1970; by 1980, it stood at $1,022, an increase of 187 percent. The relative soundness of the economy was demonstrated by the fact that Guatemala had Latin America's second lowest foreign debt.[88] Then the military governments of Lucas-García and Ríos-Montt went on a spending spree. The central bank borrowed heavily and the national debt rose from $820 million to $2.4 billion.[89] To make matters worse, these new loans were contracted with a short-term maturity and a high interest rate. Consequently, by the mid-1980s Guatemala paid back in principle and interest $504 million, an amount equivalent to about 40 percent of the total value of exports—a crushing burden.[90]

The debt service burden led to a contraction of the Guatemalan economy. Between 1980 and 1985 the gross domestic product declined 6.2 percent, a figure that translates into an 18.5 percent decline in per capita GDP. In the first five years of the decade, half the growth of the previous decade had been lost, and GDP per capita was at the level of 1971.[91] According to Guatemala's Secretariat of Economic Planning, outright unemployment rose from about 2.2 percent in 1980 to 10.5 percent in 1984. Underemployment also increased dramatically. By 1985 it was estimated that 43 percent of the economically active population—that is, one million people—were either unemployed (10.5 percent) or underemployed (32.9 percent).[92]

To deal with the crushing effects of the external debt the military government reportedly began printing quetzals and using them to buy dollars on the black market as a way to pay for its oil imports and service the debt.[93] This in turn fed inflation, which in 1985 rose to 40 percent.[94] In November 1984 after several decades of parity with the U.S. dollar, the national currency was formally depreciated and a parallel dollar market was established. In less than a year, the value of the quetzal fell 400 percent to Q4 for $1.

The economic crisis created pressure on the military to enhance its image in order to make Guatemala eligible for international assistance. Ríos-Montt became a victim of his own success: without a viable insurgency, the Guatemalan military felt that the country could afford to improve human rights conditions. In August 1983 Ríos-Montt was overthrown in a coup d'état led by his defense minister, Gen. Oscar

Humberto Mejía. Mejía moved immediately to improve Guatemala's international reputation. First, he reduced the rate of death squad activities. Under Ríos-Montt, officially tolerated killings were claiming 350 victims a month; under the new military regime the rate was reduced to 50 to 60 a month.[95] The new president also announced a timetable for a democratic transition. Elections for a Constitutional Assembly took place in July 1984, followed by presidential elections a year later.

The Guatemalan military acquiesced to the elections not from a position of weakness but from a position of strength. The victory in the counterinsurgency campaign gave the army effective control of the countryside. By 1985 the military was in a more powerful position in relation to the other political actors in Guatemala than it had ever been. Formal political power was not necessary nor probably desirable in maintaining that dominance.[96] As one analyst pointed out, "In many ways the elections were the most rational way for the military to retain its power."[97] The military needed the elections for several practical reasons: to overcome the international isolation that Guatemala had incurred during its many years as the region's worst human rights violator, to regain public sector confidence and reactivate the economy, and to establish internal stability and legitimacy.[98]

Speaking at Vinicio Cerezo's inauguration, General Mejía made clear the dominant role the military continued to play in Guatemalan politics. The general warned that the military was passing elected office to the Christian Democrats on probation; unspoken but completely understood limits were passing along as well. Any serious tampering with the military's uncontested control of rural Guatemala would clearly exceed those limits.[99]

To remain in office and survive several attempted coups against Cerezo, the Christian Democrats were forced to cede most of the authority associated with governance. Most of the military's demands were met: no talk of land reform, no meaningful dialogue with the guerrillas, no new relations with socialist countries, and no attempt to limit the activities of the right wing terrorists in or out of the security forces.[100] In fact, Cerezo went out of his way to identify himself with the army's counterinsurgency campaign, going so far as to visit war zones in a military uniform.

Cerezo tried to demonstrate his authority by expanding on the military's policy of "active neutrality" in the U.S.-Nicaraguan conflict. Beginning in the early 1980s Guatemala took the lead among the Central American states in distancing itself from Washington's effort to overthrow the Sandinista government, an initiative motivated by the military's attempt to create a right wing nationalism in Guatemala. The centerpiece of this new nationalistic rhetoric was the argument that Central American states ought to defeat communism alone. After all, in 1982 the Guatemalan army defeated its insurgency without U.S. aid. Army officials even suggested that they did not need help from a defeated army (the United States in Vietnam), and that the training they received from the United States was flawed, as it prepared the armed forces to be an army of occupation rather than a national army.[101] Behind the scenes, however, the armed forces worked with the United States in the training and arming of the contras.

Cerezo attempted to build on this position of "active neutrality" by taking the lead along with Oscar Arias of Costa Rica in the Central American peace process. Cerezo invited the Central American presidents to the border town of Esquipulas in 1986 to discuss the creation of a Central American parliament. This discussion later set the stage for the Central American peace accords. Cerezo viewed the accords, especially their provisions for regionwide free and fair elections, national reconciliation, dialogue with the armed opposition, and respect for human rights, as a strategy for tipping the political balance away from the military and toward the civilian sector. Guatemalan participation in the peace process was similar to that of Honduras, motivated by a desire to reduce the military's influence in the political system.

The Regional Crisis

The Nicaraguan revolution set off a chain reaction that transformed the political balance throughout the region. The civil war in El Salvador, the democratic transition in Honduras, and the repression in Guatemala were not isolated events; they were parts of the same general crisis that racked Central America in the 1980s. The four isthmian states were responding to the same forces of revolution and counterrevolution. Moreover, the forces of revolution and reaction throughout the region were linked by an invisible web of interdependency and alliance.

On one side of the equation were the forces of revolutionary change, the Sandinistas in Nicaragua, who had close links with both the Salvadoran guerrillas (the FMLN) and the Guatemalan rebels. These movements in turn had an extensive network of supporters in Honduras. The left also had widespread popular support among students, workers, peasants, and progressive elements in the Roman Catholic church throughout Central America. Opposing revolutionary change were the military forces of Guatemala, Honduras, and El Salvador, and the contra rebels of Nicaragua, all of which were involved with various forms of counterinsurgency or low-intensity conflict directed toward the defeat of leftist guerrillas. The military forces were aided in this campaign by their traditional allies in the oligarchy, who were intent on keeping their established privileges.

The key to the equation lay with the middle class and its centrist political parties. These centrist groups, including the Liberal party in Honduras, the Christian Democrats in Guatemala and El Salvador, and the nonviolent opposition in Nicaragua, viewed the crisis as an opportunity to break the military-oligarchic alliance that had blocked democratic avenues of change and retarded the process of economic development. These groups offered the forces of reaction a compromise in the early 1980s. The democratic center would support the violent elimination of the guerrillas in exchange for a democratic transition—in other words, a new political formula in which the old military-oligarchic alliance would be replaced by an alliance of the military with the middle class.

The civilian sectors were ultimately shortchanged in this compromise. By and large, the military establishments were able to retain their hegemony over the political system. Efforts at meaningful economic and social reform (agrarian, banking, and educational) were frustrated. Moreover, the forces of the left were not defeated. In El Salvador, after ten years of war, the guerrillas fought to a stalemate. It was this failure of the military–middle class alliance throughout Central America that created the need for a new political formula. By the mid-1980s Central American moderates were calling for a broader solution to the regional crisis, which would guarantee the evolution of democratic institutions and respect for human rights. These desires led directly to the Central American peace process.

3 *The Failure of Intervention*

The Central American peace process was shaped in part by the failure of outside powers to impose their solutions on the region. By the winter of 1986 it was clear to most observers that both the Contadora peace plan and Reagan's Central American policy had failed. Neither of these policies took into account the complicated web of alliances and relationships that were at the very heart of the crisis. Instead, both Contadora and U.S. policy were designed to serve the narrow foreign policy goals of extraregional powers.

Motivated by the desire to restore U.S. hegemony in Central America, U.S. policymakers opposed any attempt to limit their exercise of power there. The United States consistently rejected any proposal that required the Reagan administration to stop arming the contras or that imposed constraints on U.S. military exercises. President Reagan hoped that the use of economic, military, and political power would lead to the destruction of the radical Sandinista regime in Nicaragua and the leftist rebels in El Salvador.

Similarly, the Contadora process was devised to serve the national interests of the four Latin American states (Colombia, Mexico, Panama, and Venezuela) that had initiated the peace effort. Specifically, Contadora sought to legitimize the Nicaraguan regime and prevent direct U.S. military intervention in Central America. The Contadora states aimed to carve out their own sphere of influence in the region by supporting revolutionary movements.[1] They reasoned that nationalist-leftist regimes in Central America would be more inclined to ally themselves with Mexico City and Caracas than with Havana or Moscow; hence, the revolutionary process would help to replace U.S. hegemony with new regional powers.[2]

U.S. and Latin American diplomacy were designed to promote outside influence over local interests in Central America, and both would have meant sacrificing the vital interests of important Central American groups. A U.S. solution would have resulted not only in the removal of the Sandinista regime in Nicaragua, but in the defeat, if not the total destruction, of all leftist forces throughout the isthmus. Similarly, a Latin solution not only would have legitimated the Sandinista regime, but might also have assured the victory of the guerrillas in El Salvador and Guatemala. This in turn might have obliged Honduras and Costa Rica to acknowledge geographic realities and align themselves with their neighbors' policies.[3]

Central Americans were able to frustrate these efforts to impose outside solutions. The Sandinistas defeated the U.S.-sponsored contras on the battlefield, while the Salvadoran guerrillas remained a viable military force despite more than $3 billion in U.S. military aid for that country. In the United States Reagan's Central American policy was severely weakened because it lacked congressional and public support, especially after the Iran-Contra affair. The Contadora process was also frustrated by local groups in Central America. Important regional actors accused the Contadora nations, especially Mexico, of being biased toward the left.[4] Moderate and conservative Central Americans resented the pro-Sandinista tendency of the Latin American states. Regional leaders complained that Contadora was more concerned with the threat of U.S. intervention than the threat posed by the Sandinista army or communist subversion.[5]

The failure of the United States' Central America policy and the collapse of the Contadora process created a diplomatic opening for the Central Americans. Regional leaders now had the opportunity to offer a solution that took into account Central American interests. Arias of Costa Rica used this opportunity to present a peace plan that included concessions for all important regional groups. Since the Arias peace plan grew out of the failure of foreign powers to impose their solutions on Central America, it will be useful to explore in detail the reasons foreign intervention failed, enabling Central America, in the words of President José Napoleón Duarte of El Salvador, "to issue its second declaration of independence."[6]

Reagan's Central American Policy

The goal of Reagan's Central American policy was to restore U.S. hegemony in the region. Revolutionary movements, because of their alleged ties with the Soviet bloc, were viewed as a direct threat to U.S. interests in the isthmus. Having attacked Jimmy Carter during the 1980 presidential campaign for losing Nicaragua, Reagan committed himself to correcting the mistakes of past administrations by following a Latin American policy designed to restore U.S. influence in Central America. In contrast to Carter's policy, the Reagan administration emphasized U.S. military power, U.S. security assistance, and support for pro-United States regimes regardless of their human rights records.[7] Consequently, U.S. diplomacy was designed to mobilize its economic, military, and political power against the Sandinista regime in Nicaragua and radical revolutionary movements in El Salvador and Guatemala.

The Reagan administration clearly rejected Carter's policy of accommodating U.S. interests to revolutionary change in Central America in favor of the traditional policy of installing and promoting pro-United States regimes. The defeat of the communist-led insurgents in El Salvador became the centerpiece of the Reagan administration's Central American policy, and the administration increased U.S. efforts to destabilize the left wing Sandinista government. To carry out this policy in El Salvador, the United States refused to negotiate with the Salvadoran rebels and spent more than $3 billion on military assistance to El Salvador, compared to only $10 million spent by the Carter administration.[8] The United States also signaled its willingness to resort to military force by conducting large-scale military exercises in the region and providing more than $300 million in aid to the contras.

Moreover, the administration viewed all efforts to negotiate an end to the crisis (Contadora, Manzanillo, and Sapoa) in the context of a public relations problem. High-ranking officials believed that Sandinista and Salvadoran rebel offers to negotiate were nothing more than a familiar communist tactic to appear to be flexible in order to divide international public opinion.[9] Constantine Menges articulated administration thinking on this matter when he argued that the Soviets were engaged in an undeclared war against the West. "The Soviet bloc," he said, "including Cuba, has always defined both peaceful coexistence and detente to include the continuation of the struggle between the two world systems by all means short of open military attack."[10] This view of negotiations as nothing more than a communist guise for defeating the West manifested itself in the administration's rejection of dialogue with the Salvadoran guerrillas.

Five days into their so-called final offensive, the leaders of El Salvador's political and guerrilla opposition movements indicated that they were willing to start direct negotiations with Washington to avoid further bloodshed. Guillermo Ungo, civilian head of the guerrilla opposition, told reporters "we are seriously interested in talks with the United States to find a political settlement. We are saying this to the Carter and the Reagan administrations. If we wait for a military victory, the extermination of the people will be so much greater."[11] The guerrillas' military defeat in the final offensive resulted in a willingness to negotiate. Many observers urged Reagan to do so, seeing in the guerrilla failure a unique opportunity to pursue a peaceful solution to the conflict. They maintained that the final offensive had convinced the rebels and their foreign supporters that a negotiated solution was preferable to continued conflict. Former Carter officials such as Robert White, the ambassador to El Salvador, pointed out that Ungo's offer to negotiate might result in a split in opposition forces between the democratic left in the FDR (Democratic Revolutionary Front), headed by Ungo, and the Marxist guerrillas in the FMLN (Farabundo Martí Front for National Liberation).

Mexico supported White's position and offered to help Reagan open a direct line of communication with the Salvadoran rebels. According to Mexican officials, just after Reagan's first inauguration, then-National Security Adviser Richard Allen and Director of the Central Intelligence Agency William Casey agreed to a Mexican request to hold secret talks in Washington with rebel leaders.[12] But this arrangement was vetoed by Secretary of State Alexander Haig. He told the Mexican ambassador, "No longer would Washington deal secretly with insurgents, who were attempting to overthrow a legal government in the Western Hemisphere . . . Moreover, in the next four years, the Americas would see a determined United States effort to stamp out Cuban supported subversion, the days of Cuban terrorism in the Americas are over."[13]

In rebuffing the Salvadoran guerrillas' call for direct negotiations, the Reagan administration underscored its belief that the conflict between U.S. interests and Marxist-Leninist groups was not resolvable. This view was expressed by Néstor Sánchez, Reagan's deputy assistant secretary of defense: "In a long, violent, frustrating confrontation such as that in El Salvador, appeals for dialogue and accommodation have a strong attraction. Consequently, the guerrillas in El Salvador and their political leadership—even as they carry on a bloody war—have scored heavily on the public relations front by calling for negotiations. . . . A glance at history, however, shows that once their foot is in the door, communists inevitably consolidate power rather than apportion it. The Salvadoran Marxists would be no more likely to break this pattern than were their counterparts in Nicaragua."[14]

Given their view that negotiating with Marxists was useless, Reagan administration officials also proved unwilling to negotiate their differences with the Sandinista regime. The United States had three broad complaints against the Nicaraguan government: its alleged involvement in supplying military equipment to rebels in El Salvador, its militarization of Nicaragua, and the destruction of political pluralism. The Reagan administration, because it viewed Nicaraguan policy as a function of the effort to win in El Salvador, at first indicated some willingness to negotiate. The litmus test of Nicaraguan good behavior would be their restraint in supporting the Salvadoran rebels. The State Department had accused the Sandinistas of providing the staging sites for a massive Cuban-directed flow of arms for Salvadoran and Guatemalan rebels.[15] According to administration sources, from October 1980 until February 1981 several hundred tons of military equipment entered El Salvador via Nicaragua. Reagan made one of his top priorities the ending of this conduit for arms. Haig told reporters: "Our most important objective is to stop the large flow of arms through Nicaragua into El Salvador. We consider what is happening as part of the global communist campaign coordinated by Havana and Moscow to support the Marxist guerrillas in El Salvador."[16] Although Sandinista officials denied these allegations, they did concede that arms could have been smuggled from Nicaragua to leftist guerrillas in El Salvador without the knowledge of the government.[17]

U.S. Ambassador to Nicaragua Lawrence Pezzullo and Assistant Secretary of State Thomas O. Enders advocated a two-track diplomatic strategy for dealing with the Sandinistas. This strategy involved applying pressure on both Nicaraguan and Salvadoran Marxists, while at the same time negotiating with the Sandinistas to convince them to stop supplying the Salvadoran rebels and to halt their arms buildup. In return for Nicaraguan cooperation on these issues, the United States would offer economic aid and trade.[18] Though the Sandinistas responded positively to Pezzullo's effort by reducing their aid to the FDR-FMLN, hard-liners within the Reagan administration were determined to win Nicaragua's acquiescence not with the carrot of economic aid but with the stick of military action.[19] On April 1, 1981, all U.S. economic aid to Nicaragua was cut off.

Enders was able to get the president's approval, however, on a last-ditch effort to patch up differences with the Nicaraguan government. Flying to Managua in August 1981, the assistant secretary began the first of five meetings with Sandinista officials that would last until October. Pezzullo described the meetings as "a blunt exchange of views"; other U.S. diplomats said that Enders's tone was accusatory and threatening.[20] Enders made it clear that if relations were to improve, the Sandinistas had to terminate their logistical support for the Salvadoran rebels. This was the sine que non of rapprochement; without this concession, nothing else was possible. Enders offered the Sandinistas a four-point proposal: (1) Nicaragua should slow or cease their own military buildup and reduce their armed forces to fifteen thousand men; (2) the United States would renew economic aid; (3) the United States would pledge not to interfere in Nicaragua's internal affairs; and (4) the United States and Nicaragua would expand cultural relations.[21] Despite Enders's tough talk, both sides were pleased with the contacts. Pezzullo thought a deal was within reach.

However, the Pezzullo and Enders initiative soon collapsed. Both governments were constrained by officials who used events to prove that the other side was untrustworthy.[22] Hard-liners in Washington argued that the Nicaraguans could not be trusted to stop supporting the Salvadoran guerrillas. They pointed to a speech by Humberto Ortega in which the Nicaraguan defense minister declared, "We are anti-Yankee, we are against the bourgeois. . . . Sandinismo without Marxist-Leninism cannot be revolutionary." Cold warriors also pointed to the dictatorial tactics of the Sandinistas. *La Prensa*, Managua's daily opposition newspaper, was closed down on three occasions in August 1981 and twice in October 1981. Four prominent businessmen who accused the Sandinistas of leading the country toward communism were arrested on October 21, 1981.[23]

At the same time, hard-liners in Managua complained about U.S. military exercises in Central America, the cancellation of aid, and the lack of action against exile groups that were organizing military operations against Nicaragua. Moreover, the Nicaraguans did not trust the United States to meet its commitments. The Río Treaty prohibited the United States from resorting to force or the threat of force in its relations with Nicaragua, and the United States Neutrality Act already prohibited exile training camps of the sort operating in Florida and California. If the United States was not living up to existing commitments, of what value was its pledge to abide by them in the future?[24]

Thus both sides found evidence to support the argument that the other government was not serious about negotiating. In the future, both sides would choose to strike postures rather than negotiate. No progress occurred in subsequent meetings between the United States and Nicaragua, including Alexander Haig's meetings with Cuban vice-president Carlos Rafael Rodríguez and Nicaraguan foreign minister Miguel d'Escoto.[25] Instead, the Reagan administration adopted a policy of destabilizing the Sandinista regime through economic, military, and diplomatic pressure—U.S. support for the anti-Sandinista contra guerrillas being the most visible aspect of Reagan's Central American policy. Not until three years later, in 1984, would the United States and Nicaragua resume high-level contact.

The Long, Sad History of Contadora

The Reagan administration's hard-line policy toward the Sandinista regime caused widespread concern among Latin American leaders. The Latins worried that as U.S. military presence and activities in the region escalated, so would the threat of war. Specifically, they feared that the Sandinistas would retaliate against the contras and draw Honduras and the United States into open armed conflict that might eventually spill over into the rest of Central America.[26] To offset U.S. policy the leaders of Latin America established the Contadora group. Named after a resort island off Panama, the group was formed in January 1983 by the foreign ministers of Colombia, Mexico, Panama, and Venezuela. Their aim was to draw up a treaty that would reduce tensions between Nicaragua and its neighbors. Created at the initiative of Colombian president Belisario Betancúr, the initiative was intended as a diplomatic alternative to U.S. policy.

By joining forces under the Contadora umbrella, the regional powers hoped to prevent the United States from militarizing the crisis.[27] They viewed Reagan's policy, which claimed that the Central American crisis was an integral part of the Soviet-American rivalry, as fatally flawed.[28] From the perspective of the Contadora states, the root cause of the region's troubles was internal (poverty, injustice, and repression) rather than external (Cuban-Soviet subversion). Their disregard of the Soviet threat was understandable given that the United States, not the Soviet Union, has traditionally been seen as the principal danger to the countries of the region.[29] Thus the Contadora states were united in their opposition to U.S. intervention in Central America.

At the root of the Contadora process was the Latin American desire to modify the traditional hegemonic role of the United States in the hemisphere. The Latin nations hoped to replace U.S. unilateral action in the Americas with collective action by regional powers.[30] The Latin Americans realized that to challenge U.S. hegemony in the isthmus they needed a left-leaning Central America. They could only challenge the United States' power by winning the political sympathies of the area's inhabitants and governments. And they would find this sympathy on the left, not the right, of the political spectrum. The Contadora states viewed Central American revolutionaries and nationalists as their allies against U.S. power. Moreover, subsequent U.S. warnings notwithstanding, the Latin American states realized that political, social, and economic conditions in their own countries were not conducive to the guerrilla struggles that characterized the Central American crisis. The Latin states felt they had nothing to fear and much to gain from Central American revolutions.

The Contadora states came into the process with a record of successful joint efforts against U.S. hegemony. In 1976 Omar Torrijos of Panama enlisted the support of Colombia, Mexico, and Venezuela, as well as Costa Rica, to generate Latin American support for the Panama Canal treaty. Three years later these same countries came together in an international effort to aid the Sandinistas in the overthrow of Anastasio Somoza. Arms and supplies were shipped to the FSLN through Panama and Costa Rica, while San José served as a logistical base for the war against Somoza. At the same time the Mexican embassy in Managua became a haven for Sandinista militants and leaders. Money, messages, people, and goods entered and left the embassy and traveled to and from Nicaragua on Mexican government aircraft.[31] When the new Sandinista regime flew from San José to Managua to assume power, it did so in the company of the foreign ministers of what later became the four Contadora states.

The role of the Latin American states intensified in Central America after the Nicaraguan revolution. Mexico and Venezuela signaled their intention to expand their influence when they agreed to provide oil to the region at below market prices.[32] But it was Mexico that moved aggressively to consolidate its position as a key actor in the Central American scene. In May 1981 it issued a joint declaration with France that recognized Salvadoran Marxist rebels as "a representative political force."[33] The Franco-Mexican statement also called for direct negotiations between the U.S.-backed regime and the left wing guerrillas of the FMLN-FDR, giving the Salvadoran rebels an international legitimacy and standing that they would never have achieved otherwise.[34]

While the Franco-Mexican declaration outraged most of the rest of the hemisphere, it was the escalating Nicaraguan–United States conflict that became the focus of Latin American diplomacy in Central America. The presidents of Mexico and Venezuela, concerned with the activities of the U.S.-sponsored contras, wrote Reagan on September 7, 1982, warning that the "grave situation" had the potential to lead to regionwide conflict and asking for "joint exploration" of ways to reduce tensions.[35] The United States did not reply to the plea for nearly a month. When the response finally arrived, it compounded the insult by ignoring the content of the Mexican-Venezuelan initiative and arguing instead that the solution to Central America's problems was "to achieve democratic pluralism within each nation."[36]

U.S. intransigence convinced regional leaders that it was time to search for an indigenous solution to a Latin American problem. Colombia's new president, Belisario Betancúr, took the initiative in advocating a regional mediation effort. A conservative who had once been a militant rightist, Betancúr made the mission of his four-year term in office the disarming of Colombia's leftist guerrillas and their integration into the political process.[37] The new president believed that such an undertaking would not be possible while Colombia maintained close ties with the United States. Betancúr distanced himself from Washington by pursuing a progressive foreign policy that included friendly relations with Cuba and Nicaragua. He hoped that good relations with these leftist regimes would discourage them from supporting Colombia's guerrillas and encourage the guerrillas to negotiate.[38] In pursuit of his new domestic and international policy, Betancúr was fortunate in enlisting the support of Colombian Nobel Prize laureate Gabriel García Márquez. Betancúr used the novelist's ties with Fidel Castro, the Sandinista directorate, President François Mitterrand of France, and Prime Minister Felipe González of Spain to enhance Colombia's international image. Betancúr used this newly won prominence to urge the Latin American states to take the lead in resolving the Central American crisis before the United States intervened unilaterally.

The meeting of the four foreign ministers (from Colombia, Mexico, Panama, and Venezuela) at the Panamanian island of Contadora began the Latin American effort to mediate the Central American conflict. The diplomats issued a declaration that "urgently appealed to the Central American countries to uphold dialogue and negotiations as a way of reducing tensions and laying the groundwork for a permanent climate of peaceful coexistence and mutual respect among nations."[39] The Contadora communiqué contained a veiled critique of Reagan's Central American policy. It concluded "that direct or indirect foreign interference or any factors that intensify Central America's conflict must be swiftly eliminated." In this regard, the four foreign ministers stressed that it would be highly undesirable for the region's conflicts to be interpreted in the context of the East-West confrontation.[40] (See appendix 1.)

Encouraged by a positive international reaction to their January call for peace negotiations in Central America, which included support from the nonaligned movement and the European Community, the Contadora group moved to draw the Central American states into the peace process. In April 1983 the foreign ministers of the Contadora states conferred with the governments of all five Central American republics, discussing how to begin the peace process and what issues would be negotiated. At first Nicaragua rejected a multilateral setting, calling instead for direct bilateral negotiations with Washington and offering to sign a nonaggression pact with Honduras. To end the stalemate, the Contadora partners invited the isthmian states to a meeting in Panama. But the Nicaraguan envoy refused to meet the others as a group, except over dinner. The only agreement reached was to meet again.[41]

The following month, after a tour of the region by Betancúr, the foreign ministers of the five Central American states agreed to meet again in Panama City. The main accomplishment of the talks was the setting of the agenda, which included political, security, economic, and social problems as well as the machinery to implement and verify compliance with the proposed treaty. The nine representatives also agreed to set up a permanent technical commission. In July the four Contadora presidents held a summit in Cancún calling for renewed efforts to continue the peace process. The Cancún Declaration was designed to obtain Nicaragua's participation in the peace process. It called for the nations of Central America to sign ten binding treaty commitments, among them pledges to end hostilities, freeze weapons levels, eliminate foreign advisers, prohibit bases, and negotiate arms reductions.[42] But the plan failed to deal directly with either democratization or verification.

The Cancún declaration was viewed by many critics of Contadora as one-sided, and it confirmed their suspicion that the Latin American states had a pro-Sandinista bias. The Nicaraguans reacted enthusiastically to the declaration, and the Sandinista directorate quickly welcomed the "positive proposals" from Cancún as a "great step forward," announcing they would take part in multilateral negotiations.[43] They also proposed their own six-point plan focused exclusively on security issues and clearly aimed at expelling the U.S. military presence from the region and ending the contra program. The Nicaraguan proposal called for an end to all outside assistance to the two sides in El Salvador and to paramilitary forces in the region; prohibited foreign military bases and exercises; called for a Nicaraguan-Honduran nonaggression pact; promised noninterference in the internal affairs of other Central American countries; and urged an end to economic discrimination.[44]

The United States and its Central American allies, while supporting the "important contribution" of the Cancún Declaration, called for important modifications to the plan. The Reagan administration insisted that any peace process should include provisions pertaining to democracy and verification. The United States told the Contadora states that "only by ensuring free and open participation in the democratic process can the people of Central America achieve reconciliation within their societies."[45]

The other Central American republics shared the view that the

Cancún Declaration had left too much out. Honduras drew up an alternative plan called the Basis for Peace in Central America and won the backing of Guatemala, El Salvador, and Costa Rica. The Honduran proposal addressed U.S. objections to topics missing from the Cancún Communiqué: democracy, internal reconciliation, and verification. The eight points of the peace plan centered on the principle that only democratization could lead to peace and stability in the region.

Faced with a united Central American and U.S. position, the Contadora states were forced to put democratization back on the agenda. At the fourth Contadora ministerial meeting in Panama City, the final document called on the Central American states "to adopt measures conducive to the establishment . . . of democratic, representative, and pluralistic systems that will guarantee effective popular participation in the decision-making process and ensure that the various currents of opinion have free access to fair and regular elections based on the full observance of citizen rights."[46] The provisions on democratization were part of the Document of Objectives adopted by the four Contadora states. Commonly known as Contadora's twenty-one points, this document consolidated the demands of the United States, the Sandinistas, the Nicaraguan opposition, and the other Central American states. The document also called for a halt to the region's arms race, prohibited foreign military interference, bases, and advisers, and called for national reconciliation. These guidelines for a final Central American peace plan concluded with a proposal for continued negotiations to work out the agreements and mechanisms required to implement these objectives and to assure adequate systems of verification and control (see appendix 2). During the remainder of 1983 the Contadora group met repeatedly in a futile attempt to translate the Document of Objectives into a final regional peace treaty.

The peace process was overshadowed, however, by escalating tensions throughout the Caribbean basin. Less than two months after the agreement on the twenty-one points, the United States invaded the island of Grenada. Quick success and broad public support for the invasion led many observers to speculate that the Reagan administration might be emboldened to undertake a similar military intervention in Nicaragua. Equally disconcerting was Reagan's claim that the Grenada invasion was justified because the island had been transformed into a Cuban-Soviet bastion that threatened the security of its neighbors, exactly the accusation that the Reagan administration had been making for nearly two years against Nicaragua.[47] U.S. efforts to reactivate the moribund Central American Defense Council (CONDECA) in late 1984 added fuel to such suspicions, for they appeared designed to elicit an invitation similar to the one issued by the Organization of Eastern Caribbean States (OECS) in the Grenadian case.[48]

Tensions between Nicaragua and the United States continued to deteriorate in 1984, the peak of contra activity. That spring the contras conducted a series of highly visible military operations, the most publicized being the mining of the Nicaraguan harbors. Nicaragua appealed to the United Nations Security Council, charging the United States with responsibility for the mining, even though the contras had claimed credit for it.[49]

At the same time that U.S.-Nicaraguan relations were at their lowest point, the Contadora process reached an impasse. At the April 30–May 1, 1984, ministerial meeting, there was an open break between the Sandinistas and the other Central American countries. Costa Rica, El Salvador, and Honduras challenged Nicaragua to match them in agreeing to disclose military information, including sensitive matters concerning troop strength, major weapons systems, military agreements, arms deliveries from third countries, and the number of foreign military advisers. The three countries also called on Nicaragua to reduce the size of its armed forces and to eliminate trafficking in arms and the "exportation of subversion" to antigovernment guerrillas.[50] Nicaragua rejected this proposal, arguing that it could not reduce its armed forces as long as it faced U.S.-sponsored guerrillas. Afterward the Reagan administration blasted the Sandinistas for rejecting a "concrete initiative" for peace and accused them of "public relations grand-standing" in their claim to support the Contadora process.[51] Moreover, in April 1984 the U.S. Senate approved the administration's request for $21 million in aid to the contras.

The Contadora peace process was saved at this point by the stunning revelation that the CIA had been directly involved in the mining of the Nicaraguan harbors. The disclosure that the CIA was responsible for the mining led to a storm of domestic and international protest. The U.S. Congress, outraged by the administration's actions, rejected a request for $21 million in additional aid for the contras. The House refused to approve the contra aid request, and many Republican senators joined with the Democrat-controlled House in criticizing the mining operations and calling on the administration to give more than lip service to negotiations.[52]

The Republican leadership in the Senate made no effort to defend the administration, and Majority Leader Howard Baker joined forty-one Republicans on April 10, 1984, in an eight-four to twelve vote to condemn the mining.[53] Even conservative senator Barry Goldwater publicly criticized the administration and the CIA for not informing the Senate of the mining operation. In a stinging speech on the Senate floor he said "it is indefensible on the part of the administration to ask us to back its foreign policy when we don't even know what is going on because we were not briefed pursuant to the legal requirement."[54]

The mining of the harbors also led to international criticism of Reagan's policy. The action confirmed the view of Contadora countries that U.S. intransigence was the main obstacle to a peace settlement. In May 1984 following the furor in Washington over the mining, former Venezuelan president Carlos Andres Pérez complained that State Department officials "speak of support" for Contadora "but when we dig a little deeper, we find that they do not really believe in Contadora." Pérez quoted U.S. officials as saying that "Nicaragua is a communist regime and Nicaragua is not going to comply with the agreements of Contadora."[55] Additional pressure was applied by Mexican president Miguel de la Madrid during his May visit to Washington, when he appealed to Reagan to enter into bilateral talks with Managua. Mexico began its public campaign against the Reagan administration and its Central American allies on the eve of de la Madrid's visit to Washington, when a "senior Mexican official" blasted Costa Rica, Honduras, and El Salvador for trying to sabotage the Contadora process.[56] The Mexican president himself engaged in a thinly veiled criticism of Reagan's Central American policy when he addressed a joint session of Congress. He said that the Contadora states "reject, without exception, all military plans that would seriously endanger the security and development of the region."[57]

De la Madrid also lamented the absence of bilateral negotiations between Nicaragua and the United States, noting that the Sandinistas had repeatedly indicated their interest in such a dialogue. He called the mining of Nicaraguan harbors "gravely damaging" to the regional peace process and criticized the other Central American nations for their "lack of political will" in not agreeing to the Contadora proposal.[58] This statement lent credence to the argument of Reagan's congressional critics that his administration had, in the words of Sen. Edward Kennedy, "only paid it [Contadora] lip service, while pursuing actions that the Contadora group members have criticized for harming their efforts."[59]

The outcome of de la Madrid's visit was a quid pro quo between Mexico and the United States, in which both sides agreed to new initiatives in Central America.[60] Mexico agreed to upgrade its relations with El Salvador, where Christian Democrat José Napoleón Duarte had just won the presidential election. In return, Washington agreed to open talks with Nicaragua. U.S. Secretary of State George Shultz used the occasion of José Napoleón Duarte's inauguration in El Salvador to make a surprise visit to Managua. Shultz reaffirmed in his talks with Daniel Ortega the four points of U.S. concerns: "The United States wanted Nicaragua to reduce its military forces, sever its military and security ties with the Soviet Union and Cuba, end its support for Salvadoran guerrillas, and permit democratic pluralism to flourish at home."[61] Ortega responded that Nicaragua's internal affairs were not subjects for negotiations. Despite the deadlock, both sides agreed to hold further discussions. Shultz described the two-and-a-half-hour meeting as frank, without acrimony or excessive rhetoric, and concluded that "we are proceeding on the premise that a negotiated settlement is possible and that practical reason exists on all sides to reach an agreement."[62]

During the summer and fall of 1984, U.S.-Nicaraguan negotiations at Manzanillo progressed steadily, moving from procedural to substantive matters. The Sandinistas were willing to make a number of concessions on security issues in order to forestall U.S. support for the contras, but they refused to discuss Nicaragua's internal problems. During eight rounds of negotiations, the Nicaraguans agreed in principle to send home their Cuban advisers, refrain from supporting guerrilla movements in neighboring countries, and prohibit the installation of foreign bases on their territory.[63]

The talks stalled on the issues of internal reconciliation and democratization. The Sandinistas rejected the U.S. proposal on Central American democratization, because the Reagan administration placed primary emphasis on political reform within revolutionary Nicaragua.

The Nicaraguan representative at the talks made it clear that "we were not in a position to accept the involvement of the United States government in our internal matters."[64] They added that there was no need to discuss democratization because Nicaragua already had a pluralistic political system. The Sandinistas also claimed that internal reconciliation between the government and unarmed opposition groups was already occurring, but that the FSLN would never talk with the contras, who were traitors. However, both sides continued to indicate satisfaction with the talks.

Any momentum created during the bilateral talks between Washington and Managua was interrupted when the Contadora nations circulated a proposed peace treaty to the Central American nations and the Sandinistas unexpectedly agreed to sign it. This decision allowed both sides to return to striking postures rather than engaging in serious negotiations. The Sandinista representatives at the talks adopted the draft as their final position, arguing that "any substantive change would upset the delicate balance."[65] The United States objected to the September draft, pointing out that the Contadora treaty was vague on the important issues of security and verification. Security elements that would affect the United States—its military presence and maneuvers—would be subject to removal on a fixed timetable, but those aspects affecting Nicaragua were left largely to subsequent negotiations. Verification procedures had no teeth.[66] The Nicaraguans, in mid-September 1984, accepted the Contadora draft and rejected the United States' Manzanillo proposal. The United States rejected the Contadora treaty and called on Nicaragua to accept its own proposal, which required the Sandinistas to make major concessions on the size of their armed forces, sever relations with the Soviet bloc, and reorganize Nicaraguan domestic politics. The deadlock over the colliding peace plans eventually led to the United States' walkout from the Manzanillo talks in January 1985.

The failure of the Manzanillo talks led many observers to conclude that the negotiations were nothing more than a Reagan administration public relations ploy to disarm critics of U.S. Central American policy. After all, the opening of negotiations with Nicaragua had various salutary effects for the administration. By responding to the direct request of the Mexican president, the United States repaired some of the damage done to its relations with Latin America; it also produced a change in

Mexican policy toward El Salvador. The administration, by appearing to be more reasonable, also repaired some of the political damage done in Congress by the mining of Nicaragua's harbors. Finally, the negotiations allowed Reagan to defuse the unpopularity of his Central American policy just as the 1984 presidential election was getting underway.[67]

The four Latin American states had rushed forward with the Contadora Act for Peace and Cooperation in Central America (see appendix 3) in anticipation of the 1984 U.S. presidential election. President Betancúr worked with Mexican foreign minister Bernardo Sepúlveda to make a concerted push in spring 1984 to conclude the Contadora process with a grand finale on the eve of the U.S. elections. Mexico was eager for the same result. "Clearly it had to be done before the elections, or the United States would be much tougher to deal with," said a top adviser to the Mexican foreign ministry.[68]

The Contadora strategy was to bring to bear in favor of the treaty as much international and U.S. public opinion as was possible before Reagan or his Central American allies could raise serious objections to the draft. The treaty required Nicaragua to expel all Soviet bloc military advisers, halt all arms imports, reduce its 60,000-member army, end all assistance to the Salvadoran guerrillas, begin a dialogue with internal opposition groups, and permit on-site inspections by Contadora's verification commission. In return, the treaty required the United States to cease support for the contras immediately, to end military maneuvers in the region within thirty days, to shut down all military installations in Central America, and to suspend military aid programs in Honduras and El Salvador (see appendix 3).

Official U.S. reaction to the revised draft was initially positive; Shultz called the treaty an important step forward. However, the United States argued that the treaty was only a draft document to be modified and rewritten in subsequent negotiations. U.S. officials were especially critical of the vagueness of the treaty's verification procedures, which failed to specify how the proposed Commission on Verification would be funded, how inspections would be conducted, and how violations would be punished.[69] The Contadora states responded that to conclude a binding, comprehensive, verifiable agreement in treaty form was impossible; it was preferable to produce a document expressing the intentions of the signatories as a basis to press for concrete changes.[70]

The United States also objected to provisions requiring termination of military assistance to El Salvador and Honduras before an arms limitation agreement with Nicaragua was in place.[71] U.S. officials noted that the treaty put the Salvadoran and Honduran governments on a par with the contra guerrillas and, if implemented, would force the suspension of all U.S. military assistance to the two governments. Reagan administration officials viewed the September 7, 1984, "revised draft agreement" as simply too one-sided in Nicaragua's favor. They pointed out that the draft included the Sandinistas' two principal objectives: an end to U.S. assistance for the contras and to the U.S. military presence in Central America.[72] In exchange the United States received only vague promises on its two main concerns: democratization and verification.

Adding to the administration's displeasure was the fact that U.S. officials were caught off guard on September 21, 1984, when Nicaragua unexpectedly announced it was prepared to sign the treaty. The Reagan administration had assumed Nicaragua would not sign the proposed agreement because of the Sandinistas' earlier objections, especially to the language on internal political conditions. The Nicaraguans stipulated that no further changes could be introduced to the revised draft and that the United States must sign a protocol promising to abide by the agreement and to halt support for the contras.[73] Daniel Ortega wrote the presidents of the four Contadora states asserting that "the agreement between the five Central American countries to guarantee peace and security in the region will be sufficient only if it is backed by a formal and binding commitment on the part of the government of the United States. Nicaragua considers it essential, for the achievement of the lofty objectives motivating the Contadora group, for the United States to sign the additional Protocol to the Act and, as a consequence, to cease immediately the acts of aggression against Nicaragua."[74] Ortega also rejected any changes in the treaty; he told the Contadora states that "Nicaragua deems it imperative not to introduce amendments or modifications. Their submission would give rise to interminable discussions, which would serve only to hamper the attainment of the peace which our people quite rightly are urgently demanding and requiring."[75]

Endorsing the document was a public relations coup for the Sandinistas. Nicaragua's more accommodating image assured the congressional defeat of Reagan's request for an additional $21 million in military aid for the contras. It also enhanced the climate for Nicaragua at the subsequent joint Contadora–European Economic Community meeting and strengthened pro-Sandinista sentiments in the United Nations prior to Ortega's speech before the General Assembly.[76] Moreover, the four Contadora states were openly critical of Reagan's position. The Mexicans expressed their irritation with Washington's sudden discovery of major flaws in a treaty process it had previously endorsed.[77] They rejected the U.S. contention that the Revised Act was only a draft document, pointing out that after eighteen months of intense negotiations "everyone had treated it as a final document from the beginning," including the U.S. State Department.[78]

Although the revised treaty provided a much-needed public relations boost for the Sandinistas and a short-lived revival of Contadora diplomacy, it ultimately led to the demise of the negotiating process.[79] The United States was able to block acceptance of the treaty with concerted diplomatic pressure on El Salvador, Honduras, and Costa Rica. On October 19 and 20 the foreign ministers of all the Central American states except Nicaragua met in Honduras to modify the September accord. (The Sandinistas were invited but declined to attend.) The Tegucigalpa draft clearly reflected Washington's previously voiced objections. It omitted the ban on U.S. military exercises, reduced the potential limitation on U.S. aid to El Salvador, and made the foreign ministers of the Central American states themselves the judges of alleged violations of the accord.[80] The Central American draft also called for an alteration in the provisions for limitations on arms and troop levels in the region, shifting from criteria based on the defensive requirements of each country to a formula of parity among all nations of the region.[81] This proposal was rejected by the Sandinistas, who claimed that Nicaragua, unlike its neighbors, might have to defend itself against the combined forces of the contras, Honduras, and potentially the United States.[82]

The Tegucigalpa accord tilted the process against Nicaragua in the same way that the Revised Treaty was tilted against the United States. The peace process stalled when the Sandinistas refused to accept any amendments or modifications to the Revised Treaty. A dispute between Nicaragua and Costa Rica over the issue of political asylum further complicated the peace process. In February 1985 Costa Rica, El

Salvador, and Honduras refused to attend any further Contadora meetings until the Sandinistas released a man arrested outside the Costa Rican embassy in Managua. The Nicaraguan citizen, who had sought asylum in the embassy in August 1983, was apprehended outside the embassy in December 1984 despite a promise of safe conduct from Nicaraguan authorities. Costa Rican officials refused to participate in further negotiations unless the individual was allowed to emigrate to Costa Rica. After a stalemate lasting several weeks negotiations finally resumed when Nicaragua agreed to release the prisoner to Costa Rica.

To revive the peace process the Contadora states decided they needed once again to increase pressure on the United States and its Central American allies. Latin American nations had grown increasingly frustrated by U.S. opposition and their consequent inability to broker an agreement. In an effort to counterbalance U.S. pressure, Argentina, Brazil, Peru, and Uruguay formed a Contadora support group (the Grupo de Apoyo) on July 28, 1985. Initially known as the Lima group, because its first meeting was held in the Peruvian capital during President Alán García's inauguration, it hoped to demonstrate Latin American solidarity with the Contadora effort. The establishment of the support group involved the major South American democracies in the peace process in Central America, thereby lending substantial diplomatic weight to the Contadora countries, especially in their dealings with Washington.[83]

On September 12, 1985, the Contadora group unveiled yet another revised treaty. This version devoted much greater attention to issues of implementation, verification, and enforcement. And, as the United States and its Central American allies demanded, it also backed away from outright prohibition of military maneuvers and settled instead for their "regulation." More importantly, the 1985 revised treaty eliminated the requirement for an immediate end to U.S. support for the contras.

The Sandinistas refused to sign the 1985 draft. This version was denounced by the Nicaraguan foreign minister Miguel d'Escoto as "something that defends totally the interests of the United States."[84] The biggest obstacle was Nicaragua's demand that no Contadora agreement be signed without the Reagan administration's pledge to abide by it. The Sandinistas insisted that any peace treaty must include a U.S. commitment to stop aiding the contras. Ortega wrote the presidents of the Contadora countries and those of the Grupo de Apoyo on November 11, 1985, calling on them to halt U.S. support to the contras: "The interventionist and aggressive policy of the United States government is playing the central role in the Central American crisis. Given this, it is not possible to find a solution to the prevailing conflicts unless the United States government agrees to serious and detailed commitments to halt its illegal conduct."[85] Given the deadlock, the Contadora nations accepted a suggestion made by Nicaragua to suspend negotiations for five months until after the election and inauguration of new presidents in Costa Rica, Honduras, and Guatemala. Many observers concluded that if Contadora was not already dead, it clearly suffered from a terminal illness.

Contadora enjoyed a brief revival in 1986 before its final demise in 1987. It exhibited renewed life after the eight Contadora and Grupo de Apoyo nations met jointly on January 11 and 12, 1986, in Caraballeda, Venezuela. The Caraballeda Declaration was a ringing endorsement of the Latin American peace process and expressed growing frustration with U.S. Central America policy. The eight foreign ministers concluded that the only way to salvage Contadora was to end U.S. aid to the contras. The Message of Caraballeda called for the "termination of external support for irregular forces operating in the region." The message also called for the end of U.S. military maneuvers in the region and directly encouraged "the reestablishment of dialogue between the governments of the United States and Nicaragua, in order to identify possible forms of agreements." It also stated that "a respectful negotiation, which will take into account the need for mutual and equitable concessions, is the condition necessary to reduce regional tension."[86]

The Message of Caraballeda was basically a reiteration of the September 1984 Revised Draft treaty. The declaration reaffirmed the Latin American commitment to peace negotiations and offered Contadora's help to promote new steps toward "national reconciliation." But it offered no new formulas, except to call for direct talks between the United States and the Sandinistas. The Caraballeda initiative quickly faltered on the issue of bilateral talks. The United States and its regional allies simply restated that bilateral talks were an FSLN device to avoid discussion on democratization and national reconciliation, which they insisted must be the centerpiece of the peace process. Nicaraguan foreign minister Miguel d'Escoto wrote an open letter calling on the Contadora ministers to pressure the Reagan administration for the renewal of U.S.-Nicaraguan negotiations. At the same time he made it clear that the United States would have to abandon the idea that such talks could be used as an "instrument to force Nicaragua into an immoral dialogue with terrorist forces [the contras]."[87] Shultz responded that the United States would resume bilateral negotiations only if the Sandinistas would engage in talks with the contras. Shultz, meeting with the Contadora and support group foreign ministers, proposed simultaneous U.S.-Nicaraguan/Sandinista-Contra talks. The Message of Caraballeda collapsed a little more than a month after its birth.

Nonetheless, on June 7, 1986, the Contadora nations produced yet another revised treaty. The third and final version attempted to bypass the thorny issues of U.S. military maneuvers, army size, and arms limitations by proposing that they be addressed within negotiations to be held after the signing of the treaty.[88] It did, however, include guidelines for negotiating these points. Inventories detailing existing weapons systems and troop levels were to be submitted to the Verification Commission according to a precise timetable. The commission was then to draw up recommendations for maximum limits based on a point system outlined in the treaty. By tying the banning of U.S. advisers, bases, and exercises to a final accord on army sizes, the agreement contained new incentives for Nicaragua, which immediately agreed to sign the new draft.[89]

But the vagueness of the 1986 draft made it unacceptable to the other Central American states. Costa Rica's representatives rejected it because it failed to address fully the question of democratization. They also announced that they would not sign an agreement before all the negotiations were concluded, including those concerning arms limits and troop levels. Costa Rica pointed out that the draft's criteria for establishing maximum limits on military size were extremely unclear and susceptible to subjective interpretations. The Salvadorans also rejected the draft, claiming it was vague and that it ignored important provisions of the 1983 Document of Objectives. They argued that any regional treaty must be in accordance with Contadora's twenty-one points, especially in terms of arms limits and troop levels. Honduras joined its neighbors in insisting that the treaty should establish clear and rigorous obligations regarding disarmament and regional arms control. The Hondurans also argued that the treaty provisions with regard to armaments, military forces, evaluation, verification, and control could be subjectively interpreted. Guatemala also refused to sign, agreeing with its regional allies that the treaty was not sufficiently clear on security issues.[90]

The June 7, 1986, draft was the last serious attempt by the Contadora states to mediate the Central American conflict. The futility of the Contadora process was driven home with the failure of the January 1987 peace mission, when the four foreign ministers of Contadora and ministers from the support group states, accompanied by the secretaries-general of the United Nations and the Organization of American States, toured Central America and failed to obtain any concession from the regional states. After these two failures, the Contadora process began to take a back seat to efforts by the Central American states to resolve their own crisis. On May 25 and 26, 1986, the Central American presidents met in Esquipulas, Guatemala, and began a new peace process. The long, sad history of Contadora finally came to end on April 16, 1987, when the Contadora and support group foreign ministers met in Argentina and issued a communiqué expressing support for the peace initiative of the Central American states. The South American states effectively turned over the peace process to their Central American colleagues.

The Contadora process failed because it was viewed by the United States and its Central American allies as pro-Sandinista. In a speech on January 23, 1987, Elliott Abrams complained that Contadora and its support group encouraged "fake negotiations," adding, in a reference to Mexico and Peru, that the process "has tended to be led from the left." Alán García of Peru had expounded the virtues of Nicaraguan pluralism and condemned the contras, and it was this, Abrams said, that left Peru's status as a neutral in doubt.[91] Many Central American leaders also questioned the neutrality of the Contadora process. They were especially critical of Mexico's openly pro-Nicaraguan sentiments. A Honduran diplomat complained that Mexican foreign minister Sepúlveda pursued a policy whose aim was to destabilize the pro-American regimes in the region.[92] This perception that the Contadora states were not honest brokers meant that the United States and its allies viewed the peace process as a public relations problem and not as a serious forum for resolving the Central American conflict.

The Failure of U.S. Diplomacy

After the failure of both Manzanillo and Contadora, the Reagan administration felt free to concentrate on increasing pressure on Nicaragua. Despite congressional opposition, these efforts centered on maintaining the contras as a viable military threat to the Nicaraguan regime. In the aftermath of public uproar over the mining of the Nicaraguan harbors, Congress voted in 1984 to end all U.S. aid to the contras. The Boland amendment stated:

> No funds available to the Central Intelligence Agency, the Department of Defense, or any other agency or entity of the United States involved in intelligence activities may be obligated or expended for the purpose or which would have the effect of supporting, directly, or indirectly, military or paramilitary operations in Nicaragua by any nation, group, organization, movement or individual.[93]

Despite the seemingly impermeable language of the Boland amendment, the White House construed that it did not apply to the National Security Council (NSC). The president ordered the NSC to keep the contras' "body and soul together" through covert activities.[94]

The National Security Council set up a special office to aid the contras under the direction of marine Lt. Col. Oliver North. North personally directed contra operations in Central America. He also gave pep talks to organizations that were engaged in fund-raising for the rebels. Many conservative groups, led by Gen. John Singlaub's Council for World Freedom, raised money and goods for the contras. According to one source, more than $25 million was raised for the Nicaraguan rebels through these private conservative organizations.[95] The White House used its prestige and its persuasive powers with private groups to subsidize actions that Congress clearly meant to prohibit. Although House Democrats were aware that the administration was helping to raise private funds for the contras, they were not aware of the lengths the administration went to in order to circumvent congressional restrictions. Not until the scandal became public in November 1986 was it known that the NSC had secretly coordinated contra assistance efforts and later arranged the Iranian weapons deal. Between June 1984 and January 1986 the president, denied funding by Congress, raised money from third party countries; for example, conservative Islamic states contributed $42 million to the effort.

These covert activities were soon augmented by the president's effort to resume public assistance to the Nicaraguan resistance. The administration sought to take advantage of Reagan's momentum following the 1984 election by pressuring Congress to reappropriate $14 million for the contras.[96] Immediately after the election, a public education campaign was launched and directed by the president to create a national consensus on aiding the contras. In one of the most notable examples of propaganda aimed at domestic opinion, an unidentified U.S. official announced that Soviet MiG fighters were on their way to Nicaragua. The announcement proved patently false, but politicians across the political spectrum denounced the delivery of MiGs and endorsed U.S. military action to remove the security threat.[97]

The president also gave a series of emotional endorsements to the rebels during the spring of 1985, calling them "our brothers" and the "moral equivalent of the Founding Fathers." He also warned Congress that "if the Sandinistas are not stopped now, they will, as they have sworn, attempt to spread communism to El Salvador, Costa Rica, Honduras and elsewhere."[98] Initially, the campaign had little visible effect on Capitol Hill, where critics complained that the administration had not tried seriously to negotiate a settlement with Nicaragua. Implicit in congressional rejection of contra aid was the feeling articulated by Sen. Edward Kennedy that "rather than moving the region toward peace, the secret war had undermined the Contadora process and damaged the prospects for a negotiated solution to the problems of the entire region."[99] Congressional skepticism combined with Sandinista promises of democratization resulted in a stinging setback for the president when Congress voted on April 24, 1985, to reject a renewal of aid to the rebels. In a last-minute appeal, the President told the House that "the choice to be made is a fundamental one that will have a lasting effect on the prospects for democracy, economic opportunity, and peace in the region."[100] Nevertheless, the House voted 215 to 213 to reject a White House-backed amendment that would have provided $14 million in direct aid to the rebels.

The contra issue did not subside with the House vote. In an inexplicable act of political folly, the Sandinista victory on Capitol Hill was followed by a state visit by President Ortega to the Soviet Union. The administration took advantage of this Sandinista misstep to reintroduce the aid issue to Congress while simultaneously launching a new anti-Nicaraguan public relations campaign. This time Congress gave in and approved a foreign aid bill that provided $27 million in nonmilitary aid to the rebels. One year later, when the president's popularity stood at a record high of 68 percent, he asked for, and obtained, approval of $100 million in contra aid for fiscal year 1986–87.

This victory proved to be short-lived, as support for the contras quickly waned in Congress. By 1986, after the deployment of Soviet-built helicopters and the establishment of a military draft, the Sandinistas had defeated the rebels on the battlefield. Compounding the contras' military setbacks was their defeat in the political arena. The public disclosure in the Iran-Contra investigation that funds from the Iranian arms sales had been diverted to the contras led to the final erosion of congressional support for the Nicaraguan rebels. By the end of 1987 the conventional wisdom in Washington was that Reagan's Nicaraguan policy was a failure. On February 3, 1988, Congress rejected any additional aid to the Nicaraguan resistance. A month later a Democrat-sponsored aid package for the contras was rejected by House Republicans, who felt that the proposal was inadequate. Although Congress voted twice in 1988 to extend humanitarian assistance to the rebels, clearly they were no longer a serious military threat to the Sandinistas. Moreover, there was a growing consensus among U.S. officials that the contras were no longer a viable policy tool for applying pressure on the Nicaraguans.[101]

The defeat of the contras left the Reagan administration without any workable policy options for dealing with the Sandinistas. The president had previously rejected negotiations on the grounds that Nicaragua could not be trusted.[102] Thus by the end of 1986 both diplomatic and military policy options had been foreclosed. One senior State Department official observed that "after the Iran-Contra affair Reagan's Central American policy came to a virtual standstill. Those of us who believed that a diplomatic-political settlement was still possible with the Sandinistas, simply waited for the next administration."[103]

Esquipulas I

The diplomatic vacuum created by the collapse of the Contadora peace process and the failure of U.S. policy was quickly filled by the Central American presidents. The three presidents who took power in 1986 in Costa Rica, Honduras, and Guatemala shared a belief that a new diplomatic initiative was needed to settle the Central American crisis. The new presidents worried that the militarization of the region would destroy the fragile democracies in the isthmus. They rejected U.S. reliance on a military solution to the conflict, which unavoidably strengthened the armed forces in their own countries—precisely the same institution that had destroyed democracy in the past. At the same time, they feared that the consolidation of a Marxist-Leninist regime in Nicaragua would endanger their own democratic institutions. The Central American presidents sought a peace process that would strengthen regional democracy, weaken local military establishments, and reform the Sandinistas.

The impetus for a Central American solution to the crisis came first from Marco Vinicio Cerezo, the Christian Democrat who was elected president of Guatemala in December 1985. Immediately after his election Cerezo toured Central America, expressing his desire to assist in the search for regional peace. He affirmed that Guatemala would expand on the previous military regime's policy of "active neutrality" in the U.S.-Nicaraguan conflict. Cerezo called on his fellow Central American presidents to withdraw from the U.S. crusade against the Sandinistas and engage instead in intraregional diplomacy to end the crisis.[104] Cerezo seized upon the occasion of his inauguration to invite the other presidents to the border town of Esquipulas to discuss the creation of a Central American parliament.

Discussions at the presidential summit centered on the question of democracy. The five presidents agreed in principle that the solution to the Central American conflict lay in the establishment of regional democracy.[105] The final communiqué noted that the discussions were conducted in an atmosphere of "frankness" and that the Central American states still had "some differences and discrepancies" over the best way to resolve the conflict.[106] The main problem was the profound difference between Nicaragua and its neighbors over a definition of democracy. The four other Central American states insisted that Nicaragua end its state of emergency and resolve its differences with the internal opposition in order to establish a Western-style liberal democracy.

Nicaragua countered that it was already a "popular democracy" in which government policy was dedicated to furthering the interests of

all the people rather than those of any specific social class. The Sandinistas pointed out that despite the hegemonic role of their party, won by
virtue of their military triumph in 1979 and their electoral victory in
1984, formal and informal opposition groups were tolerated to a far
greater degree than in the Soviet bloc and to a degree comparable with
most liberal democracies in Latin America—and certainly beyond
anything then tolerated in Guatemala or El Salvador.[107]

Sergio Ramírez characterized the FSLN conception in July 1983 as
"effective democracy." The Nicaraguan vice-president explained that
democracy

> consists of a permanent dynamic involving the people's participation in a
> variety of political and social tasks; the people who offer their opinions and
> are listened to—the ones who make suggestions, build, and direct, organize
> themselves, who attend to community, neighborhood, and national
> problems; the people who are active in sovereignty and the defense of
> sovereignty and also teach and give vaccinations; ours is a daily democracy
> and not one that takes place every four years . . . for us democracy is not just
> a formal model, but a continual process capable of giving the people that
> elect and participate in it the real possibility of transforming their living
> conditions, a democracy which establishes justice and ends exploitation.[108]

Despite the deadlock over the question of democracy, the first
Esquipulas summit was an important watershed in regional diplomacy. The presidents established a new mechanism for negotiating the
crisis. Presidential summits among the Central American states replaced the Contadora process as the method for resolving the conflict.
Cerezo emphasized the institutionalization of consultation as the main
accomplishment of the first summit. He reported to the Guatemalan
Congress that "we created a regional organization which will permit
dialogue between the Central American states which will contribute to
regional detente."[109]

Esquipulas I established the forum for future regional negotiations.
But at the May 25–26, 1986, summit, the Central Americans lacked a
clear plan for resolving the conflict. The conference's final communiqué
made reference to a future treaty for the establishment of a Central
American parliament, but no new ideas were advanced to resolve the
conflict between Nicaragua and its neighbors. The lack of concrete
proposals was illustrated by the final communiqué, which still clung to

the hope that the Contadora process might yet produce a final treaty.[110] Nevertheless, Guatemala's initiative in calling the presidential summit did create a viable structure for future negotiations, which allowed the region's leaders to fill the political vacuum created by the failure of foreign intervention. In the following chapters, we see how Oscar Arias took advantage of the groundwork laid by Cerezo to develop a framework for the comprehensive settlement to the Central American conflict.

4 *The Arias Peace Plan*

Oscar Arias assumed the presidency of Costa Rica as the Central American conflict threatened his tranquil nation. The considerable pressure caused by the Nicaraguan revolution and the economic crisis of the 1980s put the Costa Rican political structure at risk. A polity that once commanded worldwide respect because of its long history of stable constitutional government, low levels of social conflict, welfare state, and middle-class consumer economy now threatened to be engulfed by regional violence.[1]

The vulnerability of the tiny nation was intensified because Arias's predecessors had abandoned the country's traditional policy of isolation and neutrality in Central American conflicts. Rodrigo Carazo fundamentally altered Costa Rican foreign policy by openly siding with the Sandinistas in the revolution against Somoza. This marked the first time that Costa Rica had involved itself in its neighbors' affairs since the 1920s, but Costa Rica soon grew disillusioned with the radical bent of the Sandinistas. Carazo even refused to attend the revolution's first anniversary celebration on the grounds that Cuban leader Fidel Castro would be in Managua. "I am not fond of walking on the same platform as dictators," Carazo said.[2]

Costa Rica again involved itself in the Nicaraguan civil war when it allowed counterrevolutionary groups to form on its territory. Luis Alberto Monge, who succeeded Carazo, turned a blind eye to most armed contra activities, as the implicit price for the massive U.S. economic aid that began in 1983. Contra bases in Costa Rica placed this small democracy in the eye of the Central American storm, but as the prospects for war grew more likely, Costa Rica stepped back. In the 1986 presidential election the nation rallied behind Arias and his call for a return to Costa Rica's traditional diplomacy of neutrality and pacifism. This policy allowed Arias, who would win the Nobel Peace

Prize, to take the lead in designing a Central American solution to the crisis. Taking advantage of the disintegration of the Reagan administration's Central American policy after the revelations of Iran-Contra, the Costa Rican president proposed the Arias peace plan.

Arias succeeded where the United States and the larger Latin American countries failed because he understood the complicated web of domestic and international actors with a stake in the Central American conflict. He believed that any solution to the regional crisis would have to address the severe internal strife within the individual Central American states. Arias, using the prestige of his small nation as a symbol of hope, peace, and democracy, argued that the Central American crisis could only be solved peacefully through democratization, national reconciliation, and dialogue. Costa Ricans hoped that the Arias peace plan would reduce regional tensions and thus safeguard their democracy.

The Crisis

At the time of Arias's inauguration, contras roamed through northern Costa Rica, U.S. intelligence agents ran covert activities from San José, and Costa Ricans themselves were contemplating an unprecedented military buildup.[3] The militarization of the region caused by the U.S.-Nicaraguan conflict threatened to destroy Costa Rica's tradition of pacifism. Incidents along the northern border raised the specter of a direct military confrontation with the Sandinistas. The tension along the border was manifested when two Costa Rican civil guardsmen were killed and nine others were wounded in a 1985 border clash. The incident provoked Arias's predecessor, Monge, to speed up the modernization of the civil guards, which included inviting twenty-five U.S. Green Berets to train a thousand civil guardsmen in counterinsurgency techniques.[4] The buildup gave the Costa Rican Civil Guard the same basic infantry weapons as a modern army. Costa Rica disbanded its army in 1949, and many experts have attributed the nation's relative political stability ever since to that fact.

Costa Rican democracy was also destabilized by Central American exiles and dissidents living in the country. More than 125,000 Nicaraguans sought asylum in Costa Rica after the Sandinista revolution, in addition to large numbers of Salvadorans and Guatemalans. These groups created problems for their host country as they continued their struggles against their home governments from Costa Rica. San José became a staging area for terrorist activities directed against other countries in the isthmus, especially El Salvador and Nicaragua. At least eleven acts of political terrorism were recorded in San José in 1982 and 1983.[5] The terrorism alarmed Monge, who responded by appealing for security assistance from the United States, beefing-up the nation's poorly trained and ill-equipped civil and rural guard forces, training an elite antiterrorism force, and calling for a volunteer corps of citizens to help battle terrorism.[6]

To make matters worse, there were reports that private paramilitary groups of both the extreme left and the extreme right were being armed and trained within the country. At least six right wing groups took shape during the early 1980s. Most of the groups operated with the knowledge and approval of the Costa Rican Ministry of Security, and four of the organizations were integrated into Costa Rica's national reserve.[7] Most of the groups formed in 1983 and 1984 were backed by the local economic elite, the Ministry of Security, and the contras, who used the groups to provide logistical support for their forces in Costa Rica. The groups also organized demonstrations against the Nicaraguan embassy in San José, broke up peace marches in the streets, and destroyed squatter settlements on members' land. Although the groups did not resort to the type of death-squad activities that characterized their counterparts in El Salvador or Guatemala, many leftists in Costa Rica feared that these paramilitary groups were capable of such activities. Communist party leader Arnoldo Ferreto warned that Costa Rica was not immune from right wing violence: "People talk of the Central Americanization of Costa Rica. How do they think the death squads began in El Salvador?"[8]

The political mood in Costa Rica during the height of the Central American crisis was reflected in an infamous incident that occurred on August 8, 1984. On that date the rumor that a coup d'état was in the making ran rampant through the press corps and government. The civil guard was placed on alert, streets were closed off in central San José, traffic was disrupted, and people were stunned. It turned out the rumors originated unintentionally with the Minister of Security, Angel Edmundo Solano-Calderón, who had been joking with newsmen. The political fallout from the joke forced the president to demand the resignation of his entire cabinet, as well as many other government officials. Ultimately, seven resignations were accepted, including those of four ministers, one of whom was Solano. The episode was indicative of the degree of insecurity permeating Costa Rican society.[9]

Notwithstanding these internal threats to Costa Rican stability, observers perceived the greatest challenge as emanating from outside; the country had become a battleground in the U.S.-Nicaraguan conflict. During the Monge administration (1982 to 1986), U.S. influence grew rapidly, reaching its height during his last two years in office. The Reagan administration viewed Costa Rica as an important strategic asset in its war against the Sandinista regime. Lewis Tambs, the U.S. ambassador to San José, told the Tower Commission probing the Iran-Contra affair that his main mission as ambassador was to "open the southern front" against Nicaragua.[10] Monge proved more than willing to aid in the U.S.-sponsored contra war in return for economic aid.

Monge inherited a severe economic crisis when he assumed office in 1982. Following two decades of economic growth averaging 6.4 percent per year, Costa Rica suffered negative GNP growth rates of 4.6 percent in 1981 and 8.9 percent in 1982.[11] The impact of the economic crisis from 1980 to 1982 is dramatically revealed by the following economic indicators: GNP declined by 10 percent; national income fell by 22 percent; per capita income was reduced by 25 percent; real salaries fell by 45 percent; prices increased by 180 percent; unemployment doubled to 9.4 percent while underemployment increased to 21 percent; public investment declined rapidly while foreign investment reached negative levels and in 1982 the cost of the basic market basket consumed 86 percent of the average salary; 24 percent of national income left the country through payments for debt service; and trade exports fell 13 percent as a result of deterioration of terms.[12]

Concerned over the state of the economy, Monge flew to Washington for a state visit just after his inauguration. He made it clear that he was willing to overlook Costa Rica's traditional policy of neutrality and pacifism in exchange for economic assistance. The Reagan administration responded by dramatically increasing the level of U.S. aid. Costa Rica became the second largest recipient of U.S. aid per capita in the world, exceeded only by Israel.[13] According to some experts, the collapse of the Costa Rican economic, social, and political systems was prevented by this massive infusion of aid.[14]

During the first three years of the Monge administration the U.S. channeled some $634 million in economic assistance through AID, the Agency for International Development, compared to $67 million from 1978 to 1981. In terms of all the assistance Costa Rica received from 1983 to 1984, AID accounted for 47 percent of new resources received in 1983 and 44 percent in 1984. If one includes international aid organizations over which the United States had strong influence, such as the International Monetary Fund, the Inter-American Development Bank, and the World Bank, then totals increase to 83 percent in 1983 and 65 percent in 1984.[15] Without these resources the social cost of adjustment would have been much higher and might have had an unforeseen impact on the Costa Rican political and social system.[16]

The pivotal role played by the United States in keeping the Costa Rican economy stable during the crisis greatly increased U.S. influence over Costa Rican foreign policy. Throughout his term, Monge turned a blind eye to most contra activities within his country as the implicit price for U.S. aid. Costa Rican foreign minister Carlos José Gutiérrez admitted that "we desperately needed United States aid to deal with the economic crisis. In order to get that aid we decided to play ball with the United States on the issue of the contras."[17] Thus the Reagan administration, with the cooperation of the Costa Rican government, turned the country into the second front in the war against Nicaragua. As early as 1983 more than three hundred contras were training in six farms in northern Costa Rica. Contra raids were launched against Nicaraguan targets from Costa Rican territory. Top anti-Sandinista politicians established operations in the country, including Edén Pastora, Alfonso Robelo, Alfredo César, and Pedro Joaquín Chamorro, Jr., and a powerful transmitter was built near the border to broadcast anti-Sandinista programs produced by the Voice of America into Nicaragua. The United States was even able to construct a secret air base in northern Costa Rica to resupply the contras.

Operations of contra forces from Costa Rican territory exacerbated the already difficult relations between Costa Rica and Nicaragua and continually threatened to escalate into violence along the border. By early 1985 Managua issued thirty-six and San José more than sixty-six formal protests over incursions and border incidents, and it seemed that a Nicaraguan–Costa Rican confrontation was likely. The Costa Rican political establishment was convinced that the FSLN was intent on destabilizing their little democracy.[18] These fears seemed well-founded when two Costa Rican civil guardsmen were killed in retaliation for contra raids into southern Nicaragua. The incident caused a crisis between the two neighbors. At the time a vast majority of the Costa Rican population believed that Nicaragua was their enemy. According to one public opinion poll, most Costa Ricans (77 percent) viewed Nicaragua as a major threat, while 12 percent agreed that it was a threat to some extent; a vast majority of Costa Ricans (84 percent) had a negative view of the Sandinistas.[19] Most feared that a major conflict could erupt between the two nations in the near future. Newspapers and comments heard on the street voiced the grim view that Nicaragua had plans for a massive, direct military invasion of Costa Rica. Invasion fears permeated the entire population—government workers, college professors, taxi drivers, and vendors in the market places.[20] On the eve of Arias's inauguration most Costa Ricans were convinced that their nation was about to be inundated by waves of violence from both inside and outside their country.

The Diplomacy of Democracy

The danger posed to Costa Rican democracy by the escalation of violence became a key issue in the 1986 presidential election. Although Arias was a member of the same party as Monge (Partido de Liberación Nacional), he advocated a very different policy for dealing with the Central American conflict. Arias called for a retreat from Monge's policy of belligerence and a return to Costa Rica's traditional policy of pacifism and neutrality. Arias took advantage of the fact that his opponent, Rafael Angel Calderón, was closely identified with Monge's foreign policy to transform the election into a referendum on peace. According to one of Arias's campaign advisers, the peace issue was the most effective of all the themes that Arias raised against his opponent.[21]

From the start of his administration, Arias's position was clear. Shortly after the February 2, 1986, election, he told U.S. television newsman John McLaughlin, "If I were Mr. Reagan, I would give money to Guatemala, El Salvador, Honduras, and Costa Rica for economic aid, and not military aid to the contras."[22] In his inaugural address the new president emphasized that the escalation of violence in

Central America was endangering Costa Rican democracy. "It is no longer possible," he declared, "to talk of peace and liberty, and to make decisions about our development, without first taking into account events occurring beyond our country's border."[23] To preserve democracy Arias reaffirmed his campaign promise to return Costa Rica to its traditional foreign policy:

> I affirm that thanks to the international policy implemented by Costa Rica during most of its history as an independent nation, a policy of peace and nonintervention, we have emerged in the international community stronger than we would have if we had to defend our security with weapons. Costa Rica will stay away from war. It will do so to strengthen its deep-rooted tradition of peace. It will do so to preserve its civil traditions, to maintain a climate favorable to economic development and social harmony. We will be neutral concerning regional armed conflict.[24]

To return his country to its tradition of neutrality, Arias needed to end contra operations in Costa Rica. He feared that heightened conflict in the rest of Central America, especially in Nicaragua, would spill over into Costa Rica, especially given the large number of contras operating along the northern border. Arias also worried that the Monge administration's open collaboration with the U.S. war against Nicaragua had severely undermined Costa Rica's credibility, just when the danger of war was most acute. Arias reasoned that if Costa Rica was to restore its reputation as an island of peace and democracy in a troubled region, it needed to distance itself from Washington's Central American policy.

Once Costa Rica was able to regain its international prestige, regional and international pressure would be brought to bear against the Sandinistas to compel them to democratize Nicaragua. The goals of Arias's foreign policy were clear: to democratize Central America in order to preserve Costa Rica's political structure. The key to regional democracy lay in putting pressure on Managua to accept Western-style liberalism. Arias believed that Costa Rican democracy could not survive with a Marxist Nicaragua. He told the General Assembly of the United Nations "Costa Ricans are worried about the consolidation of a regime with a Marxist ideology at our borders. Our people know that in Europe and other places on earth, geographical borders between East and West cost millions of dollars in armaments, defense systems and military alliances."[25]

In his speech to the United Nations Arias clearly stated what he believed was the solution to the Central American conflict: structural change in the Sandinista regime. Arias proposed that these reforms could be accomplished within the framework of a regionwide "pact for democracy, pluralism and liberty."[26] He left no doubt that he believed that the lack of democracy in Nicaragua was the fundamental cause of the Central American crisis. Arias told the United Nations that Nicaragua

> has taken a political course that does not respond to the people's yearning for freedom nor to the hopes of fully implementing democracy harbored by so many countries, that in their times, supported the struggle against the dictatorship. This unwanted and unforeseen political course has transformed Central America into another stage for the East-West conflict. There is no letup for anyone along the path chosen by the comandantes, who betrayed a revolution aimed at returning democracy to several generations that knew only oppression. There is no letup for people who, frustrated and disappointed, have returned to civil war. There is no letup for neighboring nations that already sense the threat from a new totalitarian dogmatism and are already suffering the consequences of a frontier of sorrow and disillusionment.[27]

Arias recognized that to force the Sandinistas to institute democracy he needed to reduce tensions by ending the contra war. Arias felt that the contras provided the Nicaraguans with an excuse for curtailing civil liberties and that the contras had allowed the FSLN to mobilize international public opinion against the other Central American states.[28] With a pending World Court suit brought by Nicaragua against Costa Rica for its support of the contras, Arias believed his country needed to recapture the diplomatic initiative. He told the United Nations: "I will not allow any armed group to use our territory to attack neighboring states. I will not permit this because Costa Rica respects international law, because the presence of armed groups in our territory threatens international security, and because we lack an army to defend ourselves."[29]

But Costa Rica had to move carefully in distancing itself from Washington's Central American policy. Like Monge before him, Arias needed U.S. aid and private investment for continuing Costa Rica's tenuous economic recovery. Nevertheless, Arias clearly understood that peace was impossible as long as Costa Rica participated in the contra war. This was driven home when Sandinista gunners downed a contra supply plane, which had taken off from a secret base in Costa Rica, and captured Eugene Hasenfus. Although the Reagan administration denied any connection to the aircraft and sought to portray it as part of a "private" contra aid effort, documents found in the wreckage and statements made by Hasenfus himself suggested the involvement of high U.S. government officials.

The incident provoked Arias to order the suspension of armed contra activities inside Costa Rica. A month earlier Arias had dispatched the civil guard to occupy a secret base that had been built by the U.S. National Security Council's contra aid network. The Reagan administration quickly brought pressure to bear on Arias after the suspension of contra activities by threatening to withhold or withdraw U.S. aid to Costa Rica. CIA director William Casey flew to San José and demanded that Arias meet him secretly in the United States embassy. Arias refused. The most blatant of these threats came from Lt. Col. Oliver North. The colonel exceeded his authority, and that of his office, by contacting Arias directly and threatening to withhold aid if Arias continued to hamper contra activities.[30] The administration froze AID funds for Costa Rica, and overall U.S. aid declined from $215 million in 1985 to $157 million during Arias's first year in power.[31]

The Reagan administration, however, was soon in no position to put pressure on Costa Rica. In late November 1986, following revelations of covert arms sales to Iran, Attorney General Edwin Meese announced that he was investigating the diversion to the contras of profits from the arms sales. In early December, in the midst of the burgeoning scandal, Arias met with President Reagan in Washington. The White House, dissatisfied with the Costa Rican president, had postponed such a visit more than once. Now Reagan's popularity was at an all-time low and his Central American policy was in shambles. Seeking to recover congressional support for his Nicaraguan policy, he strove to project the image of peacemaker and thus welcomed Arias. But Arias had his own agenda and used the opportunity to argue forcefully for a peaceful solution to the crisis, particularly in Nicaragua.[32] Arias was able to force the beleaguered Reagan to disburse the $40 million in frozen AID funds for Costa Rica.

At the same time that Arias pushed for negotiations, he also assured the Reagan administration that, unlike Contadora, his peace plan would result in the restructuring of the Nicaraguan polity. Weeks after Arias's Washington trip, Costa Rican foreign minister Rodrigo Madrigal-Nieto met in Miami with U.S. assistant secretary of state Elliott Abrams and special envoy Philip Habib. The Miami talks focused on changes to be demanded of the Sandinistas. The Costa Ricans promised they would not participate in any peace process that did not result in the democratization of Nicaragua. They assured the United States that they would not let the peace process legitimize a Marxist-Leninist regime in Central America.[33]

On February 15, 1987, President Arias convened the presidents of El Salvador, Guatemala, and Honduras (Ortega was not invited) to discuss his plan for regional peace. At the summit Arias presented his ten-point peace proposal. It called for an immediate regionwide cease-fire and the opening of talks with unarmed opposition groups, an end to outside support for insurgent forces, amnesty decrees within sixty days, a calendar of democratization including restoration of freedom of the press within sixty days, free elections according to the constitutions of each country, and arms reduction talks (see appendix 4). The other presidents supported the plan but decided to delay final approval until after Nicaragua agreed to the proposals. They agreed to present the plan to Ortega along with an invitation to a five-nation summit to be held within ninety days. The Central American presidents also issued a joint statement that implied that the solution to the regional crisis depended on the achievement of national reconciliation and democratization in Nicaragua. They declared: "The peace that is demanding its time also demands an end to the dictatorships that continue to exist. It is imperative that all of us, together, promote the substitution of such tyrannies where the people are victims of a lack of freedom in whatever form. Such a substitution should occur, preferably, as a peaceful transition, without bloodshed, towards democracy."[34]

The importance of the Arias peace plan was that by agreeing to Arias's emphasis on democratization, regional leaders discovered a formula for resolving the decade-long conflict. At the San José summit Arias restored Costa Rica's moral authority on the issue of democracy and peace. In addition to his country's legitimacy as an honest broker, Arias had another important advantage over Contadora: a shift in the balance of power in Washington.

The Iran-Contra scandal provided Arias with the political space necessary to implement his strategy for regional peace and democracy. The scandal weakened the Reagan administration and allowed the Costa Rican president and his ambassador to the United States, Guido Fernández, to forge an alliance with moderate House Democrats to pressure the Reagan administration to accept a negotiated settlement to the Central American conflict.[35] At the same time that Arias was selling his plan to regional leaders, House Speaker Jim Wright warned the White House of the erosion of congressional support for the contras.[36] Moderates in the administration argued that Reagan must accept the peace plan if he hoped to salvage his Central American policy.[37] Bending to political reality, White House Chief of Staff Howard Baker told Wright that the time was ripe for an alternative policy in Central America, and he encouraged the Speaker to undertake a bipartisan peace initiative. Wright and Baker arrived at a plan that called for three simultaneous actions: imposition of a cease-fire, an immediate halt to Soviet-bloc military aid to Nicaragua, and a lifting of the state of emergency and declaration of a general amnesty in Nicaragua. The final wording called for an election timetable but omitted the demand for a new presidential election. If the Sandinistas did not comply with these demands, the administration would be free to resume contra aid.

The Wright-Reagan plan had, at best, ambivalent support from the administration. Hard-liners argued that the contras were the only bargaining chip the United States had against the Sandinistas and feared that the Wright-Reagan proposal would be the political death warrant for the resistance. Abrams found the initiative "barely acceptable."[38] He bitterly opposed the accompanying "gag rule" under which Reagan and the Speaker agreed not to criticize each other, and the administration agreed to abstain from requesting contra aid until October 1, 1987.[39] Reagan gave the plan only lukewarm support. According to one administration official, "Reagan could not come to terms with ending United States support for the contras. He entered into Wright-Reagan in an attempt to regain the political initiative after Iran-Contra, not because he believed in negotiations."[40] The reluctant support for the plan was reflected in the manner in which the administration announced the proposal to the press. On the eve of the Central American summit, the White House issued the plan on blank paper without any indication that it was an official document. The State

Department had copies delivered to the participants at the summit, but neglected to send a top official to explain its implications.

The administration's public ambivalence outraged Wright, who felt Reagan was not complying with the spirit of the agreement. The Speaker dispatched Richard Peña, a Latin American expert formerly with the House Foreign Affairs Committee, to Guatemala to give the Central Americans the green light in regard to the Arias peace plan.[41] Peña and Guido Fernández, the Costa Rican ambassador to Washington, transformed the Wright-Reagan plan into a blank check for Arias to use as he saw fit at the summit.[42] The Wright-Reagan proposal confirmed for the Central American presidents that a shift had occurred in the balance of power between the President and the Democrat-controlled Congress.

By the time of the Guatemalan summit, Arias was in an enviable position. Guatemala, the conference host, clearly wanted the plan to succeed. The Nicaraguans, confronted with economic disaster at home and a never-ending war with the contras, were now prepared to accept the Arias peace plan. The shift in power in Washington in favor of the Democrats forced Reagan's allies in the region to reevaluate their position. El Salvador, which voiced some reservations before the summit, was supportive of the Costa Rican proposal at the Guatemala summit. Duarte, who had cultivated a special relationship with congressional Democrats, especially Wright, was well aware of the Speaker's support for Arias. Duarte feared that Salvadoran intransigence at the peace conference might endanger his relationship with the Democratic Party's leadership. The Salvadoran president recalled that Wright had been instrumental in obtaining economic and military aid for El Salvador over the objections of liberal Democrats. In explaining his unanticipated support for the Arias plan, Duarte reportedly commented: "Remember that Ronald Reagan is only President for sixteen more months. Jim Wright is going to be Speaker for the next ten years."[43]

El Salvador's support for the proposal forced the Hondurans, who were, as usual, the main holdouts, into either going along with the plan or appearing to be the spoilers; they chose the former. The Iran-Contra scandal, combined with the political implications of Wright-Reagan, had an impact on Honduras. The Honduran leadership feared that contra forces based in their country could become a national security problem. And the Honduran foreign ministry worried that Iran-Contra, and their own open collaboration with Washington, had done grave damage to their country's international standing.[44] "The scandal debilitated the standing of the United States government before the eyes of the Central American governments," said a senior Honduran diplomat. "State secrets were on page one of the newspaper. Many [top officials] got worried about what the contra program meant for future relations with a Democratic congress and a possible Democratic administration."[45]

Esquipulas II

On August 7, 1987, the five Central American presidents formally agreed to the Arias peace plan and signed an unprecedented set of agreements, known collectively as the Guatemalan Accord, the Central American Peace Accord, or Esquipulas II. The Central American presidents, sensing that the decade of violence was destroying their societies and that foreign peacemaking efforts had failed, agreed to the Arias formula. The accord was significantly different from Contadora; instead of focusing on security issues (foreign advisers, foreign military aid, military balance, etc.), Esquipulas II centered exclusively on the progressive democratization of the region. The plan recognized the powerful internal origins of the crisis. Consequently, the formula proposed by Arias to end the conflict was national reconciliation through democratization.[46] In addition to the provision on democratization, the region's leaders drew upon the logical, historically proven, last resort of agreeing to accept each other, despite sharp differences. An important element of the Guatemalan Accord was the acceptance of the legitimacy of each of the existing regimes. These provisions were extremely important for the governments of El Salvador, Guatemala, and Nicaragua, which faced civil wars.

The Central American Peace Accord also successfully dealt with the problems that had ruined the Contadora process. Esquipulas II placed no restrictions on U.S. military assistance to Honduras or El Salvador. This made the accord acceptable to the powerful militaries of these countries and removed one of the key U.S. objections to the peace process: that Contadora placed the Salvadoran government on an equal footing with the guerrilla forces and, if implemented, would have cut off all U.S. military assistance to El Salvador. Arias went out of his way to recognize the legitimacy of the Salvadoran government. The final communiqué of the first San José summit, six months earlier, clearly dismissed the Salvadoran guerrillas as a destructive force: "Clear examples of such fanatical struggles, whose motivation is to impede the development of liberty in the democracies, are the guerrillas' movements that persist in El Salvador, Peru and Colombia."[47]

Arias was also able to obtain Sandinista approval for the peace plan. Previously, Nicaragua had argued that no peace agreement was possible unless the United States pledged to abide by it. The Sandinistas insisted that the U.S. government must stop aiding the contras before they would agree to a peace treaty. They argued that since Reagan was the principal sponsor of the contras, and since rebel military operations had forced the Nicaraguan government to restrict civil liberties, the United States must halt its illegal aid to the Nicaraguan resistance before the Sandinistas could restore constitutional government. Arias countered that Reagan's contra policy was dependent on the cooperation of Washington's Central American allies, who allowed their territories to be used for covert operations. By requiring the cessation of aid to irregular forces and the denial of Central American territory to these groups, the peace plan exposed the United States' dependence on its local clients. Arias pointed out that his own government had moved to close down contra bases in Costa Rica. Arias convinced the Sandinistas that the best method for ending the contra war was pressuring Honduras (not the United States) to close down the bases.

Moreover, the Esquipulas II accord dealt with the deep distrust among the Central American states by stressing simultaneity of actions by all parties. After sixty days, on November 7, 1987, the five nations were all required *simultaneously* to: declare an amnesty for all political prisoners; negotiate a cease-fire with rebel groups within their borders; stop aiding guerrilla forces in other countries; prohibit guerrillas from using their territories to launch attacks against neighboring states; guarantee free press and free elections; and allow dissident groups to operate openly. A verification commission would meet thirty days later to review compliance, and the five presidents would meet thirty days after that to confirm that the peace process was operational.

The Central American accord had eleven articles, which closely resembled the Arias peace plan (see appendix 5). First, the agreement called for national reconciliation and dialogue. The five presidents committed themselves "to carry out urgently . . . actions toward national reconciliation that would allow popular participation with full guarantees in political processes of a democratic nature, based upon justice, freedom and democracy, and to create for these purposes the mechanisms that according to law, would allow dialogue with opposition groups."[48] To accomplish this objective the five governments were required, within twenty days of signing, to appoint national reconciliation commissions. The commissions consisted of one government representative, one leading citizen not in the government, a bishop nominated by the nation's Roman Catholic bishops' conference, and one opposition politician nominated by the internal political opposition. The presidents also recognized that to achieve national reconciliation an amnesty was necessary. Political prisoners must be released before November 7, 1987.

The second provision of the peace accord contained a strong appeal to reach a cease-fire with rebel groups. "The governments make an urgent appeal that, in those states of the region where irregular or insurgent groups are currently active, agreements must be reached to end hostilities. The governments of all those states promise to undertake all necessary steps, in accordance with their constitution, to bring about a genuine cease-fire."[49] The accord did not, however, require governments to negotiate directly with armed groups.

In the accord's third clause the Central American states also promised to take steps toward democratization. The five presidents agreed to "promote an authentic democratic process that is pluralistic and participatory, which entails the promotion of social justice and respect for human rights, the sovereignty and territorial integrity of states and the rights of every nation to choose, freely and without outside interference of any kind, its own economic, political, and social system."[50] To this end the Central American presidents committed themselves to guarantee the "complete freedom of television, radio, and the press. This complete freedom shall include freedom of all ideological groups to launch and operate communication media and to operate them without prior censorship."[51] The third provision of Esquipulas II also assured complete pluralism. The presidents guaranteed opposition groups and parties unrestricted access to the media and freedom of movement in campaigning. "Likewise, those Central American governments which are currently imposing a state of siege or emergency shall revoke it, ensuring that a state of law exists in which all constitutional guarantees are fully enforced."[52]

The agreement's fourth article called for free elections once the preconditions for democratic government had been established. The Central American states were required to hold free general elections according to timetables set by the individual countries' constitutions (1989 in El Salvador and Honduras; 1990 in Costa Rica, Guatemala, and Nicaragua). Those elections would be monitored by international observers to ensure fairness. Additionally, the accord made special reference to elections to a Central American parliament, first promised in the declaration of the five regional presidents on May 25, 1986, Esquipulas I.

The fifth point of Esquipulas II required the termination of aid to irregular forces and insurrectionist movements. The presidents requested "governments of the region and governments from outside the region which are providing either overt or covert military, logistical, financial, or propaganda support, in the form of men, weapons, munitions, and equipment, to irregular forces or insurrectionist movements, to terminate such aid; this is vital if a stable and lasting peace is to be attained in the region."[53] The appeal not only prohibited military aid, but also included restrictions on logistical, financial, and propaganda aid. The only exception was for resettlement aid.

The sixth requirement of the Central American peace accord was the nonuse of territory for aggression against neighboring states. The five governments pledged to prevent the contras or other guerrilla groups from using their territories for attacking other countries or for resupply. This provision compelled Honduras to expel the contras by November 7, 1987, and prevented resupply by the United States. "The five countries signing this document reiterate their commitment to prevent the use of their own territory by persons, organizations, or groups seeking to destabilize the government of a Central American country and to refuse to provide them with or allow them to receive military and logistical support."[54]

Esquipulas II also committed the Central American states to continue negotiations on security issues. The presidents, in the seventh article, promised to "continue negotiations on the still-pending points of disagreement with respect to security matters, verification, and control under the terms of the Contadora Agreement for Peace and Cooperation in Central America."[55] In the eighth provision the parties promised to aid refugees through relocation efforts and programs addressed to their health and safety needs. The ninth point included an agreement to seek special joint economic assistance from the international community and to cooperate in using such aid to accelerate regional development. The presidents pointed out that "the strengthening of democracy entails creating a system of economic and social well-being and justice."[56]

The tenth clause of the accord dealt with the verification process. It established an international verification commission, Comisión Internacional de Verificación y Seguimiento (CIVS), composed of the five foreign ministers of Central America, representatives of the four Contadora states (Colombia, Mexico, Panama, and Venezuela), the four Contadora support group nations (Argentina, Brazil, Peru, and Uruguay), and the secretary generals of the United Nations and the Organization of American States. It conveyed to this group the responsibility for determining compliance with the agreement and for reporting to the presidents of the five Central American nations within 150 days of the original agreement.

The final provision of Esquipulas II established the timetable. To take effect simultaneously, ninety days after the signing of the documents (November 7, 1987), were the obligations regarding amnesty, cease-fire, democratization, termination of aid to irregular forces and insurrectionist movements, and the denial of territory for the purpose of attacking other states. Thirty days after the November 7 deadline, the verification commission was to review the progress made by the parties in complying with the agreement. Sixty days after November 7, the Central American presidents were to meet again to receive the verification commission report and take appropriate action to guarantee compliance.

Compliance

Esquipulas II did not end the Central American conflict. It would take two more years, a change in U.S. administration, and three more presidential summits before all the objectives of Esquipulas would be realized. Compliance with the accord was delayed by the intransigence of the Reagan administration. Despite the fact that the Central American accord incorporated most of the U.S. demands regarding the democratization of Nicaragua and put no restrictions on U.S. military assistance to El Salvador or Honduras, the Reagan administration refused to end its support for the contras. Reagan argued that it was the military pressure created by the contras that forced the Sandinistas to the bargaining table in the first place. He pointed out that ending the contra war would deprive the Central American democracies of their only real leverage against Nicaragua. Without the contras, there would be no pressure on the Sandinistas to comply with the peace accord.[57]

The administration's unwillingness to abide by Esquipulas II led to the resignation of Philip Habib, the president's special envoy to Central America. Habib viewed the accord as a victory for the United States' Central American policy. Speaking in November, two months after his resignation, Habib complained that the United States missed a golden opportunity to settle the Central American conflict on its own terms. "I saw an opportunity to get what we wanted," he said. "I would have been down there working. I would have had a cease-fire by now."[58]

The Reagan administration's hostility to the Esquipulas II agreement became evident when, a little more than a month after the summit, it attempted to renew military assistance to the contras. On September 10, 1987, Shultz went before the Senate Foreign Affairs Committee and announced that the administration planned to request $270 million after October 1. They were forced to delay the request when, ten days later, Arias addressed a joint session of Congress at Wright's invitation and asked that the administration postpone any request for contra aid until after November 7. In a stirring conclusion to his speech, he appealed: "Let us then combat war with peace. Let us combat totalitarianism with the power of democracy. United in ideals and principles, joined by dialogue and democracy, we can and will bring hostilities to an end. We must give peace a chance."[59]

To make matters worse for the administration, President Duarte of El Salvador and President Azcona of Honduras joined Arias in speaking out against an early vote on contra aid. Both came to Washington at the invitation of the White House. On October 15, Duarte urged the vote to be deferred until after January 7, 1988, when the presidents of the five countries were to meet and evaluate the results of the peace plan to that point. A week later, Azcona said after seeing Reagan that contra aid should be suspended at least until January. These statements, along with congressional opposition, forced the administration to back away from contra aid. Shultz announced on November 10, 1987, that "to give peace every chance" the $270 million would not be requested before 1988.[60]

Nonetheless the administration continued to cling to its military strategy in Central America. Reagan put diplomatic and economic pressure on Honduras to keep the contra bases open in violation of the peace accord.[61] When Azcona returned to Tegucigalpa from the summit, he faced the displeasure of both the U.S. embassy and the Honduran military. Facing a cutoff of U.S. aid, Honduras bowed to the pressure and adopted a quiet policy of stalling the implementation of the peace plan. Azcona made Honduran compliance with the agreement contingent on that of Nicaragua. In other words, Honduras would not expel the contras until the Sandinistas reformed their regime. Asked when Honduras would dismantle the contra camps, Azcona replied: "We will fulfill this; ninety days will pass and when the ninetieth day comes, we will fulfill this. Of course, the agreement does not stipulate that one party will fulfill it and another will not. The agreement is unique in that it establishes simultaneity, in other words, that several actions must be fulfilled simultaneously."[62] In a meeting at the White House Azcona assured President Reagan that Honduras would be able to keep contra bases open and to comply with Esquipulas II, confident that Nicaragua would never live up to its obligation under the accord, especially with respect to amnesty for political opponents.[63]

Thus, although there was a substantial decrease in contra operations in Honduras after Esquipulas II, the use of Honduran territory continued in direct violation of the accord.[64] Both President Azcona and Vice-President Alfredo Fortín claimed that the only contras remaining in Honduras with the knowledge of the government were those receiving medical treatment at the Aguacate military base.[65] Honduran opposition sources and other observers disputed this claim. For example, the newspaper *Tiempo,* a frequent critic of government policy, published pictures of contra troops on a Honduran base in January 1988. The National Federation of Farmworkers (Confederación Nacional de Trabajores del Campo—CNTC) asserted that the armed Nicaraguan opposition retained control of more than five hundred square kilometers near Capire, in the Las Vegas salient, from which three thousand Honduran peasant families had been displaced.[66]

Honduras also tried to disrupt the Esquipulas II timetable at a meeting of foreign ministers convened in San Salvador on August 22, 1987, to formulate specific steps for the implementation of the peace process. Honduran foreign minister Carlos López-Contreras appeared a day late. At the meeting, the Honduran delegation succeeded in blocking the formation of specific committees to study how to implement the accord, forcing the tabling of the matter for later discussion.[67] Moreover, Honduras failed to act in concert with the other Central American republics. It did not send a representative to regional cultural and independence functions at which the other countries were present. The Honduran delegation was also absent when the region's ambassadors to the United Nations presented the plan to the secretary-general of the United Nations, Javier Pérez de Cuéllar.[68]

The U.S. administration also put pressure on El Salvador and Costa Rica to disrupt the peace process. A high-ranking Costa Rican diplomat complained that Reagan's Central American policy was single-minded in viewing the contras as the only solution to the conflict.[69] The United States' rejection of negotiations frustrated the Central Americans, and in 1987 Reagan again reduced U.S. economic and military aid in Costa Rica, this time to $120.4 million, $94 million less than Costa Rica received in the last year of the Monge administration.[70] Arias, cautious in his public criticism of the United States, was described as privately angry, hurt, and even depressed over the pressure. "We want an intelligent friend, not a stupid ally," he told an interviewer in reference to the United States.[71] Arias wondered aloud why Reagan wanted to hurt neutral Costa Rica.

While the Reagan administration rejected the Central American Peace Plan, the Sandinistas embraced it. Nicaragua viewed Esquipulas II as a mechanism for reducing U.S. influence in the region. A senior Nicaraguan diplomat wrote:

The Guatemalan accord reflected an act of national independence in contradiction with the hegemonic interest of the United States in Central America. . . . We recognized that the signing of Esquipulas II was an act of independence by the governments of Central America. We also note that in the current historic conditions in Central America, sovereignty and national independence are important factors to accelerate the political and social transformation of Central American states.[72]

The Sandinista leadership, after years of civil war and economic crisis, viewed the Esquipulas II accord as the best method for ending the contra war and economic isolation, and thus salvaging the 1979 revolution. Nicaragua's commitment to the peace process was made clear when it took early and decisive steps to comply with the accord. Four days after he returned to Managua in August 1987, Ortega became the first Central American leader to establish the National Reconciliation Commission. On August 25, the Sandinistas named their most respected critic, Archbishop Miguel Obando y Bravo, to the commission and urged that he be elected its president. In an additional olive branch to the powerful Roman Catholic Church, Ortega announced that three priests who had been forced into exile because of their alleged support for Nicaragua's armed opposition would be allowed to reenter the country. Two of the priests, Bismark Carballo and Benito Pitito, returned to Nicaragua in September 1987.

The Sandinista regime also took dramatic steps to allow an increase in opposition political activity. On September 19, 1987, the Nicaraguan government authorized the reopening of the opposition newspaper *La Prensa*. Three days later, censorship of the media was lifted, and the archdiocesan radio station, Radio Católica, was allowed to begin broadcasting again. *La Prensa* resumed publication on October 1, and Radio Católica returned to the air soon afterward.

The Sandinistas also attempted to settle their dispute with the internal opposition. On September 13 the government invited all legally recognized opposition parties to participate in a national dialogue. The purpose of these discussions was to broaden the political process. However, the talks quickly broke down. The opposition argued that democratization was not possible without sweeping constitutional reform. They viewed the 1987 Nicaraguan Constitution as hopelessly one-sided in the Sandinistas' favor. The government refused to discuss any changes in the constitution; instead they insisted that the opposition accept the legitimacy of the revolution and its constitution. The dialogue ended in a deadlock. The Sandinistas were also unsuccessful in their negotiations with the contras. On November 6 President

Ortega proposed to Cardinal Obando that he serve as mediator in cease-fire talks between the government and the armed opposition. The parties met twice in the Dominican Republic during December, but no progress was made.

Although an independent commission found that "Nicaragua has been the country in which the greatest change has occurred under the terms and timetables of the accord," its compliance was far from absolute.[73] For example, in his testimony before the Comisión Internacional de Verificación y Seguimiento (CIVS), Cardinal Obando, after reaffirming his support for what Nicaragua had accomplished, pointed to six areas where government action was still needed: (1) the continuing state of emergency; (2) the government's failure to declare total amnesty, as the Roman Catholic Church requested; (3) the lack of complete freedom of speech; (4) continuing abuse of human rights; (5) the failure to achieve a cease-fire; and (6) the collapse of national dialogue.[74]

Alajuela

The Reagan administration took advantage of the complaints of the Nicaraguan opposition to pressure the Central American states to declare Nicaragua in violation of the agreement. The focus of U.S. pressure was the upcoming summit to be held in Alajuela, Costa Rica. The meeting was designed to review progress under the original agreement, receive and review the official report from the verification commission (CIVS), and determine the future of the peace process. Days before the five presidents were scheduled to meet, National Security Adviser Colin Powell and Assistant Secretary of State Elliott Abrams toured the region to convince the Central Americans to abandon the peace process. A top Costa Rican official confirmed the existence of heavy U.S. pressure at the conference "for the peace plan to end." He described Washington as the "invisible and uninvited guest at the conference table."[75]

The United States presented its Central American allies with a dilemma: either support the peace plan or back President Reagan's call for more aid to the contras. Although the Central American presidents refused to declare Nicaragua in noncompliance and thus end the peace process, the United States was able to focus attention at Alajuela and in the international media on Sandinista compliance. The Reagan administration successfully cast the Sandinistas as the main obstacle to regional peace.

The two staunchest U.S. allies, Azcona and Duarte, unexpectedly arrived for the summit a day early, intent on enlisting Arias's support for an anti-Sandinista posture. Both vigorously attacked the Nicaraguans for not complying with the peace plan and argued that its timetable for implementation, which expired at the summit, could not be extended "for even one minute more." Their own doubtful compliance with the plan's conditions was not an issue. Duarte took the lead in demanding the immediate "democratization" of Nicaragua.[76] The other Central American presidents agreed that the contra bases in Honduras should not be closed until Nicaragua was in full compliance with Esquipulas II.[77]

The summit's final communiqué reflected Nicaragua's isolation. The presidents, while taking note of the CIVS report, expressed serious reservations over the verification procedures. The CIVS report was very favorable to Nicaragua. Azcona and Duarte felt that some of the countries participating in the CIVS committee were pro-Sandinista. They were especially suspicious of Mexico and its willingness to accept the Nicaraguan definition of democracy. "We do not need Mexicans and Panamanians teaching us about democracy," declared Azcona at the summit.[78] The Costa Rican foreign minister, Rodrigo Madrigal-Nieto, expressed similar concerns about the fairness of the CIVS report.[79] Given this unhappiness with the verification committee, the presidents decided to remove the CIVS as the verification watchdog. It was replaced by an executive committee made up of the five foreign ministers of Central America. These changes in the verification procedures left Nicaragua without any allies in the peace process, as the Contadora states were now completely removed from Central American diplomacy.

Ortega made concessions to keep the peace process alive and to make sure the United States did not renew aid to the contras. He announced at the summit that the Sandinistas would immediately lift the state of emergency that had restricted press and political freedoms, would open direct cease-fire talks with the contras, would free thousands of political prisoners, and would hold scheduled elections for the municipal government and for the Central American parliament. On the eve of the conference, he wrote in the *New York Times* that Nicaragua was willing to negotiate limits on the size of its armed forces, removal of foreign military advisers, and a ban on foreign military bases. Although Ortega did not receive what he wanted in return for this concession (a joint Central American condemnation of contra aid and a new timetable for implementation of Esquipulas II), he did attain the continuation of the peace process over the objections of the Reagan administration.[80]

Nicaraguan concessions at Alajuela did not dissuade Reagan from supporting the contras. Administration officials argued that assistance to the Nicaraguan resistance was necessary to keep the pressure on the Sandinistas. They claimed that Ortega only made the concessions at the summit to stop congressional approval of additional U.S. military aid to the contras.[81] To keep pressure on the Nicaraguans, Reagan asked Congress for $36.25 million to be put in escrow until he determined whether the Sandinistas were serious in wanting peace. He argued that it was clear that the Sandinistas had no intention of complying with Esquipulas II. They hoped merely to prevent a renewal of U.S. military aid to the contras and to wait out the final year of his administration. If they succeeded they could achieve their ambition of turning Nicaragua into a Marxist fortress with a "600,000-men army" having the capacity to sow revolutionary chaos throughout Central America. Congress refused to accept this logic, arguing instead that stability, democracy, and development in Central America would be better served by giving the peace process a chance. On February 3, 1988, the House narrowly defeated the administration's request for more contra aid.

Sapoa

The refusal of Congress to approve additional military aid to the contras created a diplomatic opportunity for the Sandinistas. If the other Central American countries would not pressure Honduras to close down the contra bases, then Nicaragua would try to persuade the contras themselves of the futility of their efforts. After years of refusing to meet face to face with the armed opposition, the Sandinistas finally agreed to hold direct talks with the contra leadership. The contras entered these negotiations in a very weak position. By 1988, after suffering a series of military defeats, they lacked the ability to conduct large-scale military operations. Political defeats had compounded the military losses. Esquipulas II not only recognized the legitimacy of the Sandinista regime, but also called for the cessation of all assistance to irregular forces. The Iran-Contra scandal also weakened the contras by damaging the influence of their most powerful patron, Ronald Reagan.

The 219-to-211 congressional vote against contra aid on February 3 was a watershed for the contras. U.S. aid deliveries ended February 29, causing an acute crisis for the rebels inside Nicaragua. Speaker Wright proposed a $30.8 million package of food and nonlethal aid, but Reagan still insisted on the restoration of military assistance and refused to negotiate with the congressional Democratic leadership. On March 3 House Republicans, backed by the White House, joined liberal Democrats to scuttle Wright's plan by an eight-vote margin. This was the final blow for the contras, who reacted bitterly and announced their final withdrawal from Nicaragua.[82] In the meantime, the Sandinistas added to the pressure against the rebels by launching an offensive in the remote Bocay valley on the Honduran border, which blocked off the principal contra supply and escape route.

The contras were forced to agree to a cease-fire in their face-to-face meeting with the government at Sapoa, a dusty village near the Costa Rican border. At Sapoa the contras promised to "halt military operations in the entire territory for a period of sixty days beginning April 1 of this year"[83] (see appendix 6). The contras also agreed to "locate themselves in zones, whose location, size and modus operandi will be mutually accorded through special commissions."[84] In exchange, the Sandinistas made major concessions to facilitate the reintegration of Nicaraguans active in the resistance into the country's political life. The government assured the rebels "that all those who have left the country for political reasons may return to Nicaragua and incorporate themselves into political, economic and social processes without any conditions beyond those established by the laws of the republic. They will not be tried, punished or persecuted for the political-military acts they have carried out."[85] The Sandinistas also promised to allow former rebels to participate in the upcoming general election and national dialogue.

The Reagan administration was quickly able to derail the Sapoa accord by taking advantage of the deep cleavages within the contra movement. The internal dispute was between those like Alfredo César,

Adolfo Calero, Walter Calderón-López, and Pedro Joaquín Chamorro, Jr., who argued that the only future for the rebels was to carry out the anti-Sandinista struggle in the political arena, and those like Enrique Bermúdez, who called for the continuation of the war. The split began when Adolfo Calero attempted, in vain, to oust top military commander Bermúdez, who had openly criticized the Sapoa agreement. The United States sided openly with Bermúdez and encouraged his faction to put pressure on the contra leadership to abandon the Sapoa agreement. In a meeting with the leadership, Assistant Secretary of State Abrams received assurances that the contras would not agree to any new concessions.[86] The administration also strengthened the position of Bermúdez within the rebel movement by giving him control of the $48 million humanitarian aid package that Reagan was able to get through Congress after Sapoa and by engineering Bermúdez's election to the contra directorate. Rebel commanders who had sided with Calero were denied assistance. Calero supporter Calderón-López charged that "Bermúdez has told our troops that the humanitarian assistance was late in arriving because of us."[87] Reagan's hard-line stance ended the dialogue between the contras and the Sandinistas.

The Nicaraguan government shifted its attention to the domestic opposition. In spring 1988 a national dialogue was begun within the framework of Esquipulas II to democratize the regime. The opposition again demanded sweeping constitutional reforms. Its most important demand was the removal of all ties between the Sandinista party (FSLN) and the state. For example, the opposition wanted the armed forces and the police transformed into national, professional, nonpartisan institutions, instead of branches of the ruling party.[88] The opposition also called for limiting the power of the presidency. Specifically, they asked that the executive be restricted to one term in office, that his relatives to the fourth degree of blood and marriage be prohibited from running for office, and that the president be removed from the nomination process for the Supreme Court and the Supreme Election Council. The opposition also demanded reforms in property rights, the educational system, and the powers of municipal government. Finally, they proposed the appointment of a human rights ombudsman, the establishment of a constitutional tribunal to resolve conflict of power among the branches and entities of government, and creation of a council to determine economic policy.[89]

While the Sandinistas refused to negotiate any changes in the constitutional order, the government did propose changes in the election laws designed to address opposition concerns over fairness. The government suggested that such issues as media access, reform in the electoral council, and the date of the presidential election were open for discussion. Despite these hopeful signs and the Sapoa agreement, deep fears and strong suspicions remained. The national dialogue of 1988 was quickly deadlocked because the domestic opposition simply did not trust the FSLN.

The political opposition in Nicaragua viewed the Sandinistas' attempts at democratization with deep suspicion. The best-known critic of the government, Violeta de Chamorro, was unimpressed with the government's move toward liberalization. She speculated that the Sandinistas' principal motivation was to win public relations points in order to end U.S. funding of the contras. Chamorro described *La Prensa* (and, by extension, Nicaragua) as "living under a precarious liberty, which the Sandinistas see themselves obliged to extend from time to time and which they can terminate at any moment."[90] Other members of the internal opposition pointed out that true democracy could not exist in Nicaragua until the structure of the regime changed. They argued that the Sandinistas were unlikely to give up control of the armed forces or the police. Leo Hernández, another government critic, predicted that the FSLN's compliance with the peace process would be partial and temporary: "They can reopen *La Prensa*, and Radio Católica, but the underlying repressive legal apparatus remains intact. At any moment they can roll us back to zero."[91] Many leaders in the domestic opposition claimed that violent opposition to the FSLN was legitimate as long as the constitutional order lacked a framework in which power could be fairly contested. A leading opposition figure expressed a common attitude in these terms: "The contra is legitimate in taking arms because the Sandinistas have closed off all peaceful avenues of opposition."[92]

The Sandinista leadership became increasingly frustrated by the refusal of the United States, the other Central American republics, and the Nicaraguan internal opposition to disavow the contras. They were especially angered by the fact that various elements of the legal opposition within the country, including leaders of the right wing Nicaragua Democratic Coordinator (usually called the *coordinadora*), the private sector, and the Roman Catholic hierarchy expressed open sympathies with the rebels. The government, to demonstrate its ability and willingness to defend the revolution, decided to take strong action in fall 1988. After an antigovernment demonstration in Augusto Sandino's hometown of Nandaime, the Sandinistas took swift action against both their internal and external enemies. After the rally the government arrested thirty-eight critics of the regime who participated in the demonstration, temporarily closed down *La Prensa*, silenced Radio Católica, and confiscated the San Antonio Sugar Mill (the single largest private enterprise in the country). The government also expelled the ambassador and eight other U.S. diplomats, accusing them of orchestrating the political opposition. The Sandinista leadership hoped that these actions would demonstrate that they still had the power to deal with their enemies.[93]

Less than a year after the signing of the peace agreement, the process appeared to break down. The Nicaraguan crackdown at Nandaime caused a crisis in the Esquipulas process. The presidential summit scheduled for summer 1988 in El Salvador was postponed. A top Costa Rican diplomat explained: "By the middle of 1988 regional tensions were so high that a presidential summit would have been disastrous. The Central American presidents were too busy accusing each other of noncompliance to talk of peace."[94] Although these actions slowed the peace process, they did not terminate the peace efforts. All the Central American republics needed peace to maintain political, social, and economic order, and the Arias peace plan was the only viable mechanism for ending the conflict. But regional leaders would have to wait for a change in the administration in Washington before renewing their peace efforts. Ironically, a year after the signing of what President Duarte called Central America's second declaration of independence, the prospects for Central American peace still depended on Washington.

5 *The Peace Process*

The Central American peace process was revived in 1989. The setbacks suffered by the Arias plan in 1988 were overcome through the slow and painful deliberations of the region's presidents. The diplomatic framework created by Oscar Arias succeeded in developing ground rules for the democratization of the Sandinista regime. In a series of summits, the Central American presidents arrived at a compromise that led to the liberalization of Nicaraguan politics in exchange for the demobilization of the contras. The Nicaraguan election of 1990 and the victory of opposition candidate Violeta Barrios de Chamorro were made possible by this arrangement.

Three developments broke the stalemate and permitted the revival of the Central American peace process. First was the end of the Reagan administration. Although George Bush shared the same general political ideology as his former boss, he entered the White House recognizing the necessity of developing a new Central American policy. The new administration viewed the settlement of the Central American conflict as one of the prerequisites for the reestablishment of a working relationship between Congress and the White House. Bush showed a strong desire to distance himself from the most controversial aspect of Reagan's Central American policy: military aid to the Nicaraguan contras. James Baker, during his confirmation hearings, told the Senate that the administration hoped to refocus its policy toward resolving the Latin American debt crisis. To this end, he said that the new administration would improve relations with Mexico and modify Nicaraguan policy to make it more acceptable to Democrats, who opposed military aid to the contras.[1]

The Bush administration also recognized that Reagan's strategy of using military pressure to oust the Sandinistas had clearly failed.[2] In its place the new administration vigorously pursued a policy of increasing diplomatic and political pressure on the Nicaraguan government to establish a democratic political process. Bush hoped that free elections would allow the United States to oust the Sandinista regime by funding opposition candidates. The key to the success of this strategy was to force the Nicaraguans to devise a system in which power could be contested.

Moreover, to build a stronger bridge with the Democrat-controlled Congress, Baker named a Democrat, Bernard Aronson, as Assistant Secretary of State for Inter-American Affairs. Baker hoped that Aronson would be the key figure in formulating a Central American policy that Congress and the public would support. Aronson quickly arranged a bipartisan accord with his fellow Democrats that included both humanitarian aid to the contras and negotiations with the Sandinistas.[3] The main elements of the March 1989 agreement included a presidential promise to support the peace process and a continuation of $4.5 million a month in nonmilitary aid to the contras through February 1990, by which time Nicaragua would hold free elections. Thus, although the Bush administration was clearly rejecting the military option and no longer considered the contras viable, it refused to completely abandon the contras. Administration officials argued against dismantling the contras until after the Nicaraguan elections, saying that "if there are no contras, what guarantees do we have that the Sandinistas will behave themselves?"[4]

By changing the emphasis of the United States' Central American policy to put diplomatic and military pressure on Nicaragua, the Bush administration created new opportunities for peace in the region. The abandonment of the military option put U.S. policy in harmony with the region's presidents. A high-ranking Costa Rican official observed that "the Bush administration support of the Arias plan was a key factor in the revival of the peace effort in 1989. Peace would have been impossible if Bush had renewed U.S. military aid to the contras."[5] Bush's willingness to give the peace process a chance created a new diplomatic climate for the region's presidents.

At the same time that hard-liners were being replaced by moderates in Washington, Managua found it impossible to maintain its intransigence against its political enemies. The deteriorating economic situation once again forced the Sandinistas to revise their economic plan along more capitalist lines and to promise their domestic critics a larger role in economic decision making.

In January 1989, in a speech designed to placate the private sector,

President Ortega announced a severe austerity program, one that would reduce government spending about 44 percent.[6] The cuts included laying off as many as twelve thousand government employees and discharging up to ten thousand army troops, as well as thirteen thousand members of the security police from the Ministry of the Interior. The austerity program was designed to offer an olive branch to the domestic opposition. Ortega touched on a key issue of concern to the opposition when he ruled out further confiscation of private property, saying "there is no reason to take an inch of land from anyone."[7] Following the speech, in a series of unusually strong statements, the Sandinistas asserted that the key component of the new austerity program would be to revitalize the country's beleaguered private business sector. Government officials pointed to their determination to stimulate new private investments by controlling inflation, ending confiscation, and returning small state-run enterprises to the private sector.[8]

The Sandinistas also concluded that economic recovery depended on rapprochement with their external enemies as well as with their domestic opponents. The most critical problem was to bring an end to the contra war, which, according to the government, had cost Nicaragua $12 billion and resulted in the displacement of more than 354,000 persons, the abandonment of 290,000 hectares of land (including 31 percent of the country's coffee-growing land), and the loss of 289,000 head of cattle.[9]

Nicaragua's economic recovery clearly depended on improving relations with the United States. The Reagan administration, as part of its strategy to destabilize the Sandinista government, had imposed an economic embargo that had forced Nicaragua to search for new markets. By 1989 it was clear that the new trading partners were unable or unwilling to take the place of the United States as the principal buyer of Nicaraguan products. Western European governments became increasingly reluctant to aid, invest in, and trade with Nicaragua. Nicaragua's exports to Western Europe declined from 54 percent of the nation's total in 1986 to 39 percent in 1987.[10] The Soviet bloc, which had made up this shortfall by giving the Sandinistas an estimated $600 million a year in aid, made it clear that Nicaragua should not expect any additional assistance.[11] In fact, the Soviets advised the Sandinistas to settle their differences with Washington.

The Sandinistas were forced to make new concessions in the peace process in order to save their country's dying economy. Economic recovery and peace depended on negotiating the end of the contra war and U.S. economic sanctions. The Nicaraguan government was now willing to arrive at a settlement with its enemies to establish the framework in which power could be fairly contested in the future.

The third factor that created new opportunities for the Central American peace process was a shift in Soviet foreign policy. Mikhail Gorbachev, in a series of dramatic actions throughout the Third World (Afghanistan, Angola, and Cambodia), limited Soviet military and economic support for revolutionary governments. The new Soviet thinking in foreign policy viewed the support of Third World radicals as a hindrance to the improvement of East-West relations. This was made clear in 1989 when Secretary of State Baker linked Soviet military aid to the Nicaraguan regime to the overall improvement of U.S.-Soviet ties. The Bush administration publicly asked the Soviets to reduce their support of the Sandinistas. During a Gorbachev visit to Cuba in April 1989, the administration indicated that Western technology, investments, and wheat would be more forthcoming if Soviet behavior in the Third World became more responsible. In a speech at Texas A&M University, Bush called on the Soviets to end their support of terrorist regimes in Central America and the Middle East as a precondition for ending the cold war.[12] Bush also sent a letter on March 30, 1989, to the Soviets asking them to suspend military shipments to the Sandinistas. Gorbachev responded to these overtures by announcing that Moscow was stopping its military aid to Nicaragua in response to the United States' policy shift in Central America from arms to diplomacy.[13]

Tesoro Beach

The new international situation allowed the Central American presidents to renew the peace process. After postponing their meeting six times, for fear of ending in failure, the presidents agreed to hold their fourth summit at the Salvadoran resort of Tesoro Beach. The summit illustrated the political will of the leaders to strengthen the peace process, despite the failure of the Central American states to comply fully with Esquipulas II. A Costa Rican diplomat explained:

Esquipulas was purposely over ambitious, especially in regards to timetables. We never expected the Central American states to comply in 180 days to such a far-reaching and comprehensive settlement. What Costa Rica wanted was an agreement to the principles of peace through democratization and national reconciliation. Once the Central American states committed themselves to this process at Esquipulas, we could move forward toward compliance at Tesoro Beach and Tela.[14]

The issue at the Tesora Beach summit was once again Nicaraguan compliance. The Sandinistas faced a great deal of pressure to open up the political process, especially after the crackdown at Nandaime. Before the February 1989 summit an aide to Arias publicly stated that the Sandinistas' failure to abide by the Esquipulas accord was the major obstacle to peace. The Costa Rican official said, "The question is whether or not the Sandinistas are ready for immediate moves toward democratization. If not, we will have to prepare ourselves for the funeral of the peace process."[15]

The process was saved as the Nicaraguans made major concessions at the summit. The Sandinistas realized that in order to meet their twin objectives of ending the contra war and U.S. economic sanctions they needed to make dramatic new proposals at Tesoro Beach.[16] At the conference Ortega announced Nicaragua's decision to call free general elections no later than February 25, 1990. He promised to amend the election laws, as well as those relating to the mass media, to assure equal access to all political parties. The Nicaraguan president also invited international observers, in particular the United Nations and the Organization of American States, to be present in all electoral districts to verify that the election process was fair at every stage. Finally, in order to create a climate for internal reconciliation, Nicaragua committed itself to release an estimated three thousand political prisoners, including members of Somoza's national guard who had been in jail for nearly ten years (see appendix 7).

In exchange for these Sandinista concessions, the Central American presidents agreed to draft a combined plan calling for the demobilization of the Nicaraguan contras based in Honduras within ninety days. In order to assure Honduran compliance, the presidents agreed to ask the United Nations to create the United Nations Observer Group in Central America (ONUCA) to monitor the border. ONUCA was to provide mobile teams of at least two members each to verify that no

Central American country harbored guerrillas from a neighboring state. This was a great victory for Nicaragua, for it meant that Honduran-based contras would violate United Nations rules if they crossed the border to fight inside Nicaragua. Sandinista officials stressed that this was the first time Honduras had agreed to international verification. "This is terrible for the contras," said Paul Reichler, a U.S. attorney for the Nicaraguan government. "The contras are not only dead, but buried."[17]

Tesoro Beach was a diplomatic triumph for the Central American presidents because it clarified and strengthened the Arias plan. However, weak compliance continued to plague the peace process. The Bush administration, intent on preserving the military option until after the Nicaraguan election, pressured the Honduran government to allow the contras to remain in their territory. The Hondurans obliged by finding a loophole in Tesoro Beach's requirement for the "demobilization, repatriation, or *voluntary* resettlement of the Nicaraguan resistance and their families within 90 days."[18] The Hondurans argued that the term "voluntary" made the entire demobilization process exactly that, and further that the contra leadership, not the Honduran government, was responsible for demobilization. Consequently, Honduras took no steps to prevent the contras from using their territory, and Honduran noncompliance in turn prevented the deployment of ONUCA. Although the five Central American states requested that the secretary-general of the United Nations establish ONUCA, the request contained a reservation by Honduras objecting to ONUCA until Nicaragua dropped its suit against it before the International Court of Justice.[19] Therefore, Pérez de Cuellar was unable to act on the request.

Nicaragua was also having difficulties implementing the agreement. In the weeks following Tesoro Beach, the Sandinistas held two rounds of negotiations with opposition parties to discuss new election laws. These discussions quickly broke down. Several parties even refused to participate, calling instead for the renewal of the national dialogue to discuss fundamental constitutional reforms. Ortega at first refused these demands, but in April 1989 he submitted reform legislation that included some seventeen points raised by opposition parties. But these reforms did not satisfy the majority of the opposition, and a group of fourteen parties (which would later become the UNO coalition) presented a new package of proposals. President Ortega refused to include them in the legislation, claiming that for six weeks the opposition had refused to respond to his request for proposals. The Sandinista-sponsored election laws passed with a few amendments on April 21, just four days before the deadline for the beginning of the four-month precampaign organizing period required by the Tesoro Beach agreement.[20]

A week after the passage of the election law, fourteen opposition parties demanded further reforms, claiming that the government had shut them out of the decision-making process. They claimed that the new election laws were nothing more than a public relations stunt designed to convince world public opinion that Nicaragua was a democracy.[21] Many parties threatened to boycott the upcoming election unless the government engaged in a national dialogue. Among other things, the opposition called for greater representation on the Supreme Election Council, a moratorium on the military draft, an opposition-controlled television station, equal public financing for all parties, voting by Nicaraguans in exile outside the country, and unrestricted financing from foreign sources.[22]

Ortega, facing the specter of an opposition boycott of the 1990 election on the eve of the fifth presidential summit in Tela, finally agreed to hold a national dialogue. The Nicaraguan government feared that the 1990 elections would suffer the same fate as the 1984 elections, which never attained the desired legitimacy because the principal opposition parties had refused to participate. Ortega agreed to make further changes in the election laws if such changes would ensure full participation by all political parties. The result was the signing of a landmark political agreement between the twenty legally constituted political parties and the government that set the ground rules for the elections.

The agreement provided that the military draft be suspended between September 1989 and election day. The public media and social communication laws were reformed to give the Supreme Electoral Council the power to guarantee equal access and to administer all matters pertaining to elections. The Law for the Maintenance of Order and Public Security, which allowed the arrest of persons suspected of subversive activity, was repealed, and it was agreed the winning presidential and vice-presidential candidates would take office in April 1990 instead of January 1991, as provided in the constitution.[23] The government also agreed to adopt a broad and unconditional amnesty law for the contras that would take effect upon completion of the demobilization. In exchange for these Sandinista concessions, the opposition called on the Central American presidents to approve the contra demobilization plan. In a pointed reference to the United States, the political agreement also called upon governments with interests in Central America to abstain from covert activities in the Nicaraguan electoral process.

At the same time that the political agreement guaranteed the full participation of the Nicaraguan opposition, the Sandinista government moved to establish the election's international legitimacy by inviting foreign observers. On July 5, 1989, the Secretary General of the United Nations and the government of Nicaragua agreed on terms for the establishment of the United Nations Observer Mission for the Verification of the Elections of Nicaragua (ONUVEN). The two parties agreed that ONUVEN had the following functions: (1) to verify that political parties were equitably represented in the Supreme Electoral Council and its subsidiary bodies (nine regional electoral councils and forty-one hundred electoral boards); (2) to verify that political parties enjoyed complete freedom of organization and mobilization, without any hindrance or intimidation; (3) to verify that all political parties had equitable access to state television and radio; (4) to verify that electoral rolls were properly drawn up; (5) to inform the Supreme Electoral Council or its subsidiary bodies of any complaints received or any irregularities or interference observed in the electoral process (where appropriate the mission could also request information on any remedial action that might be required); and (6) to submit reports to the Secretary-General, who in turn would inform the Supreme Electoral Council, where appropriate.[24]

Tela

The focus at the fifth presidential summit at Tela shifted from the democratization of Nicaragua to the demobilization of the contras. At Tela, Sandinista officials were able to argue that they had fulfilled their obligation to allow greater internal political freedom; now it was time for Honduras to close contra bases in their territory and set a timetable for demobilization.

Fearing isolation and increasingly disenchanted over the destabilizing effects of twelve thousand armed men operating in the southern part of their country, Honduras was willing to consent to a contra demobilization plan. Defying objections from the Bush administration, Azcona announced shortly before the Tela summit that he wanted the contras out of Honduras "as soon as possible."[25] The Hondurans added insult to injury when they gave orders not to allow contra leaders or their representatives to enter the Telamar Beach Hotel where the summit was being held. Azcona had earlier refused to meet with a contra delegation touring Central America to present its view to the region's democratic leaders.

Honduran foreign minister Carlos López-Contreras confirmed in an interview that "all the plans are for the contras to be demobilized as soon as possible. We are not linking that process with any event. We're going ahead with it."[26] But the Honduran government made it clear that tensions along the border with Nicaragua could be reduced if the Sandinistas dropped their World Court case against Honduras.[27] Also complicating the negotiations at Tela was the position of El Salvador's new rightist president, Alfredo Cristiani. He demanded that the demobilization of the contras be linked to the disarming of the Salvadoran guerrillas.[28]

Despite these problems, Tela produced three major breakthroughs in the peace process (see appendix 8). First, the Central American presidents agreed to "endorse the joint plan for the voluntary demobilization, repatriation or relocation in Nicaragua or in third countries of the Nicaraguan resistance."[29] The demobilization of the contras was to be completed within ninety days, by December 9, 1989. The accord called for the secretaries-general of the United Nations and the Organization of American States (OAS) to implement the plan through a new International Support and Verification Commission (CIAV). Once established, the CIAV would determine the procedures for demobilization of the contras and verify the dismantling of their camps. The CIAV would also be responsible for the distribution of humanitarian aid to the Nicaraguan rebels.[30]

The second breakthrough at Tela was the signing of an agreement between Honduras and Nicaragua that delayed the Sandinista legal action against Honduras at the World Court. This agreement committed the Sandinistas to postpone, and eventually withdraw, their complaint against Honduras, once conditions regarding implementation of the joint plan and prevention of the use of Honduran territory by irregular forces were met. Honduras, as part of this agreement, dropped its objection to the creation of ONUCA.

The final agreement at Tela was the call for a cease-fire in El Salvador. Although the other Central American presidents rejected Cristiani's attempt to link the disarming of the contras to the disarming of the FMLN, they did call on the Salvadoran guerrillas to accept the legitimacy of the Cristiani government. The Tela agreement urged the Salvadoran guerrillas "to put an immediate and effective end to hostilities so that a dialogue may be carried out that will lead to a rejection of armed struggle and the integration of FMLN members into institutional and democratic life."[31] The agreement provided for the demobilization of the guerrillas under mechanisms similar to those created to disband the contras.

The Tela summit also expanded the peace process by allowing the United Nations to play a critical role. The secretary-general established three special missions to the region to verify different aspects of the agreement. The United Nations' role in the Nicaraguan elections was mandated through ONUVEN, whose mission was to verify free and fair elections. Pérez de Cuellar guaranteed the credibility of the United Nations' role when he named Elliott Richardson as his personal representative in Nicaragua. Richardson, a prominent U.S. lawyer who had held several cabinet positions in previous Republican administrations, was a personal friend of George Bush. The Sandinistas were assured of Richardson's integrity by the secretary-general, who pointed out that the U.S. administration must be convinced of the fairness of the elections if the contra war was to end.[32]

The Tela agreement created the necessary conditions for ONUCA. The role of ONUCA was to verify the cessation of aid to irregular forces and insurrectionist movements and to make certain that no state was permitting its territory to be used for attacks against any of its neighbors. ONUCA consisted of mobile teams of at least seven unarmed military observers from Canada, Colombia, Ireland, Spain, and Venezuela. These observers were grouped in verification centers located as close as possible to sensitive areas where violations were most likely to occur. The mobile teams carried out regular patrols in jeeps, trucks, helicopters, and, in the Gulf of Fonseca and other coastal areas and rivers, patrol boats and light speedboats. In addition to their regular patrols, the mobile teams were empowered to make spot checks on their own initiative.

The International Support and Verification Commission (CIAV) was the final mission created by the United Nations to verify and implement the peace plan. Created at the request of the Central American presidents, CIAV was responsible for facilitating the demobilization of the contras, including the reception and settlement of repatriated persons at their destinations. In addition, CIAV was to ensure that repatriated persons were permitted full integration into civilian life.

An Uncertain Peace

Despite these international safeguards, the Bush administration insisted that the contras must be kept intact until after the Nicaraguan election. U.S. officials still maintained that the existence of the contras was the best guarantee of Sandinista compliance with the peace plan. The United States urged its allies in the region to delay relocating the contras until after February 25, 1990. The United States pledged to disband the contras after the Sandinistas fulfilled their promise to hold free and fair elections.

The Bush administration's position dramatically increased tensions in Central America. Honduran government officials, facing considerable pressure from the United States and their own military, in addition to being preoccupied with their own presidential election, were unable to comply with the commitments they made at Tela to demobilize the contras. Azcona was so frustrated by the bullying of the Bush administration and by U.S. interference in the Honduran elections that he refused to accept the credentials of the new U.S. ambassador. Moreover, in fall 1989 more than two thousand contra troops infiltrated Nicaragua from Honduras and launched two especially bloody attacks. On October 8 six army reservists were killed while protecting a voter registration center in Chontales, and on October 21 the contras killed thirteen peasants in Río Branco.

The renewal of contra activities inside Nicaragua created an internal crisis within the Sandinista party. Hard-liners complained that Ortega had made concessions affecting internal Nicaraguan politics without securing the disbanding of the contras in return. The peace process, according to these critics, had been nothing more than a series of unilateral Nicaraguan concessions.[33] In response to this criticism, Ortega announced on November 1 a suspension of the cease-fire with the contras, expressing frustration that the demobilization plans agreed to at Tela had not been carried out.

The decision to renew military operations resulted in a diplomatic disaster for Nicaragua. Ortega made the announcement on the eve of a hemispheric conference being held in San José, Costa Rica, to commemorate one hundred years of Costa Rican democracy. This deeply offended his host, Oscar Arias, who viewed the announcement as a Sandinista public relations ploy to upstage the conference and focus attention on the contras. The announcement, whatever its intention, led to Managua's isolation. Nicaragua's image problems were compounded when Ortega arrived at this gathering of the region's civilian leaders wearing a military uniform. The Nicaraguan president's attire seemed to confirm the view of those who held that the Sandinista regime was nothing more than a leftist military dictatorship. President Bush ridiculed Ortega's behavior at the conference by calling him "a little man" and "that unwanted animal at a garden party."[34]

Nicaragua's diplomatic problems were further complicated when, following a major rebel offensive, Salvadoran president Alfredo Cristiani alleged that Nicaragua was supplying arms to the rebels. The Salvadoran government cited evidence obtained from a Nicaraguan plane that had crashed in El Salvador loaded with surface-to-air SAM-7 missiles. Cristiani suspended diplomatic and commercial relations with Nicaragua and stated that he would not attend the Managua summit of the five Central American presidents scheduled for December unless its location was moved.

The peace process survived the crisis when the Central American presidents agreed to meet in San Isidro de Coronado, Costa Rica. Rodrigo Madrigal-Nieto, the Costa Rican foreign minister, convinced both the Salvadorans and the Sandinistas to attend the summit by warning them that whoever failed to attend would be held responsible for the death of the peace process. Madrigal-Nieto also assured the Salvadoran government that it would receive strong support from the other Central American presidents.[35]

At San Isidro de Coronado the presidents signed a thirteen-point agreement to get the three-year-old peace process back on track. The agreement explicitly recognized Salvadoran president Cristiani's government as the product of a democratic pluralistic process and called on the Salvadoran rebels (FMLN) to cease hostilities and reenter negotiations aimed at their demobilization. The summit's final communiqué declared "firm support for the president of El Salvador, don Alfredo Cristiani and his government, as demonstration of our policy of supporting governments which are products of democratic, pluralistic, and participatory processes."[36]

The Sandinistas were forced to accept the legitimacy of the Salvadoran regime that two weeks earlier they had denounced as "fascist." They also accepted for the first time the linking of the contras with the FMLN. Previously, Nicaragua held that the two rebel groups were quite different because the contras were based in a neighboring country and were a product of U.S. foreign policy, whereas the Salvadoran guerrillas were based in their homeland and received very little foreign assistance. The summit declaration clearly connected the two groups, affirming "that the demobilization of the contras and the FMLN represent a fundamental factor in the solution to the crisis."[37] The Sandinistas also agreed once again to delay their world court suit against Honduras. In return the agreement called on the United States to use the remaining funds earmarked for the contras exclusively for the demobilization, repatriation, or relocation of the rebels.

The Nicaraguan Election

The Sandinistas felt they could make these concessions because they expected that the February 25, 1990, election was going to legitimate their regime. The political agreement of August 1989 had redirected the focus of Nicaraguan politics from the war against the U.S.-backed contras to the election campaign. All parties participated in these elections, in sharp contrast to the 1984 elections, which the principal opposition parties boycotted, claiming that Sandinista monopoly over military forces and control over state resources made the election process unfair. In fact, the main opposition group, the National Opposition Union (UNO), comprised the parties that formed the abstentionist bloc in 1984. Despite minor complaints of violence against UNO supporters and misuse of state resources, the election campaign was characterized as fair. UNO presidential candidate Violeta de

Chamorro believed that by and large the election procedures were fair, conceding that her complaints were relatively minor.[38]

The Sandinistas were aware that the elections must be perceived as free and fair not only at home but abroad. Clear evidence that Nicaragua was a practicing democracy might end the U.S. economic boycott and the contra war. To this end, the Nicaraguans invited a broad group of international observers to monitor the elections. According to one United Nations official, "these are the most closely observed elections in history."[39] The Sandinistas encouraged the active participation of the European Parliament, the Center for Democracy in Washington, the Boston-based Hemisphere Initiatives, the Carter Center, the Latin American Studies Association, the Organization of America States, and the United Nations. By most accounts, including the United Nations', the election campaign proceeded in an atmosphere of fairness.[40]

Nicaraguan political reforms provided the United States with a golden opportunity to affect the outcome of the Nicaraguan election. Bush could now vigorously pursue a policy of interference in the Nicaraguan election by openly financing and backing the opposition. The U.S. role in the Nicaraguan election included: helping form an anti-Sandinista coalition out of the fragmented opposition, which included more than fourteen antigovernment parties ranging from the communist to Somoza's old Liberal National Party; finding a charismatic opposition presidential candidate; furnishing overt and covert financing to the opposition; and providing observers to monitor the election.

The key instruments in Bush's strategy for influencing the Nicaraguan election was the National Endowment for Democracy (NED). The NED was part of a private network set up in 1983 to use U.S. government funds to openly support a free press and democratic political and labor movements around the world. Congress established these networks to promote democratic institutions and processes as a means of providing an alternative to covert financial aid for political groups abroad. The NED is funded by Congress and governed by an independent sixteen-member board. The endowment has sponsored voter registration, education programs, poll-watching, and vote-counting observer delegations in elections in Panama, the Philippines, Poland, and Chile. The NED's involvement in the Nicaraguan elections was the largest project ever undertaken by endowment. Carl Gershman, president of the NED, acknowledged that the Nicaraguan election "dwarfs what the endowment has been able to spend" on elections in Chile, Panama, the Philippines or any other country.[41]

The U.S. embassy in Managua used its financial and persuasive powers to unify the twelve anti-Sandinista parties under one coalition: the United Democratic Opposition (UNO). Rumors circulated in Managua that the U.S. would spend more than $45 million in covert funding to the opposition. The administration also helped select and fund a charismatic opposition presidential candidate in the elections—newspaper publisher Violeta Chamorro.

The Bush administration originally wanted Congress to approve a $9 million aid package for the Nicaraguan opposition and to waive the prohibition against using the National Endowment for Democracy to support a particular candidate or party in order to ensure that the endowment could help UNO. After reports of ideological abuses during the Reagan administration, the Endowment's charter was amended in 1985 to bar direct aid to candidates for office. The administration's proposal included $3 million in aboveboard aid to UNO to defeat the Sandinista government in the election. Aronson described the proposal as "a modest program" to assist democratic forces in "a David versus Goliath fight."[42] Supporters of the proposal argued that the waiver was necessary because Nicaragua was a special case as there was only one genuinely democratic ticket in the running. And to have a shot at winning the democrats needed to overcome the advantages of a regime that dominated public debate while censuring and restricting opposition voices for most of the last ten years.[43]

Congress balked at granting the waiver. Sen. Christopher Dodd, Chairman of the Senate Foreign Relations Subcommittee on Western Hemisphere Affairs, argued that using the NED to fund the Nicaraguan opposition "would take an organization that has earned an excellent reputation at home and abroad and compromise it."[44] The administration, facing stiff opposition in Congress and wanting to avoid another contra-funding type battle, announced that it would not use NED money to help Chamorro. The administration assured Congress that "we [the Bush administration] believe that the National Endowment for Democracy should play an active role in insuring a free and fair election in Nicaragua. We do not intend to ask the NED to go beyond election activities permitted by the charter."[45]

By promising that NED funds were to be used to provide the opposition coalition a fair chance in the election, the administration gave itself the flexibility to provide Chamorro with substantial funds. The NED told Congress that it was still prepared to give money to the opposition coalition in Nicaragua. But it said the money would go only to assist such programs as nonpartisan voter registration campaigns, drives to increase voter turnout, election monitoring, and observers. The endowment assured Congress that "the aid would be given openly and in a manner consistent with the endowment's mandate and authorizing legislature."[46] Officials involved in distributing the aid admitted that one of their major tasks was making a distinction between strengthening the democratic process—by giving the opposition a fair chance against the entrenched Sandinistas—and simply bolstering UNO's campaign. "If somebody wants 'Violeta' for president stickers, they need to go to another shop—they won't get them from us," said Keith Schuette, of the GOP-affiliated National Republican Institute, which, working jointly with its counterpart, the National Democratic Institute, helps the NED distribute funds.[47]

The U.S. Congress approved an overt special aid package of $9 million for the February election. Specifically earmarked for the opposition (UNO) "party infrastructure" was $1.5 million for sixty-two vehicles and gasoline; $1.4 million in cash; $815,000 for party members' salaries and expenses; $600,000 to pay twenty thousand poll watchers; $300,000 for office equipment; and $50,000 for trips abroad by UNO members. Of the remaining $4 million, $1.05 million was committed for three international election-monitoring teams and the rest was designated as "flexible funds" to be used to support the electoral process.[48]

The State Department also gave $2 million to the Nicaraguan Supreme Electoral Council in compliance with the 50 percent rule on foreign donations, leaving $950,000 of flexible funds to be disbursed by the State Department. However, according to the terms of the NED charter, even UNO's $2 million was not to be spent for partisan politics.

The Central Intelligence Agency also funneled funds to Chamorro's election campaign. According to congressional sources, high-ranking State Department officials secretly paid about $530,000 to ninety-five former contras and other Nicaraguan exiles in Miami to return to their homeland and campaign for Chamorro and other opposition candidates. In the month following the bipartisan agreement, the CIA phased out payments to the Miami-based contra directorate, and U.S. officials encouraged the contras to return home and support the political opposition. The CIA then began sending money under a new covert program called the Nicaraguan Exile Relocation program, ostensibly to cover the cost of relocating to Nicaragua. According to sources who have seen the CIA records, one recipient of the funds was Alfredo Cesar, a former contra official who helped run Chamorro's presidential campaign.[49] During the congressional debate on funding the Nicaraguan opposition, Sen. Claiborne Pell asked Aronson if the administration was planning any "covert operations" to influence the Nicaraguan elections. At the time, Aronson declined to answer, saying such questions should be discussed behind closed doors by the congressional intelligence panels.[50]

The White House also acquired funding for the Nicaraguan opposition from other countries. At the United Nations, Secretary of State James Baker asked the foreign ministers of Japan and West Germany to request political parties in their countries to contribute funds to Chamorro's campaign. Baker made similar requests to other close U.S. allies, including conservative Arab regimes.

The Sandinistas were confident that the election would be deemed legitimate and that despite the massive level of U.S. intervention, the FSLN would win it. The opposition UNO coalition was composed of twelve political parties ranging from the far right to the far left, and despite a superficial appearance of unity it was deeply divided over ideological and tactical issues as well as personality conflicts. The fragility of the organization was evident when two parties, the Nicaraguan Social Christian Party and the Liberal Party of National Unity, left the original fourteen-party coalition almost immediately after UNO was formed. Moreover, some conservative elements within the coalition called for the expulsion of the leftist parties (the Communists and the left wing Social Democrats) so that UNO would have a clear conservative identity.[51]

In addition to deep divisions within the coalition, the opposition faced formidable organizational obstacles in trying to mount a serious challenge to the Sandinistas. Although some of the opposition groups had organizations and social bases in certain regions of the country (for example, the Conservatives in Granada and Liberals in León), these appeared dwarfed by the Sandinista network of mass organizations.

Most of the twelve parties in UNO had a localized, minuscule base and almost no name recognition. A U.S. political consultant brought in to advise UNO was quoted as saying that the coalition engaged in "primitive" politics with little sense of grassroots organization.[52]

UNO also lacked the necessary resources to compete with the FSLN in the elections. Despite $9 million earmarked by the Bush administration for the Nicaraguan opposition, UNO's campaign was woefully short of supplies. The funds were not approved by Congress until November 1989, and the Nicaraguan government set up bureaucratic barriers to prevent the opposition from getting the aid in a timely manner. UNO's campaign literature, posters, bumper stickers, T-shirts, and buttons were delayed for more than a month in Nicaraguan customs.[53] The campaign was forced to rely solely on campaign rallies and speeches to get its message across. By and large these rallies attracted modest crowds, and to most foreign observers the campaign seemed destined for failure.

The Sandinistas, meanwhile, had the resources of the entire Nicaraguan state at their disposal. The FSLN, while providing the opposition with a few minutes each day on government-owned television, controlled the rest of the time. This was most apparent on the nightly news, which was patently pro-Sandinista.[54] The FSLN also used government vehicles, buses, and trucks to transport their supporters to progovernment rallies. These rallies drew large crowds as the party gave away T-shirts, baseball caps, and other paraphernalia. In its use of media images, manipulation of the press, and sophisticated use of television, the Sandinista campaign closely resembled a U.S. presidential campaign.

Coming into the election, the Sandinistas confidently predicted a landslide victory for their party. They expected voters to reward a movement that had given them land, education, and democracy.[55] Public opinion polls seemed to confirm that the Sandinistas would win the election. Polls conducted by progovernment sources showed Ortega ahead by 20 to 30 percentage points, results that were confirmed in independent polls conducted by U.S. firms.[56] Only the antigovernment newspaper *La Prensa* showed Chamorro ahead.

Despite these formidable obstacles, the Nicaraguan opposition won a stunning 55 percent victory. The election-day surprise was due, in large part, to the difficulty of measuring political sentiments in a country where people were afraid. Ortega repeatedly branded the opposition as "Yankee agents." In the UNO stronghold of Jinotega Province, the word came down that the Sandinistas would know how everyone voted, a convincing rumor in a land where there had never been a peaceful transfer of power.[57] Fear led many people to hide their true opinions from pollsters and to avoid attending opposition rallies.

UNO's landslide victory may be attributed to several factors. First, the election occurred in a country in economic crisis. Inflation hit the incomprehensible figure of 35,000 percent in 1988, and unemployment was more than 20 percent. According to the government's own figures, the economy was one-third the size it had been at the time of the revolution, and the spending power of Nicaraguans was 7 percent of what it was under Somoza. The minimum wage for a state farm worker was seventy cents a day; a teacher made thirteen dollars a month. President Oscar Arias of Costa Rica pointed out that voters in democracies do not return incumbents whose terms have seen high inflation and double-digit unemployment. Indeed, he held that given the conditions in Nicaragua it was "inconceivable that the Sandinistas could win a fair election."

UNO's victory can also be attributed to the personal prestige of Violeta Barrios de Chamorro—the widow of national hero Pedro Joaquín Chamorro, a noted journalist and critic of the Somoza regime who had been murdered in 1978. Doña Violeta had impeccable anti-Somoza credentials as a member of the first revolutionary junta. She was also a veteran of the anti-Sandinista opposition. She had resigned in 1980 from the ruling junta because of its leftist orientation, and as publisher of La Prensa, following the death of her husband, she continued to be a prominent critic of the Sandinista regime. Moreover, Chamorro's personal life seemed to symbolize Nicaragua's internal divisions: two of her children joined her in opposition; two others were Sandinistas.[58] Thus Chamorro was viewed by many Nicaraguans as someone who could correct the excesses of the FSLN without reversing all the social gains of the 1979 revolution. Chamorro's personal history and prestige allowed her to be portrayed as the candidate of national reconciliation.

The opposition promise to end the war proved to be a decisive issue in the election. Public opinion polls showed that the military draft was the most unpopular of all the Sandinista policies.[59] In fact, it was widely rumored that Ortega planned to announce the end of the draft in an election-eve rally, but public opinion polls appeared so favorable that he felt he could win without such a pledge.[60] The Chamorro campaign was also aided by its promise to improve relations with the United States. UNO candidates, because of their close ties to the U.S., could claim with confidence that if they won the election the United States would end its economic embargo against Nicaragua and open the floodgate of U.S. economic assistance. As Tom Walker and Harry Vanden pointed out, "In the long run, however, it was not the Bush administration's multimillion covert and nearly $8 million [overt] support for UNO forces that tipped the scale. . . . What seems to have mattered most in shaping the outcome was the clear awareness in the minds of most Nicaraguans that they had a clear choice in 1990: Vote Sandinista and, in doing so, perpetuate the war and economic strangulation; or vote for the U.S.-sponsored candidate, and, in doing so, end the war and economic aggression. They chose the latter."[61]

Aftermath

Chamorro's victory dramatically changed Central American diplomacy. The Sandinistas and the opposition both believed that the Nicaraguan people voted for national reconciliation. Ortega immediately accepted the election results and promised to transfer power peacefully to Chamorro. The day after the election Ortega held an emotional meeting with Chamorro, and both pledged to work together to achieve the first democratic transfer of power in Nicaraguan history.[62] Transition talks between the Sandinistas and their former enemies produced a historic compromise in which the new president retained Humberto Ortega, brother of the former president, as head of the Nicaraguan armed forces. In return, the Sandinistas pledged to give the new president a hundred-day honeymoon, in which she would be given a free hand to implement economic reforms.

The Nicaraguan elections also resolved the decade-old conflict between the United States and Nicaragua. The Bush administration interpreted Chamorro's victory as a triumph for U.S. Central American policy, and it moved quickly to help the ailing Nicaraguan economy. Bush ended the five-year-old economic embargo against Managua and asked Congress to approve a $300 million aid package to the Chamorro government. The president told Congress that "we must act, and act soon, to help the people of these new democracies in two great and historic tasks: reconstruction and reconciliation."[63] The aid package was intended to help Chamorro reduce the Nicaraguan foreign debt, restore agricultural production, revive private enterprise, and provide basic services such as roads and schools.

The Bush administration also moved forcefully to dismantle the contra infrastructure. Three weeks after the election Vice-President Dan Quayle told the contra leadership that it was time for them to "become farmers instead of fighters."[64] The vice-president made it clear that the United States wanted the Nicaraguan rebels to abide by plans laid out by the United Nations observer force in Central America. The plan called for the contras to turn over their weapons to ONUCA as part of the demobilization plan accepted by the Central American presidents at Tela. Quayle also made it clear that since the United States had been closely identified with the contra side of the conflict, it favored a United Nations role in the disarmament process—"an impartial third party in there actually doing the demobilization."[65]

The newly elected president of Honduras, Rafael Callejas, placed additional pressure on the contras, announcing at a news conference that "these rebels should not continue in our territory."[66] He added that he would allow the contras to stay only until the inauguration of Chamorro on April 25: "I don't want to force circumstances in Nicaragua, which is now going through a period of political transition following a victory by the opposition at the poll."[67] In early April the contra camp at Yamales, in the southern part of the country, was dismantled and a token number of weapons were turned over to ONUCA. Two days after the inauguration Honduran forces reoccupied the base. In a televised ceremony Callejas declared that "the sovereignty of Honduras will be absolutely respected. We will never let irregular forces use our national territory again."[68]

The contras, no longer enjoying U.S. support or their Honduran sanctuaries, were forced to sign a cease-fire with the new government. On April 19 leaders of the Sandinista government, the government-elect, and the contras signed an agreement ending the eight-year civil war and calling for the complete disarming of the rebels by June 10, 1991. Earlier the contras had signed an accord in Tegucigalpa for the dismantling of the rebel bases in Honduras under international supervision. The new agreement established five security zones inside Nicaragua in which the guerrillas could safely gather to demobilize. The Sandinista army was withdrawn from the zones on April 22, monitored by ONUCA, the OAS, and the Nicaraguan Roman Catholic Church. After that, with the exception of defined air corridors, government forces were not allowed to fly over or approach within twelve miles of the security zones.

The United Nations provided food and other humanitarian services for the contras, and eight hundred U.N. troops protected the perimeter of the zones. A separate agreement, signed by contra leaders and the Chamorro government, committed the rebels to begin surrendering their weapons to international authorities (ONUCA) inside the zones the day Chamorro took power. The main contra forces were disarmed by June 10. A third agreement set similar conditions for the demobilization of the Miskito contra troops on the Atlantic coast. Their demobilization was required by May 18, 1990.

The electoral defeat of the Sandinistas and the demobilization of the contras allowed the Central American presidents to redirect the peace process toward economic development. Three presidential summits after the Nicaraguan elections (Montelimar, Nicaragua; Antigua, Guatemala; and Puntarrenas, Costa Rica) focused on the region's economic crisis and not on civil conflicts. After February 25, 1990, only lip service was paid to reducing violence in Guatemala and El Salvador. Regional leaders argued that in the final analysis violence could only be reduced through economic development. Moreover, the regional electoral trend toward the right focused economic discussion on free trade and economic growth.

After Chamorro's victory there was great hope in the region for economic reform. Many leaders confidently predicted a revival of the Central American common market. Many economists hoped that the sweep of candidates advocating free markets and a reduction in government spending in elections in Costa Rica, El Salvador, and Nicaragua signaled a new period of economic cooperation in Central America. Manuel Lasaga, chief economist with Southeast Bank in Miami, reflected the widespread optimism after the Nicaraguan election when he observed, "there's been a 180-degree turn in Latin America politically. This trend is encouraging new leaders in the region, who are democratically elected and share a common objective of a market-oriented economy. They want to open up their economies and get more involved in international trade."[69]

The presidential conference in Montelimar, Nicaragua, reflected the changing agenda in regional politics. The summit's final communiqué expressed strong support for the transition of power in Nicaragua and urged the contras to cooperate with ONUCA in the demobilization process. But the most important sections of the document were those dealing with economic issues. The Central American leaders declared that "the consolidation of democracy, once we have overcome the obstacle to peace, requires us to confront the economic challenge."[70]

The presidents clearly saw regional economic recovery as a prerequisite for stable democracy in the isthmus. Consequently, they placed four new items on the agenda for their next meeting: reactivating, restructuring, and strengthening regional economic integration; evolving an integrated production system; creating a structure to resolve the external debt problem; and establishing a more equitable system for dealing with the social cost of economic reform.[71] The Central American presidents also made an impassioned plea for international aid in resolving the region's economic problems. They were especially hopeful of economic aid from the European community and Japan.

The Central American presidents believed that the region's economic problems could be better addressed through joint actions. They felt that the framework created at Esquipulas would provide the foundations for a new Central American economic system. At the presidential summit in Antigua, Guatemala, the presidents called for the creation of a Central American Economic Action Plan (El Plan de Acción Económica de Centroamérica—PAECA).[72] However, the agreement at Antigua demonstrated the lack of consensus on economic policies among the isthmian states. Although there was general agreement on the need for a free market and the encouragement of economic integration, the plan lacked any specific instruments for re-creating the Central American Common Market. The presidents could only agree to attempt to coordinate their economic policy and develop a united approach for dealing with international lending agencies, the United States, Japan, and the European community.

The Antigua and Montelimar summits marked the end of the Esquipulas peace process. The conferences were a watershed, as the focus of regional diplomacy moved away from political and security issues and concentrated instead on common economic problems. The newly elected conservative presidents assumed that the removal of the

Sandinistas resolved the region's conflicts by eliminating its main security threat. They reasoned that the power of revolutionary groups in El Salvador and Guatemala would be vastly reduced without their Nicaraguan bases. Thus, with the fear of violent revolution removed in the wake of the Nicaraguan elections, the presidents were no longer inclined to encourage political reform in Guatemala and El Salvador. Instead, the Esquipulas peace process was transformed into a mechanism for regional economic integration.

6 *Peace in the Isthmus*

The Arias plan transformed the political situation in Central America by breaking the region's political and military stalemate and establishing the framework for peace and security. The accord's principal contribution was to end the incessant interference of the Central American states in one another's affairs; each agreed to accept the legitimacy of the other existing governments, even when it meant setting aside sharp ideological differences. The agreement also established the foundations for a regional consensus by committing the individual states to progressive democratization.

The peace accord was unique, not only because it regulated the external behavior of the Central American states, but because its most important provisions affected their domestic politics as well. Traditional concepts of sovereignty and self-determination were obsolete because of the history of Central American union, U.S. hegemony, and dependency. These strong historic links between internal and external politics meant that any viable solution to the regionwide conflict must address the internal crisis within each of the states.

The Arias plan succeeded because it was the only one of the international peace initiatives to recognize the interdependency between domestic, regional, and international politics. Its main accomplishment was to the end the spiral of escalating violence that threatened to engulf the whole isthmus. The Central American presidents, in a series of summits, were able to work out an arrangement whereby Nicaragua would establish a democratic form of government in exchange for an end to the contra war. The accord was the centerpiece in settling the dispute between the U.S. and Nicaragua. Moreover, the peace process established a regional consensus on democratization and social reform that replaced the U.S.-imposed strategy of military force-cum-reform as the linchpin of regional security.

The Lessons of Esquipulas

The Central American crisis was one of the last crises of the cold war era, and the Central American accord was one of the first settlements of a regional conflict in the post–cold war period. The lessons that emerge from the peace process clearly reflect the underlying transformation of the international system, in which the old distinctions between domestic, regional, and global politics are less important.

First, the Central American peace process exemplified the primacy of interdependency. The Central American conflict illustrates the phenomenon of cascading interdependency. It is a clear example of the close links between domestic political systems and regional and international systems. It shows how the breakdown of authority in the subsystems creates tension that interlocks with comparable tensions in other systems, and how these interact across the whole spectrum of international politics. The Sandinista revolution was not a discrete event, but an example of what James Rosenau calls "turbulence."[1] The term refers to the dynamics of systemic transformation in which old patterns of authority break down. The Nicaraguan revolution was part of a global pattern of shifting political structures in which international, national, and subnational authority relationships were being rapidly transformed.

The Sandinista victory created a chain reaction throughout Central America as it demonstrated that the region's traditional authority relationships (alliances between military and oligarchy) were hopelessly obsolete. The search for a new political formula created a region-wide crisis. The fall of Somoza was followed by a reformist coup d'état in El Salvador, the end of two decades of military rule in Honduras, and a new wave of political repression in Guatemala. In this regional crisis, long-established hierarchies presided over by narrow political elites were replaced by a multiplicity of organizations and groups that had more democratic leadership, which had a profound effect on the international system.

The very nature of the Central American conflict, with its wide array of actors competing for political power, led to the internationalization of the crisis. The crisis witnessed the evolution of a web of interdependency throughout Central America as national actors sought comparable actors across their national borders. The breakdown of the old order throughout Central America led these individuals to make alliances, wage war, and conduct campaigns on a regional and international level. The forces of revolution, reform, and reaction were linked by an invisible web of interdependency. Moreover, many of these groups had links with extraregional actors (for example, the connections between the Central American militaries and the U.S. armed forces) who were openly involved in the transformation of Central America.

The Central American peace process was part of efforts by reformist democratic elements in the isthmus to open up the region's political system. Reformers feared the extremism of popular revolutions and right wing military regimes. Believers in civil and human rights, they disapproved of popular democracy as practiced by Cuba and Nicaragua. But they also distrusted the traditional forces in their own societies. The military-oligarchy alliance had for too long violated basic human rights, limited access to economic wealth, and misused their countries' resources. Democratic reformers argued that the Nicaraguan revolution demonstrated that centrist political movements, deprived of an opportunity to participate in politics, turn to revolution. They called on their governments to open up the political and economic systems to avert a social explosion.

At first these reformist elements participated in the U.S.-sponsored strategy of controlled evolution. The centerpiece of this policy was the formation of a new alliance between the military and conservative elements in the middle class (excluding the oligarchy). The strategy of these conservative-reformist regimes consisted of two elements: social and economic reforms to co-opt the democratic left and repression of the revolutionary left to assuage the right's fear of reform.[2] Throughout Central America these regimes attempted to maintain stability in the wake of the Nicaraguan revolution through a process of democratization. This new political formula, taking advantage of public rejection of almost continuous military rule, was legitimated through the electoral process. For the first time in their history, all five of the Central American states had democratically elected governments at the beginning of the 1990s.

The challenge of consolidating the new political arrangement proved extremely difficult because in Guatemala, Honduras, and El Salvador the reformist regimes were unable to break the power of their militaries. Meaningful economic and social change (agrarian, banking, and educational) was frustrated. Moreover, although elections provided a greater degree of citizen participation, the Central American states were far from model democracies.[3] Government-sponsored death squads were active in Honduras until 1984. In El Salvador they are still active, but at reduced levels; and in Guatemala 1990 was the worst year for political murders since Ríos-Montt's dirty war.

The failure of the military-reformist alliance throughout Central America created the need for a new political formula. Reformers called for a more progressive solution, one that would not only provide for an open electoral system but also seek to guarantee extensive participatory rights and civil liberties. Most importantly, reformist civilian leaders demanded that the power of the region's military be reduced. They warned that the Central American conflict had allowed the already powerful militaries to increase their influence over political and economic affairs.

The Central American peace accord was an attempt by reformists to arrive at a new political arrangement for the region. Esquipulas II strengthened the position of reformers throughout the isthmus by creating international pressure for greater democracy. The accord's requirements that the five participating nations declare an amnesty for all political prisoners, guarantee a free press and free elections, and allow dissident groups to operate openly gave international and internal legitimacy to the reformers' domestic agenda. Revolutionary groups throughout the isthmus were weakened by the accord's provisions calling for a cease-fire with rebel groups, cessation of aid to guerrilla forces, and a ban on use of Central American territory to attack neighboring states. The Central American presidents used the peace process to delegitimate guerrilla movements in El Salvador, Guatemala, and Nicaragua. Similarly, the leaders hoped to reduce the power of their security forces by decreasing regional tensions, guaranteeing basic human rights, and moving toward an eventual demilitarization of the entire region.

The second lesson of Esquipulas was the indispensable role of democracy as a legitimating force in international politics. Central to the peace accord was the belief that the solution to the region's crisis was democratization. Arias argued that the only method for achieving national reconciliation in the deeply divided societies of El Salvador, Guatemala, and Nicaragua was through an authentic democratic process that promoted social justice and respect for human rights.

The Costa Rican president realized that to preserve his country's political structure and the embryonic democracies in the rest of Central America, international support had to be brought to bear. Democracy would protect the region from the extremes of either military coups or leftist revolutions. The progressive democratization of the region would weaken the power of the Central American militaries. The reformist regimes, under international protection, would be able to create a new political system based on civil and human rights.

Democratization would also provide legitimate and peaceful mechanisms for social transformation that would forestall the need for violent revolution. Arias designed his peace process as a mechanism for pressuring the isthmus's revolutionary forces to accept Western-style liberal democracy. Cuban-style participatory democracy was rejected as an option for the region. Throughout the eight presidential summits that made up the peace process, extraordinary pressure was brought to bear on Nicaragua to reform its political system. At first the Sandinistas resisted, arguing that Nicaragua was already a practicing democracy in which the people participated in decision making to a far greater degree than in other Latin American countries. Nicaraguans also pointed out that opposition groups were tolerated to a point comparable with most liberal democracies in Latin America and certainly beyond anything permissible in Guatemala and El Salvador.

Arias and the other Central American presidents brought an imposing array of international pressures to bear on the Sandinistas, forcing them to democratize. The Sandinistas were confronted not only with the contras and the United States' economic embargo, but also with a more skeptical Western Europe and an increasingly reluctant Soviet Union. Facing an economic nightmare and few options, Nicaragua agreed to accept the Costa Rican definition of democracy. The political agreement of August 1989 between the government and the Nicaraguan opposition signaled the Sandinistas' acceptance of Western-style liberal democracy as the accepted formula for contesting political power, a formula that resulted in their defeat in the 1990 Nicaraguan elections.

The Esquipulas peace process also strengthened the legitimacy of the Salvadoran regime. Although many observers questioned the reality of Salvadoran democracy, the other Central American presidents endorsed the progressive liberalization of El Salvador.[4] Beginning with the first presidential summit, regional leaders consistently backed both the Duarte and Cristiani regimes and dismissed the Salvadoran guerrillas as a destructive force. El Salvador's most important diplomatic victory came at the San Isidro de Coronado conference, in which all the Central American presidents, including Ortega, declared their firm support of Salvadoran democracy as practiced by the Cristiani government. The presidents also called for the demobilization of the Salvadoran guerrillas as a fundamental ingredient in the solution to the Central American crisis.[5]

The international legitimacy generated by the peace process led the Salvadoran left to reconsider participation in the electoral process. A leftist party with close links to the FMLN, Democratic Convergence, took part in the 1989 presidential election. In the 1991 legislative elections Democratic Convergence finished in third place behind the rightist ARENA party and the moderate Christian Democratic party. More importantly, in the U.N.-sponsored negotiations that ended the civil war in 1992, the guerrillas accepted the principle of Western-style elections as the mechanism for social transformation in El Salvador.

Esquipulas also underscored the United States' power in Central America. Although many Central American leaders viewed the accords as Central America's second declaration of independence, the accords were only implemented after the Bush administration endorsed the peace process. U.S. support for the peace plan was viewed as essential in the revival of the peace process in 1989. President Bush's decision to abandon the military option in Central America created the political space necessary for the Costa del Sol and Tela agreements. The Reagan administration had previously blocked all efforts to negotiate an end to the conflict. Reagan rejected negotiations with the Sandinistas on the grounds that they could not be trusted. The Reagan administration viewed all efforts at negotiations (Contadora, Esquipulas, Manzanillo, and Sapoa) in the context of a public relations problem, an attempt by the Sandinistas to manipulate public opinion in the United States and Western Europe.[6] This attitude led the administration to sabotage all efforts at negotiations. At the same time, Reagan felt he could not afford to ignore negotiations if he were to maintain at least some congressional support for his Central American policy.

The long, sad history of Contadora demonstrated the Reagan administration's strategy of paying lip service to negotiations while pursuing actions that damaged the peace process. The United States escalated the contra war against the Sandinistas, including the mining of the Nicaraguan harbors, in the middle of the negotiating process. The United States also put pressure on its Central American allies (El Salvador, Honduras, and Costa Rica) not to make any concessions in Contadora. The intransigence of the Reagan administration eventually forced the Latin American states to abandon the peace process.[7] Reagan's agreement to open bilateral negotiations with Managua in 1984 must be understood in the context of the administration's effort to gain public and congressional support for the contra war. In this context, the Manzanillo talks had various salutary effects for the administration. Reagan, by appearing to be more reasonable, repaired some of the political damage done in Congress by the mining of Nicaragua's harbor. The negotiations also allowed Reagan to defuse the unpopularity of his Central American policy just as the 1984 presidential election was getting underway.[8] The United States withdrew from the Manzanillo talks after the election, leading many critics to conclude that the negotiations were nothing more than a Reagan administration public relations stunt.

Similarly, the Reagan administration was able to delay the implementation of the Esquipulas accord. Reagan at first was forced to embrace the Arias plan as a consequence of the Iran-Contra scandal. The public disclosure that the administration had diverted to the contras profits from secret U.S. arms sales created a minicrisis for the president. Reagan's popularity plummeted and, lacking congressional support, his Central American policy was clearly in danger. To recover congressional support for his policies, the president was forced to project the image of peacemaker and support the Arias peace plan. In the summer of 1987 White House Chief of Staff Howard Baker and Speaker of the House Jim Wright proposed the Wright-Reagan plan in an effort to make the Central American accord more acceptable to the administration.

Reagan, although forced to support the plan, refused to fully embrace its provisions for ending the contra war. The president simply could not come to terms with ending U.S. support for the contras. The president's ambivalence toward his own chief of staff's plan doomed Wright-Reagan and led the frustrated Wright to support the Arias plan. Although Iran-Contra gave Arias the political space to obtain the approval of the other Central American presidents for the Esquipulas II accords, the Reagan administration was, nevertheless, able to delay compliance.

The administration, although publicly supporting the peace effort, put pressure on its Central American allies to delay implementation. President Azcona of Honduras, facing a cutoff of U.S. aid, bowed to the pressure and adopted a quiet policy of stalling the implementation of the plan. Azcona made Honduran compliance with the accord contingent on Nicaragua's compliance. The Hondurans made it clear that they would not dismantle the contra camps until Nicaragua took concrete steps towards democratization. Reagan also put pressure on Costa Rica, El Salvador, and Guatemala to abandon the peace process. Days before the Central American summit at Alajuela, Costa Rica, Gen. Colin Powell and Assistant Secretary of State Elliott Abrams toured the region complaining about Nicaragua noncompliance. They urged the Central Americans not to end the contra war. Powell and Abrams argued that assistance to the Nicaraguan resistance was necessary to keep the pressure on the Sandinistas. They claimed that Ortega only made concessions at Esquipulas II to stop U.S. assistance to the contras.

In 1987 and 1988 the Reagan administration succeeded in blocking the peace accord by refusing to end its support for the contras. U.S. pressure on Honduras prevented the Azcona government from dismantling the contra bases in the southern part of the country. Moreover, the administration was able to take advantage of Sandinista missteps, such as the crackdown at Nandaime, to center discussion in the international media on the Sandinista failure to guarantee full civil liberties. The Reagan administration successfully cast the Sandinistas as the main obstacle to regional peace.

Reagan's refusal to negotiate with the Nicaraguans or to end support for the contras prevented any further progress in the Central American peace process during the remainder of his term. Peace had to wait for Reagan's successor, George Bush. Although Bush shared the same general worldview as his former boss, he entered the White House recognizing the necessity to develop a new Central American policy. Bush's willingness to support the Arias peace plan and shift the United States' stance toward Nicaragua from military support of the contras to diplomatic pressure on the Sandinistas gave the Central American presidents the opportunity to implement the Esquipulas

Accord. Ironically, the history of the Central American peace process does not demonstrate the growing independence of the region from U.S. control; instead it illustrates the overwhelming U.S. influence in the isthmus. Peace was not possible until the United States agreed to the accord. As one Washington insider observed, "the battle for Central America was not fought in the jungles of Nicaragua. The real battle was fought inside the beltway in Washington."[9]

Endgame in Central America

The peace accord changed the political situation in Central America by providing the mechanism for national reconciliation. Esquipulas was designed to reduce international tensions by resolving the political, social, and economic conflicts within each of the isthmian states. The agreement provided the Central American states with a framework for opening up their political systems. The accord's most important provisions were those requiring each of the states to open dialogue with both armed and unarmed opposition. The Central American states were committed to create committees of national reconciliation, hold elections, respect human and civil rights, and release all political prisoners. This process of national reconciliation would allow each of the Central American states to develop political systems in which power could be fairly and peacefully contested.

Arias realized that regional peace depended on ending the civil conflict within each of the regional states. But national reconciliation proved to be a difficult procedure. The linkages between internal, regional, and international actors, which made the peace process possible in the first place, also fueled continuous conflict. The complex web of alliances and conflicts that are at the very root of the Central American crisis has made the final settlement of the conflict extremely difficult. The difficulty in resolving the internal conflicts in El Salvador, Guatemala, and Nicaragua reflects the profound polarization that occurred in these societies.

Nonetheless, the Central American peace process generated new rounds of negotiations aimed at settling these conflicts. Although neither El Salvador, Guatemala, nor Nicaragua achieved a final settlement to its internal conflict, each began the long and difficult road of negotiating new political, social, and economic ground rules. Esquipulas II pushed these three deeply divided countries into the endgame. The endgame, a metaphor from chess, refers to that stage in negotiations where the final provisions are made in the settlement. The negotiating table becomes like a chessboard at the beginning of the endgame: "the phase when both players have been reduced to a small but a comparable number of pieces. Each surviving piece becomes more valuable, its calculations over whether to trade, say, a bishop for a knight become more complex, more fraught with risk."[10] It was this endgame of negotiating the future of their societies that Nicaragua, El Salvador, and Guatemala entered in the aftermath of the Central American peace accords.

Nicaragua was the first of the Central American states to embark on the endgame. The Sandinista leadership viewed the Esquipulas accord as the best method for resolving the deep internal divisions within Nicaraguan society. They hoped that the reconciliation process would force their opponents to recognize the revolutionary order in Nicaragua while providing the framework in which power could be fairly contested. The Sandinistas' commitment to the peace process was made clear by their early compliance. They moved quickly to end press censorship, allowed the opposition greater freedom, and moved to open a dialogue with both their internal and external enemies.[11]

National reconciliation in Nicaragua, despite early progress, proved to be a long and arduous process. The Sandinistas soon grew dissatisfied with the lack of progress in ending the contra war. They were especially angered by the fact that many elements within the legal domestic opposition openly expressed sympathy with the rebels. To demonstrate that it could still deal with its enemies, the government returned to repressive actions. After an opposition rally at Nandaime, the Sandinistas arrested thirty-eight critics of the government and temporarily closed down *La Prensa* and Radio Católica.

The crackdown at Nandaime was nothing more than a temporary attempt by the Sandinistas to recapture the political initiative after a year of domestic, economic, and political setbacks.[12] The economic crisis in the country forced the regime to compromise with its internal opposition in order to forestall social and economic disaster. In a January 1989 speech designed to placate the private sector, Ortega announced a severe austerity program that reformed the economy along more capitalist lines. The government also pledged to cease confiscation of private property. In another important olive branch proffered to its enemies, the Sandinistas renewed the national dialogue. Talks with the opposition parties produced the political agreement that set the ground rules for the February 25, 1990, elections. Won by opposition leader Violeta Barrios de Chamorro, the elections were universally regarded as free and fair.[13]

The new government continued this policy of national reconciliation as Chamorro attempted to reduce the level of violence in Nicaraguan society. The centerpiece of this strategy was the rapprochement between Chamorro's government and the Sandinista-controlled army and police. The retention of Humberto Ortega as head of the armed forces was the most visible symbol of Chamorro's policy of reconciliation. The policy of cooperation with the FSLN allowed Chamorro to accomplish two very important goals. First, she was able to radically reduce the size of the Nicaraguan armed forces, including the officer corps. Once the biggest army in Central America at eighty thousand troops, the Nicaraguan military was reduced by Ortega and Chamorro to 18,500 members.[14] Second, the new president significantly reduced the level of political violence in Nicaragua. *Americas Watch* reported that "President Chamorro's leadership and strong moral authority have done much to set the country on the path of reconciliation. The government's disposition to resolve political differences through dialogue and accommodation bodes well for Nicaragua's future political stability."[15]

However, Chamorro failed to resolve Nicaragua's deepening social, political, and economic crisis. The centerpiece of the country's public life continues to be the decades-old struggle between the Sandinistas and their enemies. The polarization of Nicaraguan politics was evident in the strikes, civil unrest, and violence that marred Chamorro's first year in office. Moreover, despite expectations of a quick economic turnabout after the inauguration of the new president, the Nicaraguan economy continues to deteriorate amid large deficits and continued high military spending. The 1990 elections, which were supposed to settle so many questions regarding the framework of the new Nicaragua, only intensified the polarization of society.

The defeated Sandinistas surrendered their offices and ministries, but not their power. They continue to govern from above, through control of the security apparatus, and from below, through control of the trade unions. The Sandinista trade unions staged massive nation-wide strikes in May, July, and October 1990 in order to defend the achievements of the revolution. The government gave in to the unions on all three occasions. The Sandinista front has vigorously protected the agrarian reform program and public control of strategic industries. The Sandinistas have used their power to block the efforts of the new government to reform the economy along more capitalist lines.

Consequently, the economic recovery that most Nicaraguans expected with the end of the contra war and the lifting of the U.S. embargo failed to materialize; in fact, the economic crisis has actually deepened. The new president inherited three extremely difficult problems from the Sandinistas: inflation, low productivity, and a shortage of hard currency. These problems persisted in the Nicaraguan economy as the new government abandoned meaningful economic reform for political reasons. In order to maintain social peace and encourage national reconciliation, Chamorro kept in place most of the economic policies of the Sandinista government. Thus, despite optimistic expectations that the economy would hold steady or even grow by the end of 1990, overall production declined by as much as 5 percent—even more than the relative loss suffered in the final year of Sandinista rule—and continues to fall.

Much of the new aid, which included $300 million from the United States, was siphoned off to pay costly settlements with Sandinista unions, and the impression of chaos and weak authority kept millions of new investment dollars from ever being sent. The United States responded to this ineffective use of aid by making the aid conditional on Chamorro's restricting the power and influence of the Sandinistas. In 1992, in response to Chamorro's ties with the FSLN, Congress froze $104 million in U.S. aid. The Bush administration also used a Senate report commissioned by Jesse Helms to pressure Nicaragua to purge Sandinista officers from the police. The report blamed Chamorro for failing to return properties confiscated by her Sandinista predecessors and halt "systematic" assassinations of disarmed contras.[16] The State Department used this report to pressure Nicaragua to remove the Sandinista police chief, René Vivas.[17]

The ineffective use of U.S. aid and the political chaos effectively delayed other major foreign aid commitments. The Japanese government, which had tentatively committed large amounts of aid, continues to wait for signs that the government can make effective use of U.S. funds. European donors also await signs that the Chamorro government can get its economic house in order before committing aid.

Chamorro's policy of national reconciliation destroyed the UNO coalition that brought her to power. Former contras have staged violent protests demanding that Chamorro turn over government-owned land to the former guerrillas. Right wing members of UNO (the United Nicaraguan Opposition), the president's own party, charged that Chamorro's policies, particularly retaining Humberto Ortega as Nicaragua's military commander, allowed the Sandinistas to retain control of a huge armed organization positioned to gradually usurp the authority of an increasingly weakened government.

Feeling betrayed by Chamorro's policies of national reconciliation, which in their view have allowed the FSLN to retain its power, Nicaraguan conservatives are turning increasingly to violence. Gunfights in November 1991 over confiscated lands and street battles in the summer of 1992 between former soldiers and police foreshadow the tragedy that awaits this country if the land issue is not settled in an equitable matter. Despite government promises, some forty-five hundred to six thousand families of former rebels still have not received land, a situation that has contributed to rural violence.[18] Moreover, the private sector and Nicaraguan exiles in Miami are unlikely to aid in the reconstruction of the country if they are not given a voice in economic policy-making. The firing of Francisco Mayorga as president of the central bank in the fall of 1990 was a devastating blow to domestic and international confidence in the new government's economic policy from which the Chamorro government never recovered.

UNO's fragile ruling coalition has been torn apart by Chamorro's concessions to the Sandinistas. Vice-president Virgilio Godoy, reflecting a rising conservative opposition to the Chamorro government, was openly critical of Chamorro's conciliatory stance toward her former enemies. Cardinal Miguel Obando y Bravo, one of Chamorro's main backers in the 1990 presidential election, put the matter bluntly, stating in a September 13, 1990, interview, "I would say that right now the FSLN is running the country. . . . In Nicaragua there is no rule of law."[19] UNO's supporters have also criticized the role played by Chamorro's son-in-law and chief strategist, Antonio Lacayo-Oyanguren, who is widely suspected of having made a secret cogoverning pact with the Sandinistas.

The break between UNO and Chamorro reached the boiling point during the last four months of 1992 when Alfredo Cesar, president of the National Assembly, and other conservatives defied a Supreme Court ruling and continued holding rump sessions of the assembly despite lacking a quorum. The group passed bills to remove Sandinista army chief Humberto Ortega and roll back Sandinista land confiscations. Chamorro refused to signed these bills; worried about the stalemate and fearing that the country was becoming ungovernable she shunted aside the UNO coalition in January of 1993 and turned to the Sandinistas for support.[20] Chamorro created a new ruling coalition in the National Assembly with nine dissident UNO deputies and thirty-nine Sandinista legislators. This formalized the informal arrangement made between Lacayo and the Sandinistas.

Chamorro's inability to resolve the conflict between the Sandinistas and their enemies has raised the specter of renewed civil war. Her policies of correcting the excesses of the FSLN without reversing the gains of the 1979 revolution destroyed the coalition that elected her. The new president's dependency on a small group of advisers led by Lacayo has weakened her political base to the point that she is widely referred to as a puppet or a "rag doll." Nobody respects her, despite the fact that she is still extremely popular. Ministers ignore the orders she signs. And because of the continuing threat of civil unrest, Chamorro has been unable to attract the foreign aid or investment that many Nicaraguans expected. Thus the government is powerless to prevent the Sandinistas and their enemies from destroying each other, and despite the 1990 elections, Nicaraguans have failed to achieve a consensus on post-Somoza public life.[21]

The national reconciliation process in El Salvador, although making impressive gains from 1990 to 1992, is also far from over. After seventeen months of negotiations the parties agreed on a comprehensive peace settlement.[22] The Chapultepec peace settlement attempted to address the root causes of civil war in El Salvador. The accord was designed to "synchronize" the reintegration of former guerrilla combatants into civilian life with the government reforms affecting land tenure, political activity, institutional restructuring, and the creation of a combined (guerrilla and security force) National Civilian Police. But ten years of bloody civil war created an extremely polarized society. Moreover, although the Salvadoran peace accord established the legal framework to limit the power of the military and make it answerable to civilian authority, the Salvadoran military remains the single most powerful institution in the country.

The road to peace in El Salvador has been long and difficult. In 1985, at the first meeting between the government and the guerrillas, the FMLN adopted a hard-line position. The guerrillas at La Palma and Ayagualo ridiculed Salvadoran democracy and demanded participation in a provisional government that would arrange new elections and reorganize the military. The negotiations collapsed. Not until after Esquipulas II in 1987 did the two sides meet again in San Salvador, and their positions had changed little. The guerrillas demanded the expulsion of U.S. advisers, a territorial cease-fire, government reconstitution to include rebel leaders, and new elections.[23]

After the Nicaraguan elections progress was made in resolving the Salvadoran civil war. The rightist Cristiani government felt secure enough to renew negotiations with the guerrillas after receiving support from the other Central American presidents during the Esquipulas process. The final communiqué of the San Isidro de Coronado summit declared the Salvadoran regime "democratic, pluralistic and participatory."[24] Cristiani realized that the guerrillas were in a weakened state after the failure of their 1989 offensive and the defeat of the Sandinistas in the Nicaraguan elections. The favorable political circumstances persuaded Cristiani that the time was ripe for a political settlement of the Salvadoran conflict. Consequently, the Salvadoran government and the FMLN agreed to renew negotiations under the auspices of the United Nations in spring 1990.

Although the parties failed to achieve their September 15, 1990, deadline for a cease-fire, they made considerable progress. The government and guerrillas agreed on a process for monitoring human rights abuses. More importantly, in a stunning reversal of their previous position, the guerrillas announced that their goals would not be achieved by armed struggle, but through participation in a pluralistic, competitive democracy.[25] The military goals of the FMLN shifted from defeating or reforming the Salvadoran army to winning a permanent disarmament on both sides, under the supervision of the United Nations. Joaquín Villalobos, the FMLN senior military commander, also asserted that the rebels were no longer Marxist, calling Marxism "just one more political theory, like any other."[26] The FMLN demonstrated its new moderation by not interrupting the 1991 legislative elections. For its part the Salvadoran government conceded the need for major reforms in Salvadoran society.

During 1991 the U.N.-sponsored negotiations made impressive progress in bridging the gap between the government and the guerrillas. This was symbolized in May 1991 when Rubén Zamora, leader of the leftist Democratic Convergence, which has close links with the FMLN, was elected vice-president of the National Assembly. In the spring of 1991 the parties agreed to the establishment of a Truth Commission to investigate major human rights violations.

By the end of 1991 the Chapultepec Accord was ready for the parties' signatures. The agreement provided the legal guarantees for a cease-fire and for civil and constitutional reforms, reduced the size of the Salvadoran armed forces, and created an independent police force, which former guerrillas were invited to join. The accord also called for the demobilization of the guerrillas in five equal steps. The keystone of the accord was the "calendar of implementation," which tied the disarming of the rebels to specific government reforms. The gradual timetable was designed to build trust among the parties and permit phased implementation of other provisions.[27] Although the ten-month process moved along in fits and starts and with lots of mutual recrimination, it succeeded in ending the civil war. By December 15, 1992, most of the measures were finished or far enough along to make them seem irreversible, making it possible for the U.N.'s secretary-general, Boutros Boutros-Ghalii, to declare that "the armed conflict in El Salvador has come to an end."[28]

Salvadorans were quickly reminded of the profound polarization of their society and the power of the military, however, when key officers refused to be dismissed from their post. The dismissal of seventy-six senior officers cited on human rights violations was a key condition of the peace accord. But a group of influential officers led by Defense Minister Gen. René Emilio Ponce blocked the dismissals, forcing President Cristiani to renege on his commitment to purge the officers. Cristiani, fearing violence from the officers' corps, agreed to fire only twenty-three officers; to retain forty-five others on the active duty roster until their retirement date; and to keep eight others, including Ponce, in their commands at least until the end of Cristiani's presidential terms in May 1994.[29]

Guatemala is the Central American state least affected by the peace process. The country's first freely elected president in three decades, Vinicio Cerezo, proved too weak to control his military. During his tenure death squads continued to murder opposition politicians, trade union leaders, and human rights activists. The military high command made it clear to civilians that it would not tolerate any serious dialogue between the government and the rebels. Although Cerezo's rightist successor, Jorge Serrano Elias, is not expected to assert greater control over the military, he has made ending the thirty-year-old conflict one of his top priorities. After taking office, the new president quickly sought an unprecedented dialogue between the guerrillas and the government.[30] At the end of 1991 the guerrillas and the Serrano government began their first round of negotiations in Mexico.

The Central American peace plan did not bring peace to Central America. Although the peace process succeeded in reducing the threat of a regionwide war, Central America continues to be plagued by violence and disorder. The final settlement of the conflict awaits the resolution of the root causes of violence in the isthmus: underdevelopment and social injustice. Until the nations of the isthmus arrive at an internal consensus on the way in which political, economic, and social power is distributed in their societies, the Central American conflict will continue. The great risk of the Central American Peace Accord is that as intrastate tensions are reduced, leaders may turn away from the process of national reconciliation and their promises of social justice.

Nevertheless, the conflicts in El Salvador, Guatemala, and Nicaragua do not diminish the herculean accomplishments of Oscar Arias. His peace plan redefined regional politics by requiring the progressive democratization of Central America. The new Central American democracies, despite their many flaws, have reduced violence, guaranteed basic human rights, and initiated national reconciliation processes. Moreover, the threat of regional war and U.S. intervention was removed by ending the contra war in Nicaragua and holding elections. Today, Central American leaders are discussing the next stage of the peace process: economic integration and disarmament. Arias inaugurated a new way of settling conflicts in Central America. His place in the history of the isthmus is secure.

Appendixes

Appendix 1

REPORT ON THE CONTADORA COMMUNIQUÉ

At the end of a two-day meeting, the foreign ministers of Mexico, Colombia, Venezuela, and Panama urgently appealed to the Central American countries to uphold dialogue and negotiation as a way of reducing tensions and laying the groundwork for a permanent climate of peaceful coexistence and mutual respect among nations.

The foreign ministers, who examined the area's socioeconomic and political problems, concluded that direct or indirect foreign interference or any factors that intensify Central America's conflict must be swiftly eliminated. In this regard, the four foreign ministers stressed that it is highly undesirable for those conflicts to be included within the context of the East-West confrontation. They expressed this concern after examining the area's complex panorama, its political processes, their interrelation and their effects on the region's peace and stability.

Mexican Foreign Secretary Bernardo Sepulveda Amor, Colombian Foreign Minister Rodrigo Lloreda Caicedo, Venezuelan Foreign Minister José Alberto Zamhrano V. and Panamanian Foreign Minister Juan José Amado ended their two-day meeting on Contadora Island, which took place at the invitation of the Panamanian Foreign Minister yesterday.

The occurrence and objective of this meeting fall within the framework of the feelings of brotherhood, solidarity and mutual understanding that have traditionally linked the governments and peoples of Colombia, Mexico, Venezuela and Panama.

During their stay in Panama, the ministers met with Panamanian President Ricardo de la Espriella and other high-ranking government officials. In their working sessions, they discussed various subjects of regional interest and agreed on the need to intensify the Latin American dialogue as an effective way to confront the area's political, economic and social problems, which compromise the peace, democracy, stability and development of the continent's peoples.

The foreign ministers reiterated that all states have an obligation to refrain from using threats or force in their international relations. In this respect, they urged states to refrain from undertaking actions that could make the situation worse and create the danger of a generalized conflict that could extend throughout the region.

They also reviewed the various peace initiatives and their likely effects. In this regard, expressing their respect for the principles of nonintervention and of the self-determination of peoples, the foreign ministers analyzed possible new actions and stressed the benefits of including in those efforts the valuable contributions and the necessary support of other countries in the Latin American community. They reaffirmed their decision to continue working to strengthen the Central American and Caribbean countries economically through initiatives such as the energy cooperation program sponsored by Mexico and Venezuela and the financial cooperation plan being undertaken by Colombia. They believe that these and other similar economic cooperation measures help to achieve the objectives of political stability and social peace.

On the subject of the Nonaligned Movement Coordinating Bureau meeting to be held in Managua, Nicaragua 10-14 January, the foreign ministers stressed the importance of the meeting's success, while noting that its final conclusions should work toward the achievement of sensible and constructive solutions to the region's problems. They agreed on the importance of expanding Latin American participation in the Nonaligned Movement, either as members or observers, because this guarantees better consultation, dialogue and negotiation, thus strengthening the bases of nonalignment and political pluralism.

On examining international economic issues, the foreign ministers noted with concern the world economy's recessive tendency. They pointed out the negative effects this situation has on Latin America in terms of the flow of financing, trade, investment and employment and they stressed the need to reorganize the imbalanced international economic system, which causes great difficulties for the developing countries.

The foreign ministers also examined the contraction in world trade, the prevalence of protectionism in industrialized countries and the conditions imposed on and the insufficiency of foreign credit. They noted that to promote financing for development, domestic savings, foreign exchange resources and other complementary financial sources are necessary. These essential elements will permit, to the extent they are implemented, the consolidation of productive investment within Latin American economies, and will guarantee the creation of jobs.

The foreign ministers stressed the importance of periodic ministerial-level consultations to discuss economic subjects of interest to Latin America.

In view of the evident usefulness of coordination within SELA, the foreign ministers pointed out the relevance of the Latin American and Caribbean ministerial meeting to be held in February in Cartagena and the Group of 77 ministerial meeting to be held in Buenos Aires in March.

For this purpose, they reiterated their desire to effectively contribute so that those meetings will fully reflect the objective of coordinating and establishing the developing countries' joint negotiating position for the sixth UNCTAD meeting in Belgrade. That forum should promote the series of international negotiations that, in the UN context, should regulate international cooperation for development.

The foreign ministers agreed on the importance of the faithful fulfillment of the Panama Canal treaties and observed with approval the jurisdictional advances in their implementation. Nevertheless, they expressed concern over the negative effects resulting from the application of discriminatory legal instruments to other aspects of the Torrijos-Carter treaties' implementation process. The foreign ministers stressed the significance of the bicentennial of the birth of the liberator Simon Bolivar and the opportunity it offers to strengthen friendship and promote cooperation among all Latin American peoples.

The foreign ministers of Colombia, Mexico and Venezuela expressed thanks to Panamanian President Ricardo de la Espriella and the Panamanian Government for the hospitality shown during this meeting, which they described as highly beneficial. They also expressed thanks to the Panamanian people and authorities for the hospitality they received during their stay.

Source: Foreign Broadcast Information Service, Central America, January 11, 1983.

Appendix 2

DOCUMENT OF OBJECTIVES (ADOPTED BY THE MINISTERS OF FOREIGN AFFAIRS OF THE CENTRAL AMERICAN COUNTRIES, 9 SEPTEMBER 1983)

Considering:

The situation prevailing in Central America, which is characterized by an atmosphere of tension that threatens security and peaceful coexistence in the region, and which requires, for its solution, observance of the principles of international law governing the actions of States, especially:

—The self-determination of peoples;
—Non-intervention;
—The sovereign equality of States;
—The peaceful settlement of disputes;
—Refraining from the threat or use of force;
—Respect for the territorial integrity of States;
—Pluralism in its various manifestations;
—Full support for democratic institutions;
—The promotion of social justice;
—International co-operation for development;
—Respect for and promotion of human rights;
—The prohibition of terrorism and subversion;
—The desire to reconstruct the Central American homeland through progressive integration of its economic, legal and social institutions;
—The need for economic co-operation among the States of Central America so as to make a fundamental contribution to the development of their peoples and the strengthening of their independence;
—The undertaking to establish, promote or revitalize representative, democratic systems in all the countries of the region;

—The unjust economic, social and political structures which exacerbate the conflicts in Central America;

—The urgent need to put an end to the tensions and lay the foundations for understanding and solidarity among the countries of the area;

—The arms race and the growing arms traffic in Central America, which aggravate political relations in the region and divert economic resources that could be used for development;

—The presence of foreign advisers and other forms of foreign military interference in the zone;

—The risks that the territory of Central American States may be used for the purpose of conducting military operations and pursuing policies of destabilization against others;

—The need for concerted political efforts in order to encourage dialogue and understanding in Central America, avert the danger of a general spreading of the conflicts, and set in motion the machinery needed to ensure the peaceful coexistence and security of their peoples;

Declare their intention of achieving the following objectives:

—To promote detente and put an end to situations of conflict in the area, refraining from taking any action that might jeopardize political confidence or prevent the achievement of peace, security and stability in the region;

—To ensure strict compliance with the aforementioned principles of international law, whose violators will be held accountable;

—To respect and ensure the exercise of human, political, civil, economic, social, religious and cultural rights;

—To adopt measures conducive to the establishment and, where appropriate, improvement of democratic, representative and pluralistic systems that will guarantee effective popular participation in the decision-making process and ensure that the various currents of opinion have free access to fair and regular elections based on the full observance of citizens' rights;

—To promote national reconciliation efforts wherever deep divisions have taken place within society, with a view to fostering participation in democratic political processes in accordance with the law;

—To create political conditions intended to ensure the international security, integrity and sovereignty of the States of the region;

—To stop the arms race in all its forms and begin negotiations for the control and reduction of current stocks of weapons and on the number of armed troops;

—To prevent the installation on their territory of foreign military bases or any other type of foreign military interference;

—To conclude agreements to reduce the presence of foreign military advisers and other foreign elements involved in military and security activities, with a view to their elimination;

—To establish internal control machinery to prevent the traffic in arms from the territory of any country in the region to the territory of another;

—To eliminate the traffic in arms, whether within the region or from outside it, intended for persons, organizations or groups seeking to destabilize the Governments of Central American countries;

—To prevent the use of their own territory by persons, organizations or groups seeking to destabilize the Governments of Central American countries and to refuse to provide them with or permit them to receive military or logistical support;

—To refrain from inciting or supporting acts of terrorism, subversion or sabotage in the countries in the area;

—To establish and co-ordinate direct communication systems with a view to preventing or, where appropriate, settling incidents between States of the region;

—To continue humanitarian aid aimed at helping Central American refugees who have been displaced from their countries of origin, and to create suitable conditions for the voluntary repatriation of such refugees, in consultation with or with the co-operation of the United Nations High Commissioner for Refugees (UNHCR) and other international agencies deemed appropriate;

—To undertake economic and social development programs with the aim of promoting well being and an equitable distribution of wealth;

—To revitalize and restore economic integration machinery in order to attain sustained development on the basis of solidarity and mutual advantage;

—To negotiate the provision of external monetary resources which will provide additional means of financing the resumption of intra-regional trade, meet the serious balance-of-payments problems, attract funds for working capital, support programs to extend and restructure production systems and promote medium- and long-term investment projects;

—To negotiate better and broader access to international markets in order to increase the volume of trade between the countries of Central America and the rest of the world, particularly the industrialized countries; by means of a revision of trade practices, the elimination of tariff and other barriers, and the achievement of price stability at a profitable and fair level for the products exported by the countries of the region;

—To establish technical co-operation machinery for the planning, programming and implementation of multi-sectoral investment and trade promotion projects.

The ministers for Foreign Affairs of the Central American countries, with the participation of the countries in the Contadora Group, have begun negotiations with the aim of preparing for the conclusion of the agreements and the establishment of the machinery necessary to formalize and develop the objectives contained in this document, and to bring about the establishment of appropriate verification and monitoring systems. To that end, account will be taken of the initiatives put forward at the meetings convened by the Contadora Group.

Panama City, 9 September 1983

Source: U.N. Security Council Document S 16041 (1983).

Appendix 3

CONTADORA ACT ON PEACE AND CO-OPERATION IN CENTRAL AMERICA (REVISED VERSION)

CONTENTS

PREAMBLE

PART I:

COMMITMENTS

CHAPTER I: GENERAL COMMITMENTS

Principles

CHAPTER II: COMMITMENTS WITH REGARD TO POLITICAL MATTERS

Section 1. Commitments with regard to regional detente and confidence-building
Section 2. Commitments with regard to national reconciliation
Section 3. Commitments with regard to human rights
Section 4. Commitments with regard to electoral processes and parliamentary co-operation

CHAPTER III: COMMITMENTS WITH REGARD TO SECURITY MATTERS

Section 1. Commitments with regard to military manoeuvres
Section 2. Commitments with regard to armaments
Section 3. Commitments with regard to foreign military bases
Section 4. Commitments with regard to foreign military advisers
Section 5. Commitments with regard to the traffic in arms
Section 6. Commitments with regard to the prohibition of support for irregular forces
Section 7. Commitments with regard to terrorism, subversion or sabotage
Section 8. Commitments with regard to direct communications systems

CHAPTER IV: COMMITMENTS WITH REGARD TO ECONOMIC AND SOCIAL AFFAIRS

Section 1. Commitments with regard to economic and social matters

Section 2. Commitments with regard to refugees

PART II:

COMMITMENTS WITH REGARD TO EXECUTION AND FOLLOW-UP

1. Ad Hoc Committee for Evaluation and Follow-up of Commitments Concerning Political and Refugee Matters

2. Verification and Control Commission for Security Matters

3. Ad Hoc Committee for Evaluation and Follow-up of Commitments Concerning Economic and Social Matters

PART III:

FINAL PROVISIONS

ANNEX

ADDITIONAL PROTOCOL TO THE CONTADORA ACT ON PEACE AND CO-OPERATION IN CENTRAL AMERICA

PREAMBLE

The Governments of the Republics of Costa Rica, El Salvador, Guatemala, Honduras and Nicaragua:

1. AWARE of the urgent need to strengthen peace and co-operation among the peoples of the region, through the observance of principles and measures that would facilitate a better understanding among the Central American Governments;

2. CONCERNED about the situation in Central America, which is characterized by a serious decline in political confidence and by frontier incidents, an arms build-up, arms traffic, the presence of foreign advisers and other forms of foreign military presence, and the use by irregular forces of the territories of certain States to carry out destabilizing operations against other States in the region;

CONVINCED

3. That the tension and the present conflicts may worsen and lead to widespread hostilities;

4. That the restoration of peace and confidence in the region may be achieved only through unconditional respect for the principles of international law, particularly the principle which concerns the right of peoples to choose freely and without external interference the form of political, economic and

social organization that best serves their interests, and to do so through institutions which represent their freely-expressed will;

5. Of the importance of creating, promoting and strengthening democratic systems in all the countries of the region;

6. Of the need to create political conditions designed to guarantee the security, integrity and sovereignty of the States of the region;

7. That the achievement of genuine regional stability hinges on the conclusion of agreements on security and disarmament;

8. That, in the adoption of measures aimed at halting the arms race in all its forms, account should be taken of the national security interests of the States of the region;

9. That military superiority as a political objective of the States of the region, the presence of foreign advisers and other foreign elements and the arms traffic endanger regional security and constitute destabilizing factors in the region;

10. That the agreements on regional security must be subject to an effective system of verification and control;

11. That the destabilization of the Governments in the region, generally taking the form of encouragement or support of the activities of irregular groups or forces, acts of terrorism, subversion or sabotage and the use of the territory of a State for operations affecting the security of another State, is contrary to the fundamental norms of international law and peaceful coexistence among States;

12. That it is highly desirable to set maximum limits for military development, in accordance with the requirements of stability and security in the region;

13. That the elaboration of instruments to permit the application of a policy of detente should be based on the existence of political trust among States which would effectively reduce political and military tension among them;

14. RECALLING the provisions adopted by the United Nations concerning the definition of aggression, in particular General Assembly resolution 3314 (XXIX), and the relevant resolutions of the Organization of American States;

15. TAKING INTO ACCOUNT the Declaration on the Strengthening of International Security, adopted by the United Nations General Assembly in resolution 2734 (XXV), and the corresponding legal instruments of the inter-American system;

16. REAFFIRMING the need to promote national reconciliation in those cases where deep divisions have occurred within society, so as to permit the people to participate, in accordance with the law, in political processes of a democratic nature;

CONSIDERING:

17. That, on the basis of the United Nations Charter of 1945 and the Universal Declaration of Human Rights of 1948, various international organizations and conferences have elaborated and adopted declarations, covenants, protocols, conventions and statutes designed to provide effective protection of human rights in general, or of certain human rights in particular;

18. That not all Central American States have accepted the entirety of the existing international instruments on human rights, and that it would be desirable that they should do so in order to bring the human rights regime closer to the goal of universality in the interests of promoting the observance and guarantee of human, political, civil, economic, social, religious and cultural rights;

19. That in many cases the deficiencies of outdated or inadequate domestic legislation interfere with the effective enjoyment of human rights as defined in declarations and other international instruments;

20. That it should be the concern of each State to modernize and adapt its legislation with a view to guaranteeing the effective enjoyment of human rights;

21. That one of the most effective ways of securing the enjoyment of human rights embodied in international instruments, political constitutions and the laws of individual States lies in ensuring that the judiciary enjoys sufficient authority and autonomy to put an end to violations of those rights;

22. That, to that end, the absolute independence of the judiciary must be guaranteed;

23. That guarantee may be achieved only if judicial officials enjoy security of office and if the judiciary is ensured budgetary stability so that it may be absolutely and unquestionably independent of the other authorities;

CONVINCED:

24. Of the need to establish equitable economic and social structures in order to promote a genuinely democratic system and permit full enjoyment by the people of the right to work, education, health and culture;

25. Of the high level of interdependence of the Central American countries and the prospects which economic integration offers small countries;

26. That the magnitude of the economic and social crisis affecting the region has highlighted the need for changes in the economic and social structures that would reduce the dependence of the Central American countries and

promote regional self-sufficiency, enabling them to reaffirm their own identity;

27. That Central American economic integration should constitute an effective tool for economic and social development based on justice, solidarity and mutual benefit;

28. Of the need to reactivate, improve and restructure the process of Central American economic integration with the active and institutional participation of all the States of the region;

29. That, in the reform of the existing economic and social structures and the strengthening of regional integration, the Central American institutions and authorities are called upon to assume primary responsibility;

30. Of the necessity and appropriateness of undertaking joint programs of economic and social development which would help to promote economic integration in Central America in the context of the development plans and priorities adopted by each sovereign State;

31. Of the urgent need for substantial investment for the development and economic recovery of the Central American countries and of the efforts undertaken jointly by these countries to obtain financing for specific priority projects, and in view of the need to expand and strengthen international regional and sub-regional financial institutions;

32. That the regional crisis has provoked massive flows of refugees and that the situation demands urgent attention;

33. CONCERNED about the constant worsening of social conditions, including the situation with regard to employment, education, health and housing in the Central American countries;

34. REAFFIRMING, without prejudice to the right of recourse to other competent international forums, their desire to settle their disputes within the framework of the negotiation process sponsored by the Contadora Group;

35. RECALLING the support given by the Contadora Group to United Nations Security Council resolution S30 (1983) and General Assembly resolution 38/10, as well as to resolution AG/RES 675 (XIII-0/83) adopted by the General Assembly of the Organization of American States; and

36. BEING READY to implement fully the Document of Objectives and the norms for the implementation of the undertakings made therein, adopted by their Ministers for Foreign Affairs in Panama on 9 September 1983 and 8 January 1984 respectively, under the auspices of the Governments of Colombia, Mexico, Panama and Venezuela, which comprise the Contadora Group;

Have agreed as follows:

CONTADORA ACT ON PEACE AND COOPERATION IN CENTRAL AMERICA

PART I:

COMMITMENTS

CHAPTER I: GENERAL COMMITMENTS

Sole section. PRINCIPLES

THE PARTIES undertake, in accordance with their obligations under international law:

1. To abide by the following principles:
   (a) The principle of refraining from the threat or use of force against the territorial integrity or political independence of States;
   (b) The peaceful settlement of disputes;
   (c) Non-interference in the internal affairs of other States;
   (d) Co-operation between States in solving international problems;
   (e) The equal rights and self-determination of peoples and the promotion of respect for human rights;
   (f) Sovereign equality and respect for the rights inherent in sovereignty;
   (g) The principle of refraining from discriminatory practices in economic relations between States by respecting their systems of political, economic and social organization;
   (h) The fulfillment in good faith of obligations assumed under international law.
2. In pursuance of the foregoing principles:
   (a) They shall refrain from any action inconsistent with the purposes and principles of the Charter of the United Nations and the Charter of the Organization of American States aimed against the territorial integrity, political independence or unity of any State, and, in particular, from any such action involving the threat or use of force.
   (b) They shall settle their disputes by peaceful means in accordance with the fundamental principles of international law embodied in the Charter of the United Nations and the Charter of the Organization of American States.
   (c) They shall respect the existing international boundaries between States.
   (d) They shall refrain from militarily occupying territory of any other State in the region.
   (e) They shall refrain from any act of military, political, economic or other form of coercion aimed at subordinating to their interests the exercise by other States of rights inherent in their sovereignty.
   (f) They shall take such action as is necessary to secure their frontiers

against irregular groups or forces operating from their territory with the aim of destabilizing the Governments of neighboring States.

(g) They shall not permit their territory to be used for acts which violate the sovereign rights of other States, and shall see to it that the conditions obtaining in their territory do not pose a threat to international peace and security.

(h) They shall respect the principle that no State or group of States has the right to intervene either directly or indirectly through the use of arms or any other form of interference in the internal or external affairs of another State.

(i) They shall respect the right of all peoples to self-determination free from outside intervention or coercion by refraining from the threat or the direct or covert use of force to disrupt the national unity and territorial integrity of any other State.

CHAPTER II: COMMITMENTS WITH REGARD TO POLITICAL MATTERS

Section 1. COMMITMENTS WITH REGARD TO REGIONAL DETENTE AND CONFIDENCE-BUILDING

THE PARTIES undertake:

3. To promote mutual trust by every means at their disposal and to refrain from any action which might disturb peace and security in the Central American region;

4. To refrain from issuing or promoting propaganda in support of violence or war and hostile propaganda against any Central American Government, and to abide by and foster the principles of peaceful coexistence and friendly co-operation;

5. Towards that end, their respective governmental authorities shall:

(a) Avoid any oral or written statement which might aggravate the situation of conflict in the area;

(b) Urge the mass media to help to promote understanding and co-operation between peoples of the region;

(c) Promote increased contacts between their peoples and a better knowledge of each other's peoples through co-operation in all spheres relating to education, science, technology and culture;

(d) Consider together future action and mechanisms for bringing about and solidifying a climate of stable and lasting peace;

6. Join together in seeking a regional settlement which will eliminate the causes of tension in Central America by safeguarding the inalienable rights of its people from foreign pressure and interests.

Section 2. COMMITMENTS WITH REGARD TO NATIONAL RECONCILIATION

Each PARTY recognizes vis-à-vis the other Central American States the commitment assumed vis-à-vis its own people to ensure the preservation of domestic peace as a contribution to peace in the region, and they accordingly resolve:

7. To adopt measures for the establishment or, as the case may be, the further development of representative and pluralistic democratic systems guaranteeing effective participation by the people, through political organizations, in the decision-making process, and ensuring the different currents of opinion free access to honest and periodic elections based on the full observance of the rights of citizens;

8. Where deep divisions have come about within society, urgently to promote actions of national reconciliation which will make it possible for the people to participate, with full guarantees, in genuine democratic political processes on the basis of justice, liberty and democracy, and, towards that end, to create mechanisms making possible, in accordance with the law, dialogue with opposition groups;

9. To adopt and, as the case may be, endorse, broaden and improve legal measures for a genuine amnesty which will enable their citizens to resume full participation in political, economic and social affairs, and similarly, to guarantee the inviolability of life, the liberty and the security of person of those to whom such amnesty is granted.

Section 3. COMMITMENTS WITH REGARD TO HUMAN RIGHTS

THE PARTIES undertake, in accordance with their respective national laws and their obligations under international law:

10. To guarantee full respect for human rights and, towards that end, to comply with the obligations laid down in international legal instruments and constitutional provisions relating to human rights;

11. To set in motion the constitutional procedures necessary for them to become parties to the following international instruments:

    (a) The 1966 International Covenant on Economic, Social and Cultural Rights;

    (b) The 1966 International Covenant on Civil and Political Rights;

    (c) The 1966 Optional Protocol to the International Covenant on Civil and Political Rights;

    (d) The 1965 International Convention on the Elimination of All Forms of Racial Discrimination;

    (e) The 1951 Convention Relating to the Status of Refugees;

    (f) The 1967 Optional Protocol Relating to the Status of Refugees;

    (g) The 1952 Convention on the Political Rights of Women;

    (h) The 1979 Convention on the Elimination of All Forms of Discrimination Against Women;

    (i) The 1953 Protocol Amending the 1925 Slavery Convention;

    (j) The 1956 Supplementary Convention on the Abolition of Slavery, the Slave Trade and Institutions and Practices Similar to Slavery;

    (k) The 1953 Convention on the Civil and Political Rights of Women;

    (l) The 1969 American Convention on Human Rights, taking note of articles 45 and 62;

12. To prepare the necessary draft legislation and submit it to their competent internal organs with a view to accelerating the process of modernizing and updating their legislation, so as to make it more capable of promoting and guaranteeing due respect for human rights;

13. To prepare and submit to their competent internal organs draft legislation aimed at:

    (a) Guaranteeing the stability of the member of the judiciary, so that they can act without being subjected to political pressures, and themselves guarantee the stability of officials of lower rank;

    (b) Guaranteeing the budgetary stability of the judiciary itself, so that it may be absolutely and unquestionably independent of the other authorities.

Section 4. COMMITMENTS WITH REGARD TO ELECTORAL PROCESSES AND PARLIAMENTARY COOPERATION

Each PARTY shall recognize vis-à-vis the other Central American States the commitment assumed vis-à-vis its own people to guarantee the preservation of internal peace as a contribution to peace in the region and to that end shall resolve:

14. To adopt the appropriate measures that guarantee the participation of political parties in electoral processes on an equal footing, ensuring that they have access to the mass communication media and enjoy freedom of assembly and freedom of expression.

15. They likewise commit themselves to:

    (a) Take the following measures:

        (1) Promulgate or revise the electoral legislation with a view to the holding of elections that guarantee effective participation by the people;

        (2) Establish independent electoral organs that will prepare a reliable voting register and ensure the impartiality and democratic nature of the process;

        (3) Formulate or, where appropriate, update the rules guaranteeing

the existence and participation of political parties representing various currents of opinion;

    (4) Establish an electoral timetable and adopt measures to ensure that the political parties participate on an equal footing;

(b) Propose to their respective legislative organs that they should:

    (1) Hold regular meetings at alternating sites that would enable them to exchange experience, contribute to detente and foster better communication with a view to rapprochement among the countries of the area;

    (2) Take measures aimed at maintaining relations with the Latin American Parliament and its respective Working Commissions;

    (3) Exchange information and experience on the matters within their competence and collect with a view to comparative study, the electoral legislation in force in each country, together with related provisions;

    (4) Follow, as observers, the various stages in the electoral processes taking place in the region. To that end, the express invitation of the Central American State in which the electoral process is taking place shall be essential;

    (5) Hold periodic technical meetings in the place and with the agenda determined by consensus at each preceding meeting. The arrangements for the first meeting shall be made through consultations among the Central American Ministers for Foreign Affairs.

CHAPTER III: COMMITMENTS WITH REGARD TO SECURITY MATTERS

In conformity with the obligations they have contracted in accordance with international law, the PARTIES assume the following commitments:

Section 1. COMMITMENTS WITH REGARD TO MILITARY MANOEUVRES

16. To comply with the following provisions as regards the holding of military manoeuvre:

(a) When national or joint military manoeuvres are held in areas less than 30 (thirty) kilometers from the frontier, the appropriate prior notification to the neighboring countries and the Verification and Control Commission, mentioned in Part II of this Act, shall be made at least 30 (thirty) days beforehand.

(b) The notification shall contain the following information:

    (1) Name;

    (2) Purpose;

    (3) Participating forces;

    (4) Geographical location;

(5) Timetable;

(6) Equipment and weapons to be used.

Invitations shall be issued to observers from neighboring countries.

17. To prohibit the holding of international military manoeuvres in their respective territories. Any manoeuvre of this kind which is currently under way shall be suspended within a period of not more than thirty days after the signing of this Act.

Section 2. COMMITMENTS WITH REGARD TO ARMAMENTS

18. To halt the arms race in all its forms, and begin immediately negotiations on the control and reduction of the current inventory of weapons and the number of troops under arms;

19. Not to introduce new weapons systems that alter the quality or quantity of current inventories of war material;

20. Not to introduce, possess or use chemical, biological, radiological or other weapons which may be deemed to be excessively injurious or to have indiscriminate effects;

21. To send to the Verification and Central Commission their respective current inventories of weapons, installations and troops under arms within a period of not more than 30 (thirty) days from the date of the signing of this Act. The inventories shall be prepared in accordance with the definitions and basic criteria agreed on in the Annex and in paragraph 21 of this section. On receiving the inventories, the Commission shall carry out within a period of not more than 30 days the technical studies that will be used for the purpose of setting maximum limits for the military development of the States of the region, taking into account their national security interests, and of halting the arms race.

On the basis of the foregoing, the PARTIES agree on the following implementation stages:

First stage: Once they have submitted their respective inventories, the PARTIES shall acquire no more military material. The moratorium shall continue until limits are agreed on in the following stage.

Second stage: The PARTIES shall establish within a maximum period of thirty days limits for the following types of armaments: fighter aircraft and helicopters, tanks and armored vehicles, artillery, short-, medium- and long-range rockets and guided missiles and launching equipment, ships or vessels that are of a military nature or can be used for military purposes.

Third stage: Once the preceding stage has been completed and within a period of not more than thirty days, the PARTIES shall establish limits for military forces and for installations that can be used in military actions.

Fourth stage: The PARTIES may begin negotiations concerning those matters with which it is considered essential to deal notwithstanding the foregoing, the PARTIES may, by mutual agreement, change the periods set for the negotiation and establishment of limits.

22. The following basic criteria shall determine the levels of military development of the Central American States, in accordance with the requirements of stability and security in the region:

    (a) No armed institution shall have as a political objective the pursuit of hegemony over the other forces considered individually;

    (b) The definition of national security shall take into account the level of economic and social development attained at a given time, and the level which it is desired to attain;

    (c) For the purpose of formulating that definition, studies shall be carried out covering the following aspects in a comprehensive manner:

        (1) Perception of the internal and external security needs of the State;
        (2) Area of the territory;
        (3) Population;
        (4) Nation-wide distribution of economic resources, infrastructure and population;
        (5) Range and characteristics of land and sea boundaries;
        (6) Military expenditure in relation to gross domestic product (GDP);
        (7) Military budget in relation to public expenditure and other social indicators;
        (8) Geographical features and position, and geopolitical situation;
        (9) Level of advanced military technology suited to the region.

23. To initiate constitutional procedures so as to be in a position to sign, ratify or accede to treaties and other international agreements on disarmament, if they have not already done so.

Section 3. COMMITMENTS WITH REGARD TO FOREIGN MILITARY BASES

24. Not to authorize the installation in their respective territories of foreign bases or foreign military schools.

25. To close down any foreign bases or foreign military schools in their respective territories within six months of the signing of this Act.

Section 4. COMMITMENTS WITH REGARD TO FOREIGN MILITARY ADVISERS

26. To provide the Verification and Control Commission with a list of any foreign military advisers or other foreign elements participating in military and security activities in their territory, within 30 days of the signing of this Act. In the preparation of the list the definitions contained in the annex shall be taken into account.

27. With a view to the removal of foreign military advisers and other foreign elements, to set a timetable for phased withdrawals, including the immediate withdrawal of any advisers performing operational and training functions. To that end, the studies and recommendations of the Verification and Control Commission shall be taken into account.

28. As for advisers performing technical functions related to the installation and maintenance of military equipment, a control register shall be maintained in accordance with the terms laid down in the respective contracts or agreements. On the basis of that register, the Verification and Control Commission shall seek to set reasonable limits on the number of such advisers.

Section 5. COMMITMENTS WITH REGARD TO THE TRAFFIC IN ARMS

29. To stop the flow of arms, within and outside the region, towards persons, organizations, irregular forces or armed bands trying to destabilize the Governments of the States Parties.

30. To establish for that purpose internal control mechanisms at airports, landing strips, harbors, terminals and border crossings, on roads, air routes, sea lanes and waterways, and at any other point or in any other area likely to be used for the traffic in arms.

31. On the basis of presumption or established facts, to report any violations to the Verification and Control Commission, with sufficient evidence to enable it to carry out the necessary investigation and submit such conclusions and recommendations as it may consider useful. Whenever appropriate, the following elements, among others, shall be taken into account for the purpose of establishing the facts:
    (a) Source of the arms traffic;
    (b) Persons involved;
    (c) Type of armaments, munitions, equipment and other military supplies;
    (d) Extra-regional means of transport;
    (e) Extra-regional transport routes;
    (f) Storage bases for arms, munitions, equipment and other military supplies;
    (g) Areas and routes in the intra-regional traffic;
    (h) International means of transport;
    (i) Receiving unit.

Section 6. COMMITMENTS WITH REGARD TO THE PROHIBITION OF SUPPORT FOR IRREGULAR FORCES

32. To refrain from giving any political, military, financial or other support to individuals, groups, irregular forces or armed bands advocating the over-

throw or destabilization of other Governments, and to prevent, by all means at their disposal the use of their territory for attacks on another State or for the organization of attacks, acts of sabotage, kidnapping or criminal activities in the territory of another State.

33. To exercise strict control over their respective borders, with a view to preventing their own territory from being used to carry out any military action against a neighboring State.

34. To disarm and remove from the border area any group or irregular force identified as being responsible for acts against a neighboring state.

35. To dismantle, and deny the use of, installations, equipment and facilities providing logistical support or serving operational functions in their territory, if the latter is used for acts against neighboring Governments.

Section 7. COMMITMENTS WITH REGARD TO TERRORISM, SUBVERSION OR SABOTAGE

36. To refrain from giving political military, financial or any other support for acts of subversion, terrorism or sabotage intended to destabilize Governments of the region.

37. To refrain from organizing, instigating or participating in acts of terrorism, subversion or sabotage in another State, or acquiescing in organized activities within their territory directed towards the commission of such acts.

38. To abide by the following treaties and international agreements:

    (a) The Hague Convention for the Suppression of Unlawful Seizure of Aircraft;

    (b) The Convention to prevent and punish the acts of terrorism taking the form of crimes against persons and related extortion that are of international significance;

    (c) The Convention for the Suppression of Unlawful Acts against the Safety of Civil Aviation;

    (d) The Convention on the Prevention and Punishment of Crimes against Internationally Protected Persons, including Diplomatic Agents;

    (e) The International Convention against the Taking of Hostages.

39. To initiate constitutional procedures so as to be in a position to sign, ratify or accede to the treaties and international agreements referred to in the preceding paragraph, if they have not already done so.

40. To respect the commitments referred to in this section, without prejudice to compliance with treaties and other international agreements relating to diplomatic and territorial asylum.

41. To prevent in their respective territories participation in criminal acts committed by individuals belonging to foreign terrorist groups or organi-

zations. To that end, they shall strengthen co-operation between the competent migration offices and police departments and between the corresponding civilian authorities.

Section 8. COMMITMENTS WITH REGARD TO DIRECT COMMUNICATIONS SYSTEMS

42. To establish a regional communications system which guarantees immediate and timely liaison between the competent government and military authorities with a view to preventing incidents.
43. To establish Joint Security Commissions in order to prevent and settle Conflicts between neighboring States.

CHAPTER IV: COMMITMENTS WITH REGARD TO ECONOMIC AND SOCIAL AFFAIRS

Section 1. COMMITMENTS WITH REGARD TO ECONOMIC AND SOCIAL MATTERS

With a view to intensifying the process of Central American economic integration and strengthening the institutions representing and supporting it, the PARTIES undertake:

44. To reactivate, perfect and restructure the process of Central American economic integration, harmonizing it with the various forms of political, economic and social organization of the countries of the region.
45. To ratify resolution 1/84, adopted at the thirtieth Meeting of Ministers responsible for Central American Economic Integration held on 27 July 1984, which is designed to re-establish the institutional basis of the Central American economic integration process.
46. To support and promote the conclusion of agreements designed to intensify trade between Central American countries within the legal framework and in the spirit of integration.
47. Not to adopt or support any coercive or discriminatory measures detrimental to the economy of any of the Central American countries.
48. To adopt measures designed to strengthen the financial agencies in the area, including the Central American Bank for Economic Integration, supporting their efforts to obtain resources and diversify their operations, while safeguarding their decision-making powers and the interests of all the Central American countries.
49. To strengthen the multilateral payments machinery within the Central American Common Market Fund and to reactivate the machinery already in operation through the Central American Clearing House. In order to attain these objectives, recourse may be had to available international financial assistance.
50. To undertake sectoral co-operation projects in the area, such as those pertaining to the power production and distribution system, the regional

food security system, the Plan for Priority Health Needs in Central America and Panama and others which would contribute to Central American economic integration.

51. To examine jointly the problem of the Central American external debt through an evaluation taking into account the domestic circumstances of each country, its payments capacity, the critical economic situation in the area and the flow of additional resources necessary for its economic and social development.

52. To support the elaboration and subsequent application of a new Central American tariff and customs regime.

53. To adopt joint measures to protect their exports, integrating as far as possible the processing, marketing transport of their products.

54. To adopt the necessary measures to confer equal status on the Central American Monetary Council.

55. To support, at the highest level, the efforts CADESCA is making, in co-ordination with sub-regional agencies, to obtain from the international community the financial resources needed to revitalize the Central American economy.

56. To implement the international norms governing labor and, with the cooperation of International Labor Organization, to adapt their domestic laws to these norms, particularly those which are conducive to the reconstruction of Central American societies and economies. In addition, to carry out, with the co-operation of the aforesaid agency, programs to create jobs and provide vocational training and instruction and also for the application of appropriate technologies designed to make greater use of the manpower and natural resources of each country.

57. To request the support of the Pan-American Health Organization and UNICEF, and of other development agencies and the international financial community, to finance the Plan for Priority Health Needs in Central America and Panama, adopted by the Ministers of Health of the Central American Isthmus at San Jose on 16 March 1984.

Section 2. COMMITMENTS WITH REGARD TO REFUGEES

THE PARTIES undertake to make the necessary efforts:

58. To carry out, if they have not yet done so, the constitutional procedures for accession to the 1951 Convention relating to the Status of Refugees and the 1967 Protocol relating to the Status of Refugees.

59. To adopt the terminology established in the Convention and Protocol referred to in the foregoing paragraph with a view to distinguishing refugees from other categories of mini-grants.

60. To establish the internal machinery necessary for the implementation,

upon accession, of the provisions of the Convention and Protocol referred to in paragraph 58.

61. To ensure that machinery is established for consultation between the Central American countries and representatives of the government offices responsible for dealing with the problem of refugees in each State.

62. To support the work performed by the United Nations High Commissioner for Refugees (UNHCR) in Central America and to establish direct co-ordination machinery to facilitate the fulfillment of his mandate.

63. To ensure that any repatriation of refugees is voluntary, and is declared to be so on an individual basis, and is carried out with the co-operation of UNHCR.

64. To ensure the establishment of tripartite commissions, composed of representatives of the State of origin, of the receiving State and of UNHCR, with a view to facilitating the repatriation of refugees.

65. To reinforce programs for protection of and assistance to refugees, particularly in the areas of health, education, labor and safety.

66. To ensure that programs and projects are set up with a view to ensuring the self-sufficiency of refugees.

67. To train the officials responsible in each State for protection of and assistance to refugees, with the co-operation of UNHCR and other international agencies.

68. To request immediate assistance from the international community for Central American refugees, to be provided either directly, through bilateral or multilateral agreements, or through UNHCR and other organizations and agencies.

69. To identify, with the co-operation of UNHCR, other countries which might receive Central American refugees. In no case shall a refugee be transferred to a third country against his will.

70. To ensure that the Governments of the area make the necessary efforts to eradicate the causes of the refugee problem.

71. To ensure that, once agreement has been reached on the bases for voluntary and individual repatriation, with full guarantees for the refugees, the receiving countries permit official delegations of the country of origin, accompanied by representatives of UNHCR and the receiving country, to visit the refugee camps.

72. To ensure that the receiving countries facilitate, in co-ordination with UNHCR, the departure procedure for refugees in instances of voluntary and individual repatriation.

73. To institute appropriate measures in the receiving countries to prevent the participation of refugees in activities directed against the country of origin, while at all times respecting the human rights of the refugees.

PART II:

COMMITMENTS WITH REGARD TO EXECUTION AND FOLLOW-UP

The PARTIES decide to establish the following mechanisms for the purpose of executing and following up the commitments contained in this Act:

1. Ad Hoc Committee for Evaluation and Follow-up of Commitments concerning Political and Refugee Matters
   (a) Composition

   The Committee shall be composed of five (5) persons of recognized competence and impartiality, proposed by the States members of the Contadora Group and accepted by common agreement by the Parties. The members of the Committee must be of a nationality different from those of the Parties.
   (b) Functions

   The Committee shall receive and evaluate the reports which the Parties undertake to submit on the ways in which they have proceeded to implement commitments with regard to national reconciliation, human rights, electoral processes and refugees.

   In addition, the Committee shall be open to any communications on these subjects, transmitted for their information by organizations or individuals, which might contribute useful data for evaluation. On the basis of the aforesaid data, the Committee shall prepare a periodic report which, in addition to the evaluation, shall contain proposals and recommendations for improving implementation of the commitments . This report shall be submitted to the Parties and to the Governments of the Contadora Group.
   (c) Rules of procedures

   The Committee shall draw up its own rules of procedure, which it shall make known to the Parties.

2. Verification and Control Commission for Security Matters
   (a) Composition

   The Commission shall be composed of:

   —Four Commissioners, representing States of recognized impartiality and having a genuine interest in contributing to the solution of the Central American crisis, proposed by the Contadora Group and accepted by the PARTIES, with the right to participate in decisions of the Commission. Co-ordination of the work of the Commission shall be by rotation.

   —A Latin American Executive Secretary appointed by the Contadora Group by common agreement with the PARTIES, with the right to participate in the decisions of the Commission, who shall be responsible for its ongoing operation.

—A representative of the Secretary-General of the United Nations and a representative of the Secretary-General of the Organization of American States, as observers.

(b) Establishment

The Commission shall be established not more than thirty (30) days after the signing of this Act.

(c) Functions

—To receive current inventories of armaments, installations and troops under arms of the PARTIES, prepared in accordance with the provisions of the Annex.

—To carry out technical studies to be used to establish maximum limits for the military development of the PARTIES in the region in accordance with the basic criteria established in commitment 22 of this Act.

—To verify that no new weapons are introduced which would qualitatively and quantitatively alter current inventories, and to verify the non-use of weapons prohibited in this Act.

—To establish a register of all commercial transfers of weapons carried out by the PARTIES, including donations and other transactions carried out in the framework of military assistance agreements with other Governments.

—To verify the dismantling of foreign military installations, in accordance with the provisions of this Act.

—To receive the census of foreign military advisers and to verify their withdrawal in accordance with the agreed timetable.

—To verify compliance with this Act in respect of traffic in arms and to consider any reports of non-compliance. For that purpose, the following criteria shall be taken into account:

(1) Origin of the arms traffic: this criterion calls for determination of the port or airport of embarkation of the arms, munitions, equipment or other military supplies intended for the Central American region.

(2) Personnel involved: persons, groups or organizations participating in the organization and conduct of the traffic in arms, including the participation of Governments or their representatives.

(3) Type of weapon, munitions, equipment or other military supplies: describing, under this heading, the category of weapons, their calibre and the country of manufacture, if the country of origin is not the same as the country of manufacture, and the quantities of each type of weapon, munitions, equipment or other military supplies.

(4) Means of transport: listing the means of land, maritime or air transport, including the nationality.

(5) Extra-regional transport routes: indicating the traffic routes used before arrival in Central American territory, including stops or intermediate destinations.

(6) Bases for the storage of weapons, munitions, equipment and other military supplies.

(7) Intra-regional traffic areas and routes: describing the areas and routes and participation or consent by Governments or governmental or political sectors, for the conduct of the traffic in arms, including frequency of use of these areas and routes.

(8) International means of transport: specifying the means of transport used, the ownership of the vehicles and the facilities provided by Governments or governmental or political sectors, indicating whether war material is being unloaded by clandestine flights, whether packages are being dropped by parachute or whether small launches, loaded on the high seas, are being used.

(9) Receiving unit: determining the identity of the persons, groups or organizations receiving the weapons.

—To verify compliance with this Act with regard to irregular forces and the non-use of their own territory in destabilizing actions against another State, and to consider any reports in that connection.

—To verify compliance with the procedures for notification of national or joint military manoeuvres provided for in this Act.

(d) Rules and procedures

—The Commission shall receive any duly substantiated report concerning violations of the security commitments assumed under this Act, shall communicate it to the PARTIES involved and shall initiate such investigations as it deems appropriate.

—The Commission shall carry out its investigations by making on-site inspections, gathering testimony and using any other procedure which it deems necessary for the performance of its functions.

—In the event of any reports of violations or of non-compliance with the security commitments of this Act, the Commission shall prepare a report containing recommendations addressed to the Parties involved.

—The Commission shall transmit all its reports to the Central American Ministers for Foreign Affairs.

—The Commission shall be accorded every facility and prompt and full cooperation by the PARTIES for the appropriate performance of its functions. It shall also ensure the confidentiality of all information elicited or received in the course of its investigations.

(e) Rules of procedure

After the Commission is established it shall draw up its own rules of procedure and shall make them known to the PARTIES.

3. Ad Hoc Committee for Evaluation and Follow-up of Commitments concerning Economic and Social Matters

(a) Composition

—For the purposes of this Act, the Meeting of Ministers responsible for Central American Economic Integration shall constitute the Ad Hoc Committee for Evaluation and Follow-up of Commitments concerning Economic and Social Matters.

(b) Functions

—The Committee shall receive the reports of the PARTIES concerning progress in complying with commitments concerning economic and social matters.

—The Committee shall make periodic evaluations of progress made in complying with commitments with regard to economic and social matters, using for that purpose the information produced by the PARTIES and by the competent international and regional organizations.

—The Committee shall present, in its periodic reports, proposals for strengthening regional cooperation and promoting development plans, with particular emphasis on the aspects mentioned in the commitments contained in this Act.

PART III:

FINAL PROVISIONS

1. The commitments made by the PARTIES in this Act are of a legal nature and are therefore binding.

2. This Act shall be ratified in accordance with the constitutional procedures established in each of the Central American States. The instruments of ratification shall be deposited with the Governments of the States members of the Contadora Group.

3. This Act shall enter into force when the five Central American signatory States have deposited their instruments of ratification.

4. The PARTIES, as from the date of signature, shall refrain from any acts which would serve to frustrate the object and purpose of this Act.

5. Thirty (30) days after the date of signature of this Act, the machinery referred to in Part II shall enter into operation on a provisional basis. The Parties shall take the necessary measures, before the end of that period, to ensure such provisional operation.

6. Any dispute concerning the interpretation or application of this Act which cannot be settled through the machinery provided for in Part II of this Act, shall be referred to the Ministers for Foreign Affairs of the PARTIES for consideration and a decision, requiring a unanimous vote in favor.

7. Should the dispute continue, it shall be referred to the Ministers for Foreign Affairs of the Contadora Group, who shall meet at the request of any of the PARTIES.

8. The Ministers for Foreign Affairs of the States forming the Contadora Group shall use their good offices to enable the parties concerned to resolve the specific situation brought to their attention. After this venue has been tried, they may suggest another peaceful means of settlement of the dispute, in accordance with Article 33 of the Charter of the United Nations, and article 24 of the Charter of the Organization of American States.

9. This Act shall not be subject to reservation.

10. This Act shall be registered by the Parties with the Secretary-General of the United Nations and with the Secretary-General of the Organization of American States in accordance with Article 102 of the Charter of the United Nations, and article 118 of the Charter of the Organization of American States DONE in the Spanish language, in nine original copies, at . . ., on . . . 1984.

ANNEX

THE PARTIES hereby agree on the following definitions of military terms:

1. Register: Numerical or graphical data on military, paramilitary and security forces and military installations.

2. Inventory: Detailed account of nationally- and foreign-owned arms and military equipment, with as many specifications as possible.

3. Census: Numerical data on foreign military or civilian personnel acting in an advisory capacity on matters of defence and/or security.

4. Military installation: Establishment or infrastructure including airfields, barracks, forts, camps, air and sea or similar installations under military jurisdiction, and their geographical location.

5. Organization and equipment chart (OEC): Document describing the mission, organization, equipment, capabilities and limitations of a standard military unit at its various levels.

6. Military equipment: Individual and collective, nationally- or foreign-owned material, not including weapons, used by a military force for its day-to-day living and operations.

7. Classification of weapons:
   (a) By nature:
      (i) Conventional.
      (ii) Chemical.

(iii) Biological.

(iv) Radiological.

(b) By range:

    (i) Short: individual and collective portable weapons.

    (ii) Medium: non-portable support weapons (mortars, howitzers and cannons).

    (iii) Long: rockets and guided missiles, subdivided into:

        (a) Short-range rockets, with a maximum range of less than twenty (20) kilometers;

        (b) Long-range rockets, with a range of twenty (20) kilometers or more;

        (c) Short-range guided missiles, with a maximum range of one hundred (100) kilometers;

        (d) Medium-range guided missiles, with a range of between one hundred (100) and five hundred (500) kilometers;

        (e) Long-range guided missiles, with a range of five hundred (500) kilometers or more.

(c) By calibre and weight:

    1. Light: one hundred and twenty (120) millimeters or less;

    2. Medium: more than one hundred and twenty (120) and less than one hundred and sixty (160) millimeters.

    3. Heavy: more than OK hundred and sixty (160) and less than two hundred and ten (210) millimeters;

    4. Very heavy: more than two hundred and ten (210) millimeters.

(d) By trajectory:

    (i) Weapons with a flat trajectory.

    (ii) Weapons with a curved trajectory.

        (a) Mortars;

        (b) Howitzers;

        (c) Cannons;

        (d) Rockets;

(e) By means of transportation:

    1. On foot;

    2. On horseback;

    3. Towed or drawn;

    4. Self-propelled;

    5. All weapons can be transported by road, rail, sea or air;

    6. Those transported by air are classified as follows:

        (a) Transported by helicopter;

        (b) Transported by aeroplane.

8. Characteristics to be considered in different types of aeroplane and helicopters:
   (a) Model;
   (b) Quantity;
   (c) Crew;
   (d) Manufacture;
   (e) Speed;
   (f) Capacity;
   (g) System of propulsion;
   (h) Whether or not fitted with guns;
   (i) Type of weapons;
   (j) Radius of action;
   (k) Navigation system;
   (l) Communications system;
   (m) Type of mission performed.
9. Characteristics to be considered in different ships or vessels:
   (a) Type of ship;
   (b) Shipyard and year of manufacture;
   (c) Tonnage;
   (d) Displacement;
   (e) Draught;
   (f) Length;
   (g) System of propulsion;
   (h) Type of weapons and firing system;
   (i) Crew.
10. Services: logistical and administrative bodies providing general support
for military, paramilitary and security forces.
11. Military training centers: establishments for the teaching, instruction and
training of military personnel at the various levels and in the various areas
of specialization.
12. Military base: land, sea or air space which includes military installations,
personnel and equipment under a military command. In defining a foreign
military base, the following elements should be taken into account:
—Administration and control;
—Sources of financing;
—Percentage ratio of local and foreign personnel;
—Bilateral agreements;
—Geographical location and area;
—Transfer of part of the territory to another State;
—Number of personnel.

13. Foreign military installations: those built for use by foreign units for the purposes of manoeuvres, training or other military objectives, in accordance with bilateral treaties or agreements; these installations may be temporary or permanent.

14. Foreign military advisers: military and security advisers means foreign military or civilian personnel performing technical training or advisory functions in the following operational areas: tactics, logistics, strategy, organization and security, in the land, sea, air or security forces of Central American States, under agreements concluded with one or more Governments.

15. Arms traffic: arms traffic means any kind of transfer by Governments, individuals or regional or extra-regional groups of weapons intended for groups, irregular forces or armed bands that are seeming to destabilize Governments in the region. It also includes the passage of such traffic through the territory of a third State, with or without its consent, destined for the above-mentioned groups in another State.

16. National military manoeuvres: these are exercises or simulated combat or warfare carried out by troops in peacetime for training purposes. The armed forces of the country participate on their own territory and may include land, sea and air units, the object being to increase their operational capability.

17. International military manoeuvres: these are all operations carried out by the armed forces—including land, sea and air units—of two or more countries on the territory of one of their countries or in an international area, with the object of increasing their operational capability and developing joint co-ordination measures.

18. The inventories drawn up in each State, a separate one being made for each of their armed forces, shall cover the personnel, weapons and munitions, equipment and installations of the forces mentioned below, in accordance with their own organizational procedures:

    (a) Security Forces:
        1. Frontier guards;
        2. Urban and rural guards;
        3. Military forces assigned to other posts;
        4. Public security force;
        5. Training and instruction center;
        6. Other.

    (b) Naval Forces:
        1. Location;
        2. Type of base;

3. Number of vessels and characteristics of the naval fleet. Type of weapons;
4. Defence system. Type of weapons;
5. Communications systems;
6. War material services;
7. Air or land transport services;
8. Health services;
9. Maintenance services;
10. Administrative services;
11. Recruitment and length of service;
12. Training and instruction centers;
13. Other.

(c) Air Forces:
1. Location;
2. Runway capacity;
3. Number of aircraft and characteristics of the air fleet. Type of weapons;
4. Defence system. Type of weapons;
5. Communications system;
6. War material services;
7. Health services;
8. Land transport services;
9. Training and instruction centers;
10. Maintenance services;
11. Administrative services;
12. Recruitment and length of service;
13. Other.

(d) Army Forces:
1. Infantry;
2. Motorized infantry;
3. Airborne infantry;
4. Cavalry;
5. Artillery;
6. Armored vehicles;
7. Signals;
8. Engineers;
9. Special troops;
10. Reconnaissance troops;
11. Health services;
12. Transport services;

13. War material services;
14. Maintenance services;
15. Administrative services;
16. Military police;
17. Training and instruction center;
18. Precise information on system of induction, recruitment and length of service must be given in this document;
19. Other.
(e) Paramilitary forces.
(f) Information required for airports: existing airfields:
1. Detailed location and category;
2. Location of installations;
3. Dimensions of take-off runways, taxi ways and maintenance strips;
4. Facilities: buildings, maintenance installations, fuel supplies, navigational aids, communications systems.
(g) Information required for terminals and ports:
1. Location and general characteristics;
2. Entry and approach lanes;
3. Piers;
4. Capacity of the terminal.
(h) Personnel: Numerical data must be given for troops in active service, in the reserves, in the security forces and in paramilitary organizations. In addition, data on advisory personnel must include their number, immigration status, specialty, nationality and duration of stay in the country, and any relevant agreements or contracts.
(i) Weapons: munitions of all types, explosives, ammunition for portable weapons, artillery, bombs and torpedoes, rockets, hand grenades and rifle grenades, depth charges, land and sea mines, fuses, mortar and howitzer shells, etc., must be included.
(j) Domestic and foreign military installations: military hospitals and first-aid posts, naval bases, air fields and landing strips must be included.

ADDITIONAL PROTOCOL TO THE CONTADORA ACT ON PEACE AND CO-OPERATION IN CENTRAL AMERICA

THE UNDERSIGNED PLENIPOTENTIARIES, invested with full powers by their respective Governments:

CONVINCED that the effective co-operation of the international community is necessary to guarantee the full force, effectiveness and viability of the Contadora Act on Peace and Co-operation in Central America adopted by the countries of that region,

Have agreed as follows:

1. To refrain from any acts which would serve to frustrate the object and purpose of the Act.
2. To co-operate with the Central American States on the terms they request by mutual consent, in order to achieve the object and purpose of the Act.
3. To lend all support to the Verification and Control Commission for Security Matters in the performance of its functions, when the Parties so require.
4. This Protocol shall be open to signature by all States desiring to contribute to peace and co-operation in Central America. It shall be signed in the presence of any of the Depositary Governments of the Act.
5. This Protocol shall enter into force for each signatory State on the date on which it has been signed by all of them.
6. This Protocol shall be deposited with the Governments of the States which comprise the Contadora Group.
7. This Protocol shall not be subject to reservation.
8. This Protocol shall be registered with the United Nations Secretariat in accordance with Article 102 of the United Nations Charter.

DONE in the Spanish language, in four original copies, at . . . on . . . , 1984.

For the Government of Colombia For the Government of Mexico
For the Government of Venezuela For the Government of Panama

Source: UN General Assembly/Security Council Doc. A/39/562 and S/16775 of October 9, 1984.

Appendix 4

PEACE PLAN BY OSCAR ARIAS,
15 FEBRUARY 1987

The introductory part of the proposal was signed by all the presidents. It was agreed that the proposed measures should be considered at a further meeting, to be held at Esquipulas, Guatemala, within 90 days.

THE TIME FOR PEACE

Peace in the Americas can be maintained only through independence for each of the nations concerned, political and economic cooperation among the peoples of the Americas, exercise of the broadest freedoms, the functioning of stable democratic regimes, fulfillment of the basic requirements of the populations concerned and progressive disarmament.

The time for peace has come. The dictatorships that for so many year determined the fate of many peoples in the Americas systematically violated human rights and engulfed the populations concerned in poverty, exploitation, servitude, inequality, and injustice.

The time for peace has come. There are still dictators in a few countries in the Americas, and under them contempt for the principal human values persists. This peace whose time has come therefore calls for an end to the dictatorships that continue to exist. Joint action must be taken to bring about the removal of tyrants wherever people are deprived of freedom in any form. Preferably such removal should take the form of a peaceful transition—without bloodshed—to democracy.

This peace whose time has come also calls for an end to extreme poverty and for the realization of equal opportunity for all. Without such a commitment to justice, there will continue to be conflict.

This peace whose time has come also calls for strengthening democracies throughout the Americas. In situations where the doors to freedom and democracy have been opened, where men and women can elect freely and at regular intervals those who govern them, where political pluralism, dialogue, and freedom of expression prevail, armed struggle can be regarded as only a desire to establish another dictatorship; armed struggle does not represent a struggle for freedom but rather an endeavor by fanatics to impose the beliefs of a minority—whatever its ideology—by means of force. A clear example of such fanatical struggles, whose goal is to prevent the development of freedom in democracies, is provided by continuing guerrilla warfare in El Salvador, Peru, and Colombia.

In the case of Central America, the governments of Costa Rica, El Salvador, Guatemala, and Honduras assert that the time for peace has come. They desire a stable, lasting peace, which can be attained only under a democratic form of government committed to helping the neediest. The governments in question seek reconciliation between people, so that brothers do not continue to kill one another. They reaffirm their faith in political solutions to problems and declare that where there is freedom and democracy, dialogue replaces guns, security banishes fear, and cooperation takes the place of selfishness.

Central America is not alone in its endeavor to bring about the triumph of peace. For four years now, the Contadora Group has—through its mediation—expressed the sentiment of a Latin America that seeks peaceful solutions to conflicts between its people. The Contadora Support Group is a manifestation of fraternal peoples who, having taken the path to democracy once again, proclaim that there is no substitute for freedom and democracy in the endeavor to achieve reconciliation in Central America. The Organization of American States has witnessed solemn promises to bring about peace and has taken many initiatives to promote peace and fulfill the undertakings of the parties concerned. The United Nations has taken a keen interest in the Central American problems, in keeping with its responsibility to promote world peace.

The Central American governments have played an active role in the process designed to achieve security and peaceful coexistence in the region. This process prompted the five states in question to reach agreement on the Document of Objectives of the Contadora Group and on the Esquipulas Declaration.

The democratic governments of Central America are aware of the fact that the Central American countries have a political duty to resolve their conflicts. They therefore believe that it is urgent to determine what definitive and verifiable action is required in order to promote a settlement of the regional conflict within a clearly defined time frame.

Thought must be transformed into action, and agreements into reality. The time to act has come. Implementation of agreements expands dialogue and restores trust among peoples, and prevents violence and war.

The governments of Costa Rica, El Salvador, Guatemala and Honduras—inspired by the charter of the Organization of American States (charter of Bogota) and by the charter of the United Nations—with a view to promoting the peaceful settlement of disputes and prevailing on states to prevent and eliminate threats to peace and security, make the proposal set forth below to the government of Nicaragua for implementation in the context of mediation by the Contadora Group.

In view of the critical situation in Central America and the urgent need jointly to take the path toward peace, the Nicaraguan government is urged to accept the proposal within the next two weeks. The governments of Costa Rica, El Salvador, Guatemala, and Honduras believe that prompt action is indispensable in order to deal with differences that could lead to an even more serious conflict.

PROCEDURE FOR ESTABLISHING A STABLE AND LASTING PEACE IN CENTRAL AMERICA

The governments of the five Central American states undertake to follow the procedures set forth in this proposal, with a view to achieving the principal purposes of the Charter of the United Nations, the Charter of the Organization of American States, the Guatemala Declaration, the Punta del Este Declaration, the Panama City communiqué, the Document of Objectives of the Contadora Group, the Caraballeda Message for Peace, Security and Democracy in Central America, the draft Contadora Act on Peace and Cooperation in Central America, and the Esquipulas Declaration. To that end, they shall proceed as follows.

1. National Reconciliation

a. Amnesty
In the 60 days following the signing of this document by all the governments of the Central American states, a general amnesty for political and related offenses shall be decreed in those Central American countries where armed struggles are being waged. The corresponding amnesty decrees shall establish all necessary provisions guaranteeing the inviolability of life, freedom in all its forms, property and security of person.

Such decrees shall also set up, in each of those states, a National Commission for Reconciliation and Dialogue made up of representatives of the government, the domestic political opposition, the Catholic church and the Inter-American Commission on Human Rights, which shall be responsible for testifying to the genuine implementation of the process of national reconciliation. Within a maximum of six months following the signing of this document, all provisions of the amnesty decree must be judged by the above commission to have been genuinely and effectively implemented.

b. Dialogue

The governments of those Central American states where armed struggles are being waged shall, as of the signing of this document, initiate or reinforce, as the case may be, a broad dialogue with all the domestic political opposition groups that have laid down their arms, as a means of strengthening civilian society and promoting "national reconciliation efforts wherever deep divisions have taken place within society, with a view to fostering participation in democratic political processes in accordance with the law" (Document of Objectives).

2. Cease-fire

Simultaneously with the launching of a dialogue, warring parties in each country shall suspend military actions.

3. Democratization

As of the signing of this document, an "authentic democratic process that is pluralistic and participatory, which entails the promotion of social justice and respect for human rights, the sovereignty and territorial integrity of the States and the right of every nation to choose, freely and without outside interference of any kind its own economic, political and social system" (Esquipulas Declaration) shall be launched and "measures conducive to the establishment and, where appropriate, improvement of democratic, representative and pluralistic systems that will guarantee effective popular participation in the decision-making process and ensure that the various currents of opinion have free access to fair and regular elections based on the full observance of citizens' rights" (Document of Objectives) shall begin to be adopted in a way that can be verified. In order to ensure good faith in the implementation of this process of democratization, it shall be understood that

(a) Within 60 days from the signing of this document, there must be complete freedom of television, radio, and the press. This complete freedom shall include freedom for all ideological groups, without any exceptions, to launch and operate communication media and operate them without prior censorship.

(b) Within the same period, complete pluralism of political parties must be established. Political groupings shall, in this connection, have broad access to the communication media and full enjoyment of the rights of association and the power to hold public demonstrations, as well as unrestricted exercise of the right to publicize their ideas orally, in writing, and on television.

4. Free Elections

Once the conditions inherent in any democracy have been created, free, pluralistic, and fair elections shall be held.

The first joint expression of the Central American states on achieving reconciliation and lasting peace for their peoples shall be the holding of elections for the Central American Parliament proposed in the Esquipulas Declaration of 25 May 1986.

Such elections shall be held simultaneously in all the countries of Central America in the first six months of 1988, at a date to be determined in due course by the presidents of the Central American states. They shall be subject to supervision by the Organization of American States in order to guarantee to the whole world the fairness of the process, which shall be governed by the strictest rules of equal access for all political parties to the communication media and by broad opportunities for organizing public demonstrations and any other type of political propaganda.

Once elections for the Central American Parliament have been held, equally free and democratic elections for the appointment of popular representatives to municipalities, Parliament and the office of the President of the Republic shall be held in each country, subject to the same international guarantees and supervision and within the time limits established in their respective constitutions.

5. Suspension of Military Aid

Simultaneously with the signing of this document, the governments of the five Central American states shall request those governments from outside the region that are providing either overt or covert military aid to insurgents or irregular forces to suspend such aid, which the Central American governments regard as running counter to peace efforts in the Central American region. At the same time they shall request irregular forces and insurgent groups operating in Central America to refrain from receiving such aid in order to demonstrate a genuine spirit of Latin Americanism. These requests shall be made pursuant to the provision of the Document of Objectives, which calls for eliminating "the traffic in arms, whether within the region or from outside it, intended for persons, organizations or groups seeking to destabilize the Governments of Central American countries."

6. Nonuse of Territory to Attack Other States

The five countries signing this document reiterate their commitment to "prevent the use of their own territory by persons, organizations or groups seeking to destabilize the Governments of Central American countries and to refuse to provide them with or allow them to receive military or logistical support" (Document of Objectives).

7. Weapons Reduction

Within a period of 60 days from signing this document, the governments of the five Central American states shall begin "negotiations for the control and reduction of current stocks of weapons and on the number of troops under arms" (Document of Objectives). To this end the five countries agree to the procedure outlined in the joint proposal by Costa Rica and Guatemala presented in the course of the deliberations of the Contadora Group. Such negotiations shall also cover measures for disarming irregular forces operating in the region.

8. National and International Supervision

a. Follow-up committee
Within a period of 30 days from signing this document, a Follow-up Committee shall be established consisting of the secretary-general of the United Nations, the secretary-general of the Organization of American States, foreign ministers of the Contadora Group and foreign ministers of the Support Group. This committee shall be responsible for supervising and verifying compliance with commitments set forth in this document. Its follow-up functions shall apply even in cases where other organs of supervision and compliance are established.
b. Support and facilities to supervisory bodies
In order to reinforce the efforts of the Follow-up Committee, the governments of the five Central American states shall issue statements of support for its work. All nations interested in promoting the cause of freedom, democracy, and peace in Central America may adhere to these statements.

The five governments shall provide all necessary facilities for the proper conduct of the work and investigations of the National Commission for Reconciliation and Dialogue in each country and the Follow-up Committee.

9. Evaluation of the Progress Toward Peace

The presidents of the five Central American states shall, at a date to be determined by them in due course but within six months following the signing of this document, meet at Esquipulas, Guatemala, to evaluate progress made in the commitments undertaken herein.

10. Democracy and Freedom for Peace and Development

In the climate of freedom guaranteed by democracy, the Central American countries shall adopt such agreements as will help to speed up development, in order to make their societies more egalitarian and free from misery.

The elements set forth in this document form a harmonious and indivisible whole. By signing it, the Central American states accept in good faith the obligation to comply, within the established time limits, with all the elements of this procedure for establishing a stable and lasting peace in Central America.

This document shall enter into force on the date of its signature by the presidents of the governments of the five Central American states.

Source: International Legal Materials, February 26, 1987.

Appendix 5

ESQUIPULAS II: PROCEDURE FOR THE ESTABLISHMENT OF A FIRM AND LASTING PEACE IN CENTRAL AMERICA

Voces tendidas y gravidos vientos de esperanzas
quieren la paz alegre para todos.
—Arturo Echeverria Loria

PREAMBLE

We, the Presidents of the Republics of Guatemala, El Salvador, Honduras, Nicaragua and Costa Rica, meeting at Guatemala City on 6 and 7 August 1987, encouraged by the far-sighted and unfailing determination of the Contadora Group and the Support Group to achieve peace, strengthened by the steady support of all the Governments and peoples of the world, their main international organizations and, in particular, the European Economic Community and His Holiness John Paul II, drawing inspiration from the Esquipulas I Summit Meeting and having come together in Guatemala to discuss the peace plan presented by the Government of Costa Rica, have agreed as follows:

To take up fully the historical challenge of forging a peaceful destiny for Central America;

To commit ourselves to the struggle for peace and the elimination of war;

To make dialogue prevail over violence and reason over hatred;

To dedicate these peace efforts to the young people of Central America whose legitimate aspirations to peace and social justice, freedom and reconciliation have been frustrated for many generations;

To take the Central American Parliament as the symbol of the freedom and independence of the reconciliation to which we aspire in Central America.

We ask the international community to respect and assist our efforts. We have our own approaches to peace and development but we need help in making them a reality. We ask for an international response which will guarantee development so that peace we are seeking can be a lasting one. We reiterate firmly that peace and development are inseparable.

We thank President Vinicio Cerezo Arevalo and the noble people of Guatemala for having hosted this meeting. The generosity of the President and people of Guatemala were decisive in creating the climate in which the peace agreements were adopted.

PROCEDURE FOR THE ESTABLISHMENT OF A FIRM AND LASTING PEACE IN CENTRAL AMERICA

The Governments of the Republics of Costa Rica, El Salvador, Guatemala, Honduras and Nicaragua, determined to achieve the principles and purposes of the Charter of the United Nations, the Charter of the Organization of American States, the Document of Objectives, the Caraballeda Message for Peace, Security and Democracy in Central America, the Guatemala Declaration, the Punta del Este Communiqué, the Panama Message, the Esquipulas Declaration and the draft Contadora Act of 6 June 1986 on Peace and Co-operation in Central America, have agreed on the following procedure for the establishment of a firm and lasting peace in Central America.

1. National Reconciliation

(a) Dialogue
Whenever deep divisions have taken place within society, the Governments agree to urgently undertake actions of national reconciliation which permit popular participation, with full guarantees, in genuine democratic political processes on the basis of justice, freedom and democracy and, to that end, to create mechanisms permitting a dialogue with opposition groups in accordance with the law.

To this end, the Governments in question shall initiate a dialogue with all the domestic political opposition groups which have laid down their arms and those which have availed themselves of the amnesty.

(b) Amnesty
In each Central American country except those where the International Verification and Follow-up Commission determines this to be unnecessary, amnesty decrees shall be issued which establish all necessary provisions guaranteeing the inviolability of life, freedom in all its forms, property and security of person of those to whom such decrees are applicable. Simultaneously with the issue of amnesty decrees, the irregular forces of the countries in question shall release anyone that they are holding prisoner.

(c) National Reconciliation Commission

To verify fulfillment of the commitments with regard to amnesty, a cease-fire, democratization and free elections entered into by the five Central American Governments signing this document, a National Reconciliation Commission shall be set up in each country, responsible for verifying genuine implementation of the process of national reconciliation and also unrestricted respect for all the civil and political rights of Central American citizens guaranteed in this document.

The National Reconciliation Commission shall be composed of: a representative of the executive branch and his alternate; a representative and an alternate proposed by the Conference of Bishops and chosen by the Government from a list of three bishops. This list shall be submitted within 15 days following receipt of the formal invitation. Governments shall make this invitation within five working days following the signing of this document. The same procedure of proposing three candidates shall be used to choose a representative and an alternate representative of legally registered opposition political parties. The list of three candidates shall be submitted within the same period as indicated above. Each Central American Government shall also choose an eminent citizen belonging to neither the Government nor the government party, and his alternate, to serve on the Commission. The agreement or decree setting up the corresponding National Commission shall be communicated immediately to the other Central American Governments.

2. Appeal for an End to Hostilities

The Governments make an urgent appeal that, in those States of the region where irregular or insurgent groups are currently active, agreement be reached to end hostilities. The Governments of those States undertake to take all necessary steps, in accordance with the constitution, to bring about a genuine cease-fire.

3. Democratization

The Governments undertake to promote an authentic democratic process that is pluralistic and participatory, which entails the promotion of social justice and respect for human rights, the sovereignty and territorial integrity of States and the right of every nation to choose, freely and without outside interference of any kind, its own economic, political and social system. They shall adopt, in a way that can be verified, measures conducive to the establishment and, where appropriate, improvement of democratic, representative and pluralistic systems that will guarantee the organization of political parties and effective popular participation in the decision-making process and ensure that the

various currents of opinion have free access to fair and regular elections based on the full observance of citizens' rights. In order to ensure good faith in the implementation of this process of democratization, it shall be understood that:
(a) There must be complete freedom of television, radio and the press. This complete freedom shall include freedom for all ideological groups to launch and operate communication media and to operate them without prior censorship;
(b) Complete pluralism of political parties must be established. Political groupings shall, in this connection, have broad access to the communication media and full enjoyment of the rights of association and the power to hold public demonstrations in unrestricted exercise of the right to publicize their ideas orally, in writing and on television, and members of political parties shall enjoy freedom of movement in campaigning for political support;
(c) Likewise, those Central American Governments which are currently imposing a state of siege or emergency shall revoke it, ensuring that a state of law exists in which all constitutional guarantees are fully enforced.

4. Free Elections

Once the conditions inherent in any democracy have been created, free, pluralistic and fair elections shall be held.

As a joint expression by the Central American States of their desire for reconciliation and lasting peace for their peoples, elections will be held for the Central American Parliament proposed in the Esquipulas Declaration of 25 May 1986.

In the above connection, the Presidents expressed their willingness to move ahead with the organization of the Parliament. To that end, the Preparatory Commission for the Central American Parliament shall complete its deliberations and submit the corresponding draft treaty to the Central American Presidents within 150 days.

Elections shall be held simultaneously in all the countries of Central America in the first six months of 1988, at a date to be agreed in due course by the Presidents of the Central American States. They shall be subject to supervision by the corresponding electoral bodies, and the Governments concerned undertake to invite the Organization of American States, the United Nations and the Governments of third States to send observers to verify that the electoral process has been governed by the strictest rules of equal access for all political parties to the communication media and by ample opportunities for organizing public demonstrations and any other type of political propaganda.

With a view to enabling the elections to the Central American Parliament to be held within the period indicated, the treaty establishing the Parliament shall be submitted for approval or ratification in the five countries.

Once the elections for the Central American Parliament have been held, equally free and democratic elections for the appointment of popular representatives to municipalities, congress, the legislative assembly and the office of the President of the Republic shall be held in each country, with international observers and the same guarantees, within the established time-limits and subject to time tables to be proposed in accordance with each country's current constitution.

5. Termination of Aid for Irregular Forces and Insurrectionist Movements

The Governments of the five Central American States shall request Governments of the region and Governments from outside the region which are providing either overt or covert military, logistical, financial or propaganda support, in the form of men, weapons, munitions and equipment, to irregular forces or insurrectionist movements to terminate such aid; this is vital if a stable and lasting peace is to be attained in the region.

The above does not cover aid for the repatriation or, failing that, the relocation and necessary assistance with reintegration into normal life of former members of such groups or forces. The Central American Governments shall also request the irregular forces and insurgent groups operating in Central America to refrain from receiving such aid in order to demonstrate a genuine spirit of Latin Americanism. These requests shall be made pursuant to the provision of the Document of Objectives which calls for eliminating the traffic in arms, whether within the region or from outside it, intended for persons, organizations or groups seeking to destabilize the Governments of Central American countries.

6. Nonuse of Territory to Attack Other States

The five countries signing this document reiterate their commitment to prevent the use of their own territory by persons, organizations or groups seeking to destabilize the Governments of Central American countries and to refuse to provide them with or allow them to receive military and logistical support.

7. Negotiations on Security Verification and the Control and Limitation of Weapons

The Governments of the five Central American States, with the Contadora Group acting as mediator, shall continue negotiating on the points outstanding in the draft Contadora Act on Peace and Co-operation in Central America with regard to security, verification and control.

These negotiations shall also cover measures for disarming irregular forces prepared to avail themselves of amnesty decrees.

8. Refugees and Displaced Persons

The Central American Governments undertake to attend, as a matter of urgency, to the flows of refugees and displaced persons caused by the crisis in the region, providing them with protection and assistance, particularly in the areas of health, education, work and safety, and to facilitate their repatriation, resettlement or relocation provided that this is voluntary and carried out on an individual basis.

They also undertake to seek assistance from the international community for Central American refugees and displaced persons, to be provided either directly, through bilateral or multilateral agreements, or indirectly, through the Office of the United Nations High Commissioner for Refugees (UNHCR) and other organizations and agencies.

9. Cooperation, Democracy and Freedom for Peace and Development

In the climate of freedom guaranteed by democracy, the Central American countries shall adopt such agreements as will help to speed up development, in order to make their societies more egalitarian and free from misery.

The strengthening of democracy entails creating a system of economic and social well-being and justice. To achieve these goals, the Governments shall jointly seek special economic assistance from the international community.

10. International Verification and Follow-up

(a) International Verification and Follow-Up Commission
An international verification and follow-up commission shall be established consisting of the Secretary-General of the United Nations, or his representative, and the Minister of Foreign Affairs of Central America, the Contadora Group and the Support Group. The Commission shall be responsible for verifying and monitoring fulfillment of the commitments set forth in this document.
(b) Support and Facilities for Reconciliation and Verification and Follow-up Bodies
In order to reinforce the efforts of the International Verification and Follow-up Commission, the Governments of the five Central American States shall issue statement in support of its work. All nations interested in promoting the cause of freedom, democracy and peace in Central America may adhere to these statements.

The five governments shall provide all the necessary facilities for proper conduct of the verification and follow-up functions of the National Reconciliation Commission in each country and the International Verification and Follow-up Commission.

11. Timetable for Fulfillment of Commitments

Within a period of 15 days from the signing of this document, the Central American Ministers for Foreign Affairs shall meet as an Executive Commission to regulate, encourage and facilitate compliance with the agreements contained in this document and to organize working commissions so that, as of that date, the processes leading to fulfillment of the agreed commitments within the stipulated periods can be set in motion by means of consultations, negotiations and other mechanisms which are deemed necessary.

Ninety-days after the signing of this document, the commitments with regard to amnesty, a cease-fire, democratization, termination of aid to irregular forces or insurrectionist movements, and the non-use of territory to attack other States, as defined in this document, shall enter into force simultaneously and be made public.

One hundred and twenty days after the signing of this document, the International Verification and Follow-up Commission shall review the progress made in complying with the agreement set forth in this document.

One hundred and fifty days after the signing of this document, the five Central American Presidents shall meet to receive a report from the International Verification and Follow-up Commission and shall take the relevant decisions.

FINAL PROVISIONS

The elements set forth in this document form a harmonious and individual whole. By signing in, the Central American States accept in good faith the obligation to comply simultaneously with what has been agreed within the established time-limits.

We, the Presidents of the five Central American States, having the political will to respond to our peoples' desire for peace, sign this document at Guatemala City on 7 August 1987.

The Presidents of the Republics of Honduras and Nicaragua, convinced of the need to strengthen this regional peace plan by taking measures to restore mutual trust, have agreed to instruct their respective Ministers for Foreign Affairs to request the International Court of Justice to agree to the postponement, for a period of three months, of the oral phase of the ruling on competence which, inter alia, is being heard by that high tribunal, on the understanding that they will review the aforementioned judicial situation on the occasion of the meeting of Central American Presidents which is to take place within 150 days, in accordance with the commitment established in this plan, with a view to agreeing to waive recourse to international judicial action on the situation in Central America.

Signed at the Esquipulas II Summit meeting, at Guatemala City, on 7 August 1987.

Source: United Nations Department of Public Information, November 1989.

Appendix 6

SAPOA CEASE-FIRE AGREEMENTS

The Constitutional Government of Nicaragua and the Nicaraguan Resistance meeting in Sapoa, Nicaragua on March 21, 22, and 23 with the aim of contributing to national reconciliation in the framework of the Esquipulas II Accord, and in the presence of witnesses His Eminence Cardinal Miguel Obando y Bravo, president of the Nicaraguan Episcopal Conference, and His Excellency Ambassador João Clemente Baena Soares, Secretary General of the Organization of American States, have reached the following agreement.

(1) To halt military operations in the entire national territory for a period of 60 days beginning on April 1 of this year, during which an integral process of negotiation will be carried out for a definitive cease-fire to end the war, to be carried out effectively together with the other commitments contained in the Esquipulas II Accord.

Both parties agree to meet at the highest level in Managua next April 6, to continue negotiations for a definitive cease-fire.

(2) During the first 15 days, the Resistance forces will locate themselves in zones, whose location, size and modus operandi will be mutually accorded through special commissions at a meeting in Sapoa to begin Monday, March 28.

(3) The Government of Nicaragua will decree a general amnesty for those tried and convicted for violation of the public security law, and for members of the army of the previous regime for crimes committed before July 19, 1979.

In the case of the first group, the amnesty will be gradual. Taking into account the religious sentiments of the Nicaraguan people on the occasion of Holy Week, on Palm Sunday the first 100 prisoners will be freed. Later, when it is verified that Nicaraguan Resistance forces have entered the mutually accorded zones, 50 percent of the remaining prisoners will be freed. The other 50 percent will be freed at a date following the signing of a definitive cease-fire, which will be agreed at the meeting in Managua on April 6.

In the case of the prisoners mentioned in the final part of the first paragraph of this numeral: Their release will begin at the moment of signing a definitive cease-fire, following judgment by the Inter-American Human Rights Commission of the Organization of the American States.

The Secretary General of the Organization of American States shall be guarantor and depository for the compliance of this amnesty.

(4) With the aim of guaranteeing food and basic supplies for the irregular forces, exclusively humanitarian aid channeled through neutral organizations may be solicited in conformity with Numeral 5 of the Esquipulas II Accord.

(5) The Government of Nicaragua will guarantee unrestricted freedom of expression, as contemplated in the Esquipulas II Accord.

(6) Once the Resistance forces are concentrated in the mutually accorded zones, they will send to the national dialogue as many representatives as they have constituent political groups, up to a maximum of eight. In the national dialogue, the matter of military service will be taken up among others.

(7) It is guaranteed that all those who have left the country for political or any other reasons may return to Nicaragua and incorporate themselves into political, economic and social processes without any conditions beyond those established by the laws of the republic. They will not be tried, punished or persecuted for the political-military acts they have carried out.

(8) The Government of Nicaragua pledges that people who return to peaceful life will be able to participate with equal conditions and guarantees in the election for Central American Parliament, in municipal elections on the date they are held, and in national elections on the dates established by the political constitution.

(9) To verify compliance with this agreement, a verification commission will be created, made up of the president of the Nicaraguan Episcopal Conference. His Excellency Cardinal Miguel Obando y Bravo, and the Secretary General of the Organization of American States, His Excellency João Clemente Baena Soares.

The technical assistance and services necessary to allow the expeditious functioning of this commission will be sought from and entrusted to the Secretary General of the Organization of American States.

TRANSITORY

Both parties agree to prolong until April 1 of this year the halt to offensive military operations that was agreed by both parties on March 21.

With faith in the above, those who sign below accept this agreement in four copies of the same original, in Sapoa, Rivas, Nicaragua, on March 23, 1988.

Source: James Malloy and Eduardo Gamarra, *Latin America and Caribbean Contemporary Record*, vol. 8 (New York: Holmes & Meier, forthcoming).

Appendix 7

TESORO BEACH ACCORD

The Presidents of El Salvador, Guatemala, Honduras, Nicaragua and Costa Rica meeting in the Department of La Paz, Republic of El Salvador, on 13 and 14 February 1989 analyzed the peace process in Central America and adopted decisions necessary to keep process current, with the understanding that the compromises entered into in the framework of Esquipulas II and the Declaration of Alajuela constitute a common and indivisible whole.

The Presidents of Costa Rica, El Salvador, Guatemala, and Honduras understood the willingness of the Constitutional President of Nicaragua Daniel Ortega Saavedra to develop a democratization and national reconciliation process in his country, within the framework of the Esquipulas II Accords, and in conformity, among others, with the following actions:

Once reforms to electoral legislation and to legislation regulating freedom of expression, information, and public opinion norms are completed, in a manner that guarantees political organization and political action in the broadest sense, a four month initial period will begin for the preparation, organization, and mobilization of the parties.

This period will be followed by a new six-month period of political activity; at the end of said period elections will be held for President, Vice President, Representatives of the National Assembly, Municipalities, and the Central American Parliament.

The elections must take place no later than 25 February 1990, unless after a common agreement, the government and the opposition political parties decide on another date. The government of Nicaragua will be a member of the Supreme Electoral Council with the equal participation of opposition political parties. In this sense, the presidents call on the political parties of Nicaragua to participate in the electoral process. International observers will be invited to participate, especially delegates from the Secretary General of both the United Nations and the Organization of American States, and to make themselves present in all electoral districts during the two stages previously mentioned to assure the purity of the process.

The government of Nicaragua will guarantee the free functioning of the communication media through a revision and modification of the Media Law, and equal access by all political parties to state owned radio and television stations. The government of Nicaragua will authorize all media channels to avail themselves inside or outside of the country, of all material, equipment, and instruments necessary to carry out their job.

In accordance with the proposal of the president of Nicaragua and the initiative from the president of Honduras, the Central American presidents agree to elaborate, within 90 days, a joint plan for the de-mobilization, voluntary repatriation or relocation in Nicaragua and in third countries of members of the Nicaraguan Resistance and their families. To that end, the (presidents) request technical assistance from specialized organisms of the United Nations. With the objective of creating the conditions for the demobilization, repatriation or relocation of Nicaraguans who have been involved directly or indirectly in armed activities and who are in Honduran territory, the government of Nicaragua has decided to release prisoners, in conformity with Inter American Human Rights Commission provisions.

Said plan also contemplates assistance for the demobilization of all persons who were involved or are involved in armed actions in all countries of the region, when they request voluntarily. To comply with the provisions of the security verification accords, an Executive Commission will be charged with calling technical meetings to establish a more efficient and appropriate mechanism along the lines of conversations held in New York with the Secretary General of the United Nations.

The presidents reaffirmed the faculties of the National Reconciliation Commissions to continue the development of specific verification functions in the areas indicated by the Guatemala procedures and the Declaration of Alajuela and to inform the Executive Commission periodically about the results of its efforts.

The presidents reiterated firmly their request number 5 of the Esquipulas Accord that regional and extra regional governments who overtly or covertly provide aid to irregular forces or insurrectional movements in the areas, cease that aid immediately, with the exception of humanitarian aid which contributes to the goals of this document.

The presidents request all sectors, especially insurrectional movements and irregular forces in the region to enter into the constitutional political processes in each country. In this sense, they call all sectors of Salvadoran society to participate in the next elections.

The presidents reiterated the importance of the Central American Parliament as a forum for the peoples of the area which, through their directly and freely elected representatives, can discuss and formulate appropriate recommendations about the political, economic, social, and cultural problems of Central America.

The presidents make an urgent call to the international community to support the economic recovery of the central American nations both in the short and medium term, taking into account the grave foreign debt problem and the need to recuperate the levels of intra regional commerce as a basic factor of the strengthening of the integration process.

[The presidents] particularly request support from the European Economic community for a program to restructure, reactivate, and strengthen the process of economic integration of the Central American Isthmus, which was presented officially in Guatemala during the past month of January.

Similarly, the presidents were pleased by the report from the International Commission for the Recovery and Development of Central America which constitutes a significant contribution for the consolidation of democracy and the creation of a welfare system and social and economic justice in the region.

The presidents agree to search for solutions negotiated directly to overcome the conflicts that emerged as a result of the Central American Crisis.

The presidents agreed to establish the Central American Environment and Development Commission as a regional cooperation mechanism for the optimal and rational utilization of the natural resources, the control of contamination, and the re-establishment of ecologic equilibrium in the region. At its next meeting the Executive Commission will name said commission and will convoke it immediately to elaborate the project /agreement to regulate its functioning and nature.

Similarly, the presidents gave their decided support to the celebration of the International Conference on Central American Refugees (CIREFCA—Conferencia Internacional sobre Refugiados Centroamericanos) in May 1989 in Guatemala because it will aid positively in the finding of solutions for the flow of refugees and people displaced by the crisis in the region.

[The presidents] agreed to promote a regional cooperation accord for the eradication of the illegal drug trafficking. To that end, the Executive Commission will elaborate a project for an accord which must be delivered to the affected governments.

They also expressed the willingness of their governments to support the initiative to formulate the Convention on the Rights of Children within the framework of the United Nations.

The Presidents agreed to meet in the Republic of Honduras at a date that will be established in the future.

The Presidents of Guatemala, Honduras, Nicaragua, and Costa Rica thank the people and the government of El Salvador, especially President José Napoleon Duarte for the hospitality that provided an adequate framework for the celebration of this meeting.

Department of La Paz, El Salvador, 14 February 1989.

Source: United Nations Department of Public Information, November 1989.

Appendix 8

THE TELA AGREEMENTS

The Central American Presidents, meeting at the port city of Tela, Honduras, on 5, 6 and 7 August 1989, bearing in mind and recognizing the important work done by the Executive Commission at its ninth meeting and by the Technical Working Group, whose efforts have made this meeting possible,

Considering:

That the measures agreed in the Esquipulas 11 agreement for the establishment of a firm and lasting peace must be implemented and the commitments made subsequently by the Presidents in their declarations and agreements at Alajuela and Costa del Sol fulfilled,

Agree:

1. To confirm their determination to promote all efforts aimed at implementing points 5 and 6 of the Esquipulas agreement in order to prevent the use of their own territory to destabilize the Governments of Central American countries. Accordingly, they have endorsed the Joint Plan for the voluntary demobilization, repatriation or relocation in Nicaragua or third countries of the Nicaraguan resistance and their families and for assistance in the demobilization of all those involved in armed actions in the countries of the region when such persons voluntarily request it.
2. To promote, by direct means, concerted solutions to any disputes that may arise directly between the various countries of Central America. Accordingly, they have endorsed the agreement between Honduras and Nicaragua regarding the application filed with the International Court of Justice, which enjoys the moral support of the Presidents of Guatemala, El Salvador and Costa Rica.
3. To endorse the appeal to armed groups in the region, particularly to FMLN, that still persist in its use of force, to halt such activities. Accordingly, they have endorsed chapter 111 on assistance in the voluntary demobilization of FMLN, whereby FMLN is strongly urged to put an immediate and effective end to hostilities so that a dialogue may be carried out that will lead to a

rejection of armed struggle and the integration of FMLN members into institutional and democratic life.

4. The Presidents acknowledge the efforts made by the Government of Guatemala to strengthen its process of national reconciliation through a wide-ranging, ongoing dialogue in which the National Reconciliation Commission is a leading participant. They also express their hope that this dialogue will be used to strengthen the democratic, pluralistic and participatory process, in keeping with point 1 of the Esquipulas Procedure and internal legislation. They reiterate the appeal to armed groups to abandon their activities, which violate the spirit of this agreement, and to enter political life through the national reconciliation process.

5. To request the United Nations to take the necessary steps for the establishment of the security machinery by virtue of which Honduras and Nicaragua have reached an agreement in which, inter alia, Honduras agrees to withdraw its reservation to implementation of the Plan. They also reiterate the request by Honduras concerning the dispatch of an international peacekeeping force to Honduran territory.

6. To confirm the decision taken by the Executive Commission at its ninth meeting to convene the Central American Commission on Environment and Development for the first time at Guatemala City on 30 and 31 August 1989, so that it can begin work on the draft convention setting out its nature and functions.

7. To reiterate the importance of the Central American Parliament as a forum in which the peoples of the region can discuss and make recommendations on political, economic, social and cultural problems in Central America. Accordingly, it is imperative that the treaty establishing the Parliament enter into force as soon as possible.

8. To condemn vigorously drug trafficking and use. The Central American Presidents agree to promulgate laws and take drastic measures to prevent the countries of Central America from becoming bases for drug trafficking. To this end, regional and international co-operation shall be sought and agreements concluded with nations affected by such illegal traffic, and activities for the effective control of drug trafficking shall be carried out.

9. The Central American Presidents agree to entrust the Executive Commission with the task of considering and adopting the document on political monitoring, which shall be ratified by the Presidents no later than at their next meeting.

As two years have passed since the signing of the Esquipulas II peace plan, the Presidents of Costa Rica, El Salvador, Guatemala, Honduras and Nicaragua reiterate their firm commitment to implement fully all commitments and agreements set out in the Guatemala Procedure and the Alajuela and Costa del

Sol Declarations, particularly those which refer to the strengthening of democratic processes. Accordingly, strict compliance with these agreements is of fundamental importance.

The Central American Presidents agree to meet before the end of the year in Nicaragua.

The Central American Presidents express their gratitude to the people and Government of Honduras, and especially to its President, Mr. José Azcona Hoyo, for their hospitality.

Tela, Honduras, 7 August 1989

Source: United Nations Department of Public Information, November 1989.

Notes

Chapter One

1. Figures are cited in John A. Booth and Thomas W. Walker, *Understanding Central America*, p. 2.

2. Author's interview with Horacio Boneo, deputy chief of the United Nations mission to the Nicaraguan elections, Managua, Nicaragua, November 23, 1989.

3. Thomas L. Karnes, *The Failure of Union: Central America, 1824–1875*, p. 246.

4. The best account of Barrios's attempt at Central American Union under his leadership is told in John D. Martz, *Justo Rufino Barrios and Central American Union*.

5. The similarities between Barrios and Zelaya are noted in Mario Rodríguez, *Central America*, 106–7.

6. Karnes, *Failure of Union*, pp. 183–210.

7. Richard V. Salisbury, "Costa Rican Relations with Central America: 1900–1934," pp. 5–6.

8. Charles L. Stansifer, "Application of the Tobar Doctrine to Central America."

9. Salisbury, "Costa Rican Relations with Central America," p. 29.

10. *Papers Relating to the Foreign Relations of the United States, 1907*, 2: 696.

11. Ibid.

12. The introduction of more stringent recognition provisions, far from being a United States diktat, represented a genuinely independent and completely understandable Costa Rican diplomatic initiative. Richard V. Salisbury, "Domestic Politics and Foreign Policy," p. 457.

13. See Stansifer, "Application of the Tobar Doctrine to Central America."

14. For an excellent account of the demise of the Tobar Doctrine see Kenneth J. Grieb's "American Involvement in the Rise of Jorge Ubico" and "The United States and the Rise of General Maximiliano Hernández Martínez."

15. John Patrick Bell, *Crisis in Costa Rica*, pp. 146–47.

16. Cited in Richard H. Immerman, *The CIA in Guatemala*, p. 49.

17. Ibid., p. 120.

18. Stephen Schlesinger and Stephen Kinzer, *Bitter Fruit*, p. 114.

19. Ibid.

20. Karnes, *Failure of Union*, p. 241.

21. Ibid.

22. Ibid., p. 244.

23. Thomas Anderson, *The War of the Dispossessed*.

24. Victor Bulmer-Thomas, *The Political Economy of Central America since 1920*, p. 195.

25. For an account of the historic animosity between Costa Rica and Nicaragua see Charles D. Ameringer, "The Thirty Year War between Figueres and the Somozas."

26. Mitchell A. Seligson and William J. Carroll, "The Costa Rican Role in the Sandinista Victory," pp. 332–36.

27. Warren Hoge, "Costa Rica Supporting Sandinistas," *New York Times*, June 29, 1979.

28. Mario Ojeda, "Mexican Policy toward Central America in the Context of U.S.-Mexico Relations," p. 142.

29. Latin American Studies Association, *Extraordinary Opportunities and New Risks: Final Report of the LASA Commission on Compliance with the Central America Peace Accord*, (Pittsburgh: Latin American Studies Association) March 15, 1988, p. 2.

30. Joseph B. Lockey, "Diplomatic Futility," p. 265.

31. It should be noted that this lack of official interest did not quell the spirit of imperialism, as private citizens, especially southern adventurers, proved eager to acquire additional slave territory in Central America and the Caribbean. These adventurers hoped to take advantage of the chronic civil wars in the region to make their fame and fortune. William Walker was the most notorious of these filibusters. In May 1855 he and fifty-seven ruffians arrived in Nicaragua and enlisted in the forces of the Liberal army. After successes in the field Walker was promoted to commander of the Nicaraguan army and later had himself elected president. Walker declared slavery legal, executed his opponents, and laid plans to take over the rest of Central America. However, his plans came to naught: the Costa Rican army invaded in 1857, with British support, and toppled him from power. Walker's career ended three years later when he attempted to wrest the Bay Islands from the government of Honduras. He was executed by a firing squad on September 12, 1860.

32. An analysis of Mahan's works is given in Margaret J. Sprout, "Mahan: Evangelist of Sea Power," and in Russell J. Weigley's "A Strategy of Sea Power and Empire."

33. Lester D. Langley, *The Banana War*, p. 56.

34. Eduardo Crawley, *Dictators Never Die*, pp. 45–46.

35. Ibid., p. 53.
36. Richard Salisbury, "Mexico, the United States, and the 1926–1927 Nicaraguan Crisis," pp. 320–21.
37. John Booth, *The Ends and the Beginning,* pp. 40–41.
38. Grieb, "American Involvement in the Rise of Jorge Ubico," p. 5.
39. Thomas P. Anderson, *Matanza: El Salvador's Communist Revolt of 1932,* p. 130.
40. Ibid., p. 135.
41. John Patrick Bell, *Crisis in Costa Rica,* p. 57.
42. For a good account of the U.S. role in the Costa Rican civil war see Jacobo Schifter, *Las Alianzas Conflictivas.*
43. Schlesinger & Kinzer, *Bitter Fruit,* pp. 75–76.
44. Both Immerman and Parkinson accept the primacy of strategic and political motivation on United States–Latin American policy. Schlesinger and Kinzer, however, emphasized the role of the United Fruit Company in convincing the Eisenhower administration that the Arbenz government presented the United States with a security risk in Latin America.
45. James Dunkerley, *Power in the Isthmus,* p. 236.
46. Richard Feinberg, "The Recent Rapid Redefinitions of U.S. Interests and Diplomacy in Central America," p. 62.
47. Darío Moreno, *U.S. Policy in Central America,* p. 5.
48. Feinberg, "Recent Rapid Redefinitions of U.S. Interests," p. 63.
49. Moreno, *U.S. Policy in Central America,* p. 61.
50. Victor Bulmer-Thomas, *Political Economy of Central America,* p. 17.
51. Ibid., p. 1.
52. Thomas Anderson, *Matanza,* p. 9.
53. Bulmer-Thomas, *Political Economy of Central America,* p. 275.
54. Ibid.
55. Ibid., p. 278.
56. James Rosenau, "A Pre-Theory Revisited," p. 256.
57. Ibid., p. 257.
58. James Rosenau, "Patterned Chaos in Global Life," p. 339.

Chapter Two

1. The role of the Central American elections in legitimating the new political order in the region is explored in John A. Booth and Mitchell A. Seligson, *Elections and Democracy in Central America.*
2. Figures are from the United States Embassy in Managua, "Foreign Economic Trends," January 1988.
3. Ricardo Chavarría, "The Social and Economic Impact of the War" (Lec-

ture delivered at the Latin American Studies Association's Research Seminar on Nicaragua in Managua, June 20, 1988.)

4. Author's interview with Jaime Bengochea and Nicolás Bolaños of COSEP (Superior Council of Private Enterprise), Managua, Nicaragua, June 23, 1988.

5. Lance Taylor, "Report of an Economic Mission to the Government of Nicaragua" (Unpublished report, April 5, 1989).

6. Ibid.

7. "Ortega Enacts Drastic Cuts to Ease Crisis." *Miami Herald*, January 31, 1989.

8. Mary Speck, "Managua Gets Tough on Farmers," *Miami Herald*, June 29, 1989.

9. David Close, *Nicaragua: Politics, Economics, and Society*, p. 165.

10. Author's interview with Mario del Amico, April 29, 1990, Tegucigalpa, Honduras. Del Amico claims that the moving force behind the early organization of the contras was the Guatemalan military. The role of Honduras and the Argentines is well documented in Roy Gutman, *Banana Diplomacy*, pp. 39–40, 49–57.

11. Christopher Dickey, *With the Contras: A Reporter in the Wilds of Nicaragua*, p. 119.

12. Wayne Smith, "Lies About Nicaragua," pp. 87–113.

13. *Washington Post*, May 8, 1983.

14. Defense Intelligence Agency, "Weekly Intelligence Survey," July 16, 1982, pp. 21–22.

15. Ibid.

16. *Washington Post*, April 18, 1984.

17. Peter Kornbluh, "The Covert War," pp. 30–31.

18. Ibid., p. 31.

19. *Mesoamerica*, March 1985, pp. 1–2; Reed Brody, *Contra Terror in Nicaragua; Nicaraguan Revolutionary Justice*, (New York: Lawyers Committee for International Human Rights, April 1985), pp. 152–61.

20. Gabriela Selser, "Contra Military Offensive," *Barricada Internacional*, November 11, 1989, pp. 3–4.

21. Author's conversation with Arturo Cruz, University of Miami, Coral Gables, Florida, January 1989.

22. Hemisphere Initiatives, "Establishing the Ground Rules: A Report on the Nicaraguan Electoral Process," p. 8.

23. *Miami Herald*, March 17, 1989.

24. Arms Control and Foreign Policy Caucus, "Special Alert: Funds for the Nicaraguan Opposition," October 3, 1989, p. 2.

25. Hemisphere Initiatives, "Nicaraguan Election Update No. 2: Foreign Funding of Internal Opposition," p. 3.

26. Enrique Baloyra, *El Salvador in Transition*, pp. 1–2.

27. Ibid., p. 2.

28. Moreno, *U.S. Policy in Central America*, p. 71.

29. Baloyra, *El Salvador in Transition*, p. 85.

30. *New York Times*, October 17, 1979.

31. Moreno, *U.S. Policy in Central America*, p. 71.

32. Frank Smyth, "Consensus or Crisis?" p. 30.

33. Mark Hatfield, Jim Leach, and George Miller, *Bankrolling Failure*, pp. 1–2.

34. Ibid., p. 12.

35. A. Bacevich, J. Hammulas, R. White, and T. Young, *American Military Policy in Small Wars*, p. 8.

36. Ibid.

37. Sara Miles and Bob Ostertag, "El Salvador: The Offensive in Perspective," p. 7.

38. Ibid.

39. See Rubén Zamora and Shafix Handel, "Proposal of the FMLN/FDR," 481–86.

40. Sam Dillon, "Dateline El Salvador," pp. 164–65.

41. Timothy Wickham-Crowley, "Understanding Failed Revolution," p. 523.

42. Joaquín Villalobos, "Popular Insurrection," p. 5.

43. Miles and Ostertag, "El Salvador: The Offensive in Perspective," pp. 7–8.

44. Enrique Baloyra, "Negotiating War in El Salvador," pp. 123–48.

45. Dillon, "Dateline El Salvador," p. 152.

46. James LeMoyne, "El Salvador's Forgotten War," p. 113.

47. Dillon, "Dateline El Salvador," p. 156.

48. Hatfield, Leach, and Miller, *Bankrolling Failure*, p. 17.

49. Ibid., p. 1.

50. Author's interview with Efraín Díaz-Arrivallaga, president of the Honduran Christian-Democratic Party, April 30, 1990, Tegucigalpa, Honduras.

51. Author's interview with Jaime Guell-Borgan, sub-secretary of Honduran foreign relations, May 2, 1990, Tegucigalpa, Honduras.

52. Gutman, *Banana Diplomacy*, pp. 49–57.

53. Philip Shepherd, "Honduras," p. 129.

54. Ibid.

55. Ibid.

56. Ibid.

57. Ibid, p. 130.

58. Gutman, *Banana Diplomacy*, pp. 49–57.

59. Mark Rosenberg, "From Transition to Consolidation in Honduras," p. 51.

60. Ibid., p. 44.

61. Victor Meza, "Honduras: The War Comes Home," p. 50.

62. Author's interview with Manuel Gamero, director of *Tiempo*, January 19, 1988, Tegucigalpa, Honduras.

63. Author's interview with Victor Meza, director, Honduran Research Center, January 19, 1988, Tegucigalpa, Honduras.

64. Mark Rosenberg, "Toward a Redefinition of U.S.-Honduran Relations? Alternatives and Options" (Paper presented at the Inter-American Dialogue, September 1988), p. 5.

65. Ernesto Paz, "Foreign Policy and National Security of Honduras," p. 186.

66. Rosenberg, "Toward a Redefinition of U.S.-Honduran Relations?" p. 5.

67. Leticia Salomon, "La Doctrina de la Seguridad Nacional en Honduras," *Boletín Informativo Honduras* (Tegucigalpa: Centro de Documentación de Honduras, May 1984).

68. Meza, "Honduras: The War Comes Home," p. 16.

69. Ibid.

70. Americas Watch, "Honduras: Without the Will," p. 1.

71. *Tiempo*, December 22, 1981.

72. Gregoria Selser, *Honduras: República Alguilada* (Coyoacán, Mexico: Mex Sur, 1982).

73. Ernesto Paz, "Foreign Policy and National Security," p. 193.

74. Quoted in Meza, "Honduras: The War Comes Home," p. 18.

75. "Visita de Suazo Cordova a USA" *Boletín Informativo Honduras* 49 (May 1985).

76. *Tiempo*, October 18, 1984.

77. Quoted in Guillermo Molina, "The Politics of Democracy in Honduras," p. 33.

78. Shelton Davis, "Introduction: Sowing the Seeds of Violence," p. 6. Also for an excellent description of conditions in the highlands during the height of the counterinsurgency campaign see Jonathan Evan Muslow, *Bird of Life, Bird of Death*.

79. Jonathan Powers, "Guatemala: Stirring of Change," p. 34.

80. George Black, *Garrison Guatemala*, p. 133.

81. Ibid., p. 135.

82. Quoted in Michael McClintock, *The American Connection*, p. 258.

83. *New York Times*, December 6, 1982.

84. *New York Times*, July 20, 1982.

85. Susanne Jonas, "Contradictions of Guatemala's 'Political Opening,' " p. 27.

86. Americas Watch Committee, "Creating a Desolation and Calling it Peace," April 1982 supplement of the human rights report on Guatemala.

87. *Washington Post*, March 10, 1977.

88. Louis S. Sergesvary, *Guatemala: A Complex Scenario*, p. 3.

89. "Special Report: The Recent Evolution of the Guatemalan Economy," *Central American Report*, October 10, 1986.

90. Piero Gleijeses, "Guatemala," p. B 302.

91. Ibid.

92. Ibid.

93. "Who Would Want to be President," *Economist* 296, no. 7410 (September 4, 1985), p. 44.

94. Gleijeses, "Guatemala," p. B 302.

95. "Guatemala: Please Keep Your Promise," *Economist* 296, no. 7376, (January 12, 1985), p. 23.

96. Jim Handy, "Resurgent Democracy and the Guatemalan Military," p. 408.

97. Jonas, "Contradictions of Guatemala's 'Political Opening,' " p. 30.

98. Ibid., p. 31.

99. Handy, "Resurgent Democracy and the Guatemalan Military," p. 408.

100. Susanne Jonas, "Guatemala: Keeping the Lid On," p. 7.

101. Jonas, "Contradictions of Guatemala's 'Political Opening,' " p. 42.

Chapter Three

1. Jorge E. Castañeda, "Don't Corner Mexico!" *Foreign Policy* 60 (Fall 1985), p. 76.

2. Ibid., p. 78.

3. Ibid.

4. Author's interview with José Azcona, President of Honduras, Tegucigalpa, Honduras, January 18, 1988.

5. This view was held by various foreign ministry officials in Costa Rica and Honduras. Author's interview with Jaime Guell-Borgan, sub-secretary of Honduran foreign relations, Tegucigalpa, Honduras, May 2, 1990; Rodrigo Madrigal-Nieto, Costa Rican foreign minister, San José, Costa Rica, November 14, 1990; and Carlos Riveria-Bianchini, Costa Rican vice-minister of foreign affairs, San José, Costa Rica, September 18, 1990.

6. Duarte made this statement at the presidential summit in Alajuela, Costa Rica, January 18, 1988.

7. Moreno, *U.S. Policy in Central America*, p. 86.

8. Center for Defense Information, Press Briefing Package, November 1985.

9. Author's interview with Luigi Einaudi, U.S. ambassador to Organization of American States, Washington, D.C., March 18, 1985.

10. Author's interview with Constantine Menges, adviser to the National Security Council, Washington, D.C., March 15, 1985.

11. *Washington Post*, January 15, 1981.

12. Castañeda, "Don't Corner Mexico!" p. 83.

13. Alexander M. Haig, *Caveat: Realism, Reagan, and Foreign Policy*, p. 99.

14. Néstor Sánchez, "The Communist Threat," p. 45.

15. Department of State, Press Briefing, December 14, 1981.

16. *New York Times*, February 21, 1981.

17. Moreno, *U.S. Policy in Central America*, p. 97.

18. Ibid., p. 96.

19. William LeoGrande, "Roll-back or Containment?" p. 91.

20. Gutman, *Banana Diplomacy*, p. 67.

21. The account of Enders's offer is given in Shirley Christian, *Nicaragua: Revolution in the Family*, pp. 198–99; Gutman, *Banana Diplomacy*, pp. 66–73; and Robert Pastor, *Condemned to Repetition*, pp. 233–35.

22. Pastor, *Condemned to Repetition*, p. 235.

23. *Washington Post*, December 21, 1981.

24. LeoGrande, "Roll-back or Containment?" p. 92.

25. Moreno, *U.S. Policy in Central America*, p. 100.

26. Susan Kaufman Purcell, "Demystifying Contadora," p. 75.

27. Ibid.

28. The point is made by Purcell in "Demystifying Contadora"; by Bruce Bagley in "Contadora: The Failure of Diplomacy"; and by Castañeda in "Don't Corner Mexico!"

29. Bagley, "Contadora: The Failure of Diplomacy," p. 5.

30. Purcell, "Demystifying Contadora," p. 76.

31. Robert Pastor and Jorge G. Castañeda, *Limits to Friendship*, p. 179.

32. The Energy Cooperation Program for Central American and Caribbean Countries was established by Venezuela and Mexico on August 3, 1980; it provided up to 160,000 barrels of oil a day, and the two regional powers also pledged to contribute financially to the recipient nations.

33. "Joint Franco-Mexican Declaration on El Salvador." United Nations Security Council Document S/14659.

34. Pastor and Castañeda, *Limits to Friendship*, p. 180.

35. Gutman, *Banana Diplomacy*, p. 160.

36. Ibid.

37. Ibid.

38. Purcell, "Demystifying Contadora," p. 84.

39. *La Estrella de Panama*, January 10, 1983.

40. Ibid.

41. Gutman, *Banana Diplomacy*, p. 163.

42. Ibid., p. 164.

43. Ibid.

44. Inforpress Centroamericana, *Compendio: Proceso de Paz en Centro America,* January 5, 1988.

45. "President Reagan's Letter to the Presidents of the Contadora Four, July 26, 1983." U.S. Department of State, *Bulletin* 83 (September 1983), p. 83.

46. "Document of Objectives," United Nations Security Council Document S/16041.

47. LeoGrande, "Roll-back or Containment?" p. 102.

48. Bagley, "Contadora: The Failure of Diplomacy," p. 7.

49. "U.S. Vetoes Resolution on Mines in Nicaragua," *Washington Post,* April 5, 1984.

50. Bagley, "Contadora: The Failure of Diplomacy," p. 7.

51. LeoGrande, "Roll-back or Containment?" p. 104.

52. Bagley, "Contadora; The Failure of Diplomacy," p. 7.

53. Cynthia J. Arnson, *Crossroads,* p. 161.

54. Ibid.

55. Cynthia J. Arnson, "Contadora and the U.S. Congress," p. 129.

56. Dan Oberdofer, "Obstruction of Contadora Efforts is Charged," *New York Times,* May 13, 1984.

57. *Congressional Record,* May 18, 1984, p. S5795.

58. LeoGrande, "Roll-back or Containment?" p. 105.

59. *Congressional Record,* May 15, 1984, p. S5758.

60. *Wall Street Journal,* June 4, 1984.

61. Ron Greenberger, "Shultz Nicaragua Trip Is Faulted by Some as Step to Quiet Critics," *Wall Street Journal,* June 4, 1984.

62. Gutman, *Banana Diplomacy,* p. 211.

63. Purcell, "Demystifying Contadora," p. 92.

64. Gutman, *Banana Diplomacy,* p. 222.

65. Ibid., p. 230.

66. Ibid., p. 228.

67. LeoGrande, "Roll-back or Containment?" p. 105.

68. Carlos Rico, as quoted in Gutman, *Banana Diplomacy,* p. 225.

69. Bagley, "Contadora: The Failure of Diplomacy," p. 9.

70. Gutman, *Banana Diplomacy,* p. 227.

71. Paul Taumur, "Latin Peace Plan, Why the U.S. Balks," *New York Times,* October 3, 1984.

72. United States Government, Department of State, *Negotiations in Central America: A Chronology,* 1981–1987, Washington, D.C.: Department of State Publication (May 1987), p. 4.

73. *Washington Post,* October 3, 1984.

74. "Letter Dated 21 September 1984 from the Co-ordinator of the Government Junta of National Reconstruction of Nicaragua," United Nations Security Council, Doc S/167756.

75. Ibid.

76. Bagley, "Contadora: The Failure of Diplomacy," p. 10.

77. J. Omans, "U.S. Plays Contadora Catch-up," *Washington Post*, October 3, 1984.

78. Ibid.

79. This is Roy Gutman's position. See Gutman, "The United States, Nicaragua, and Consensus Decision Making," p. 151.

80. LeoGrande, "Roll-back or Containment?" p. 108.

81. Bagley, "Contadora: The Failure of Diplomacy," p. 11.

82. Ibid.

83. LeoGrande, "Roll-back or Containment?" p. 112.

84. "Central America: The Long Sad History of Contadora," *Economist* 300, no. 7462 (September 5, 1986), p. 32.

85. "Letter from the President of Nicaragua," United Nations, General Assembly Document A/40/894.

86. "The Caraballeda Message on Central America's Peace, Security, and Democracy," United Nations General Assembly Document A/40/1095.

87. United States Department of State, *Negotiations in Central America*, p. 7.

88. "Contadora Act on Peace and Cooperation in Central America, June 7, 1986."

89. Bagley, "Contadora: The Failure of Diplomacy," p. 19.

90. United States Department of State, *Negotiations in Central America*, p. 9.

91. "Contadora: Have No Hope, Will Travel," *Economist* 302, no. 7483 (January 31, 1987), p. 35.

92. Author's interview with Jaime Guell-Borgan, sub-secretary of Honduran foreign relations, Tegucigalpa, Honduras, May 2, 1990.

93. Arnson, *Crossroads*, pp. 167–68.

94. U.S. Congress, *Report of the Congressional Committee Investigating the Iran-Contra Affair*, p. 104.

95. Ibid., pp. 48–49.

96. Moreno, *U.S. Policy in Central America*, p. 126.

97. Arnson, *Crossroads*, p. 166.

98. *New York Times*, April 22, 1985.

99. *Congressional Record*, April 4, 1984, p. S3761.

100. *New York Times*, April 25, 1985.

101. Moreno, *U.S. Policy in Central America*, pp. 127–28.

102. Ibid., p. 128.

103. Author's interview with Chris Arcos, U.S. ambassador to Honduras, Tegucigalpa, Honduras, May 3, 1990.

104. For a discussion of Cerezo foreign policy see Gabriel Aguilar, "La Neutralidad Guatemala ante el Conflicto Centroamericano," pp. 41–50.

105. Francisco Rojas-Aravena, *Costa Rica: Política Exterior y Crisis Centroamericana*, p. 176.

106. "Declaración de Esquipulas," Esquipulas, Guatemala, May 25, 1986, p. 1.

107. Dunkerley, *Power in the Isthmus*, p. 228.

108. Quoted in Gary Ruchwarger, "The Sandinista Mass Organization and the Revolutionary Process," p. 89.

109. Quoted in Rojas-Aravena, *Costa Rica: Política Exterior*, p. 177.

110. *Declaración de Esquipulas*, Esquipulas, Guatemala, May 25, 1986, p. 1.

Chapter Four

1. The exceptional character of Costa Rica is attributed by local political scientists and historians to some combination of the following five factors: colonial poverty, the absence of precious metals, the isolation of the colony, the small size of the Indian population, and the system of land ownership and labor. See Chester Zelaya, Daniel Camacho, Oscar Aguilar-Bulgarelli, Adolfo Cerdas, and Jacobo Schifter, *Democracia en Costa Rica? Cinco Opiniones Polémicas*, p. 26.

2. *Miami Herald*, June 15, 1980.

3. Marc Edelman and Joanne Kenen, *The Costa Rican Reader*, p. 269.

4. *Washington Post*, June 10, 1985.

5. William L. Furlong, "Costa Rica: Caught between Two Worlds," p. 125.

6. *Tico Times*, 1982 Review, p. 5.

7. Jean Hopfensperger, "Costa Rica's Right-Wing Paramilitary Groups," p. 24.

8. Ibid., p. 27.

9. Furlong, "Costa Rica," pp. 125–26.

10. Quoted in Peter Kornbluh, *Nicaragua: The Price of Intervention*, p. 132.

11. Juan Manuel Villasuso, "Crisis, Políticas de Ajuste y Desarrollo Agrícola en Costa Rica" (San José, Costa Rica: Mimeo, December 1982), p. 26.

12. Programa de Seguridad Alimentaria, *Breve Análisis del Sector Agropecuario con Enfasis en los Granos Básicos* (San José, Costa Rica: Midiplan, 1988), p. 5.

13. Sol W. Sanders, *The Costa Rican Laboratory*, p. 45.

14. Miguel B. Gómez and Mitchell A. Seligson, "Ordinary Elections in Extraordinary Times: The Political Economy of Voting in Costa Rica" (Paper delivered at the 14th meeting of the Latin American Studies Association, Boston, October 23–25, 1986), pp. 9–28.

15. Villasuso, "Crisis, Políticas de Ajuste y Desarrollo Agrícola en Costa Rica," p. 57.

16. Gregg L. Vunderink, "Peasant Participation and Mobilization during an Economic Crisis" (Paper delivered at the 15th meeting of the Latin American Studies Association, Miami, December 4–6, 1989), p. 6.

17. Author's interview with Carlos José Gutiérrez, Costa Rican foreign minister (1983–86), San José, Costa Rica, November 15, 1990.

18. Ibid.

19. Encuesta de Opinión Pública, "Costa Rica" no. 23, San José, Costa Rica: Consultoria Interdisciplinaria en Desarrollo, July 1986.

20. Furlong, "Costa Rica," p. 126.

21. Guido Fernández, *El Primer Domingo de Febrero: Crónica Interior de la Elección de Oscar Arias*, p. 310.

22. Quoted in Edelman and Kenen, *Costa Rican Reader*, p. 273.

23. Oscar Arias, "Inaugural Speech by President Oscar Arias-Sanchez."

24. Ibid.

25. Oscar Arias, "Address to the United Nations, September 24, 1986."

26. Ibid.

27. Ibid.

28. Author's interview with Rodrigo Madrigal-Nieto, Costa Rican foreign minister (1986–90), San José, Costa Rica, November 14, 1990.

29. Oscar Arias, "Address to the United Nations, September 24, 1986."

30. Furlong, "Costa Rica," p. 139.

31. Carlos Sojo, "Impacto de la Política Centroamericana de Arias en las Relaciones con Estados Unidos," pp. 8–9.

32. Edelman and Kenen, *Costa Rican Reader*, pp. 274–75.

33. Author's interview with Rodrigo Madrigal-Nieto, Costa Rican foreign minister (1986–90), San José, Costa Rica, November 14, 1990.

34. "A Declaration of Principles Signed February 25, 1987, by the Presidents of Costa Rica, El Salvador, Guatemala, and Honduras." In United States Department of State, *Negotiations in Central America: A Chronology 1981–1987*, p. 17.

35. Author's interview with Carlos Riveria-Bianchini, Costa Rican vice-minister of foreign affairs, San José, Costa Rica, September 18, 1990.

36. Gutman, *Banana Diplomacy*, p. 343.

37. Author's interview with Chris Arcos, U.S. ambassador to Honduras, Tegucigalpa, Honduras, May 3, 1990.

38. Gutman, *Banana Diplomacy*, p. 347.

39. Ibid.

40. Author's interview with Chris Arcos, U.S. ambassador to Honduras, Tegucigalpa, Honduras, May 3, 1990.

41. Ibid.

42. Gutman, *Banana Diplomacy*, p. 347.

43. Author's interview with José Azcona-Hoyo, president of Honduras, Tegucigalpa, Honduras, January 18, 1988.

44. Author's interview with Jaime Guell-Borgan, sub-secretary of Honduran foreign relations, Tegucigalpa, Honduras, May 2, 1990.

45. Quoted in Gutman, *Banana Diplomacy*, p. 348.

46. Rojas-Aravena, *Costa Rica: Política Exterior*, p. 180.

47. "Declaration of Principles Signed February 15, 1987," p. 17.

48. "Procedures for the Establishment of a Firm and Lasting Peace in Central America (Esquipulas II)," United Nations Press Kit, p. 3.

49. Ibid.

50. Ibid., pp. 3–4.

51. Ibid., p. 4.

52. Ibid.

53. Ibid, p. 5.

54. Ibid.

55. Ibid.

56. Ibid, p. 6.

57. Author's interview with Jon Glassman, foreign policy assistant to the vice-president, Washington, D.C., April 4, 1990.

58. Gutman, *Banana Diplomacy*, p. 357.

59. Oscar Arias, "Let's Give Peace a Chance," (Speech delivered before Joint Session of Congress, Washington, D.C., September 22, 1987).

60. Gutman, *Banana Diplomacy*, p. 357.

61. United States pressure on the Azcona government to violate and derail the Central American peace plan was a constant theme of the author's interviews in Tegucigalpa, Honduras, January 19–21, 1988, and April 23–May 6, 1990, with the internal opposition: Manuel Acosta-Bonilla, director of the Legal Affairs Committee, Honduran Bar Association; Rafael Alegría, project secretary, National Farmworkers Association (CNTC); Efraín Díaz-Arrivallaga, president of the Honduran Christian-Democrats; Manuel Gamero, director, *Tiempo*; and Victor Meza, director, Honduran Research Center.

62. *Tiempo*, August 15, 1987.

63. *New York Times*, October 22, 1987.

64. This was one of the findings of the *Final Report of the LASA Commission on Compliance with the Central American Peace Accord*, (Pittsburgh: Latin American Studies Association, 1988), p. 6.

65. Author's interview with José Azcona-Hoyo, president of Honduras, January 18, 1988; and with Alfredo Fortín-Inestrosa, vice-president of Honduras (1986–90), member National Reconciliation Commission, January 18, 1988, Tegucigalpa, Honduras.

66. Author's interview with Rafael Alegría, project secretary, National Farmworkers Association, January 18, 1988, Tegucigalpa, Honduras.

67. *New York Times*, August 21, 1987.

68. "Honduras and the Arias Plan," *Central American Bulletin* 6, no. 12 (November 1987), p. 5.

69. Author's interview with Carlos Riveria-Bianchini, Costa Rican vice-minister of foreign affairs, September 18, 1990, San José, Costa Rica.

70. Carlos Sojo, "Impacto de la Política," p. 9.

71. Martha Honey and Michael Emergy, "The Patchwork of Peacework," *Los Angeles Times*, January 24, 1988.

72. Victor Hugo Tinoco, *Conflicto y Paz: El Proceso Negociador Centroamericano*, p. 36.

73. *Final Report of the LASA Commission*, p. 36.

74. Ibid., p. 27.

75. *Los Angeles Times*, January 24, 1988.

76. Author's interview with Rodrigo Madrigal-Nieto, Costa Rican foreign minister (1986–90), San José, Costa Rica, November 14, 1990.

77. Ibid.

78. Author's interview with José Azcona-Hoyo, president of Honduras, January 18, 1988, Tegucigalpa, Honduras.

79. Author's interview with Rodrigo Madrigal-Nieto, Costa Rican foreign minister (1986–90), San José, Costa Rica, November 14, 1990.

80. Moreno, *U.S. Policy in Central America*, p. 133.

81. Jeane Kirkpatrick, "Making Aid to the Contras the Only Answer," *Miami Herald*, January 25, 1988.

82. Gutman, *Banana Diplomacy*, p. 359.

83. "Sapoa Cease-Fire Agreement, March 23, 1988," United Nations Press Kit.

84. Ibid.

85. Ibid.

86. *Miami Herald*, May 1, 1988.

87. *Miami Herald*, May 2, 1988.

88. Author's interview with Virgilio Godoy, vice-president of Nicaragua, Managua, Nicaragua, June 14, 1988.

89. Nina M. Serfino, "Dateline Managua: Defining Democracy," 167–86.

90. Testimony of Violeta Barrios de Chamorro before the Comisión Internacional de Verificación y Seguimiento (CIVS), January 15, 1988.

91. *Washington Post*, September 13, 1987.

92. Author's interview with Joaquín Mejía, editor of *La Prensa*, Managua, Nicaragua, June 22, 1988.

93. Darío Moreno, "Peace and the Nicaraguan Revolution."

94. Author's interview with Carlos Riveria-Bianchini, Costa Rican vice-minister of foreign affairs, San José, Costa Rica, September 18, 1990.

Chapter Five

1. Senate Committee on Foreign Relations, *Nomination of James Baker* (Washington, D.C.: Government Printing Office, 1989).

2. Author's interview with Chris Arcos, U.S. ambassador to Honduras, Tegucigalpa, Honduras, May 3, 1990.

3. Jorge Sarmiento, "Bernard Aronson: La Correcta Elección para América Latina?" p. 7.

4. *New York Times*, May 11, 1989.

5. Author's interview with Carlos Riveria-Bianchini, Costa Rican vice-minister of foreign affairs, San José, Costa Rica, September 18, 1990.

6. *Miami Herald*, January 31, 1989.

7. Ibid.

8. *New York Times*, February 2, 1989.

9. Carlos Vilas, "Crisis, Ajuste y Perspectivas de Reactivación Económica de Nicaragua," p. 24.

10. Figures are from the U.S. embassy, Managua, "Foreign Economic Trends Toward Nicaragua," January 1988.

11. Voytek Zubek, "Soviet 'New Thinking' and the Central American Crisis," p. 102.

12. *New York Times*, May 11, 1989.

13. *Miami Herald*, May 13, 1989.

14. Author's interview with Carlos Riveria-Bianchini, Costa Rican vice-minister of foreign affairs, San José, Costa Rica, September 18, 1990.

15. *Miami Herald*, February 13, 1989.

16. Tinoco, *Conflicto y Paz*, p. 63.

17. *Miami Herald*, February 15, 1989.

18. "Joint Declaration of the Central American Presidents," Costa del Sol, El Salvador, February 14, 1989.

19. Rojas-Aravena, *Costa Rica: Política Exterior*, pp. 219–20.

20. Hemisphere Initiatives, "Establishing the Ground Rules," p. 4.

21. Author's interview with Virgilio Godoy, vice-president of Nicaragua, Managua, Nicaragua, May 4, 1988.

22. Hemisphere Initiatives, "Establishing the Ground Rules", p. 4.

23. Ibid., p. 5.

24. "Establishment and Terms of Reference of the United Nations Observer

Mission to Verify the Electoral Process in Nicaragua," United Nations Press Kit.

25. *Miami Herald*, August 8, 1989.

26. *Miami Herald*, August 7, 1989.

27. Tinoco, *Conflicto y Paz*, p. 80.

28. *Miami Herald*, August 6, 1989.

29. "Joint Declaration of Central American Presidents," Tela, Honduras, August 7, 1989.

30. Ibid.

31. Ibid.

32. Author's interview with Mariano Fiallos, president of the Supreme Election Council, Managua, Nicaragua, November 22, 1989.

33. Author's interview with Trish O'Kane, researcher with CRIES, Managua, Nicaragua, November 25, 1989.

34. *Miami Herald*, November 5, 1989.

35. Author's interview with Rodrigo Madrigal-Nieto, Costa Rican foreign minister (1986–90), San José, Costa Rica, November 14, 1990.

36. "Joint declaration of Central American Presidents," San Isidro de Coronado, Costa Rica, December 13, 1989.

37. Ibid.

38. Author's interview with Violeta Barrios de Chamorro, president of Nicaragua, Managua, Nicaragua, November 23, 1989.

39. Author's interview with Horacio Boneo, deputy chief of the United Nations mission to the Nicaraguan elections, Managua, Nicaragua, November 23, 1989.

40. United Nations, General Assembly, Forty-fourth Session, agenda item 34. "Evolution of the Electoral Process in Nicaragua: First Report of the United Nations Observer Mission to Verify the Electoral Process in Nicaragua to the Secretary-General," October 17, 1989.

41. Robert Pear, "U.S. to Pare Aid in Nicaragua Vote," *New York Times*, September 29, 1989.

42. Ibid.

43. *New York Times*, September 14, 1989.

44. Thomas L. Friedman, "U.S. Drops a Plan to Finance Nicaraguan Opposition Leader," *New York Times*, September 16, 1989.

45. Ibid.

46. Ibid.

47. Martin McReynolds, "Nicaragua Election Aid in Limbo," *Miami Herald*, October 30, 1989.

48. Hemisphere Initiatives, "Nicaraguan Election Update No. 2," p. 2.

49. Christopher Marquis, "CIA Aid to Chamorro Alleged: Envoy's Posting held up in probe," *Miami Herald*, June 26, 1992.

50. Robert Pear, "U.S. to Pare Aid in Nicaragua Vote," *New York Times*, September 29, 1989.

51. Hemisphere Initiatives, "Establishing the Ground Rules," pp. 6–7.

52. Author's interview with John Boardman, first political officer U.S. Embassy, Managua, Nicaragua, November 23, 1989.

53. Author's interview with Violeta Barrios de Chamorro, president of Nicaragua, Managua, Nicaragua, November 23, 1989.

54. Hemisphere Initiatives, "Establishing the Ground Rules," p. 17.

55. Author's interview with Bayardo Arce, member of Sandinista Directorate, Managua, Nicaragua, November 22, 1989.

56. William Bolinger, "Pollsters Invade Nicaragua," p. 5.

57. *Miami Herald*, February 24, 1990.

58. An excellent account of the role of Violeta Barrios de Chamorro and her children in Nicaraguan politics is Patricia Taylor Edmisten, *Nicaragua Divided: La Prensa and the Chamorro Legacy*.

59. Hemisphere Initiatives, "Nicaragua National Election Survey," December 11, 1989.

60. *Miami Herald*, February 24, 1990.

61. Harry E. Vanden and Thomas W. Walker, "The Reimposition of U.S. Hegemony over Nicaragua," p. 171.

62. Lindsey Gruson, "Chamorro and Sandinista Rulers Begin Delicate Transition Talks," *New York Times*, February 28, 1990.

63. Martin McReynolds, "U.S. Lifts Managua Trade Embargo," *Miami Herald*, March 14, 1990.

64. Martin McReynolds, "Quayle to Contras: Farm, Don't Fight," *Miami Herald*, March 17, 1990.

65. Ibid.

66. Dennis Hevesi, "Honduras President Asks Contras to Leave Soon," *New York Times*, February 28, 1990.

67. Ibid.

68. *Tiempo*, April 28, 1990.

69. Christopher Marquis, "A Central American Common Market?" *Miami Herald*, April 23, 1990.

70. "Joint Declaration of the Central American Presidents," Montelimar, Nicaragua, April 4, 1990.

71. Ibid.

72. Manuel Araya, "La Declaración de Antigua de Guatemala: Economía, Política y la Vaguedad del Consenso," p. 1.

Chapter Six

1. James N. Rosenau, *Turbulence in World Politics: A Theory of Change and Continuity*, p. 107.

2. Moreno, *U.S. Central American Policy*, pp. 63–65.

3. A good discussion of the failure of the electoral process to bring democracy to Central America is John Booth, "Elections and Democracy in Central America: A Framework for Analysis," pp. 7–39.

4. For a review of the problems facing Salvadoran democracy see José Z. García, "El Salvador: Recent Elections in Historical Perspective," 60–92.

5. "Joint Declaration of Central American Presidents," San Isidro de Coronado, Costa Rica, December 13, 1989.

6. Moreno, *U.S. Policy in Central America*, p. 128.

7. See Bagley, "Contadora: The Failure of Diplomacy" and LeoGrande's "Roll-back or Containment?"

8. LeoGrande, "Roll-back or Containment," p. 105.

9. Author's interview with Jon Glassman, foreign policy assistant to the vice-president, Washington, D.C., April 4, 1990.

10. The metaphor for chess was used by Strobe Talbott in his *Endgame: The Inside Story of SALT II*, p. 17.

11. *Final Report of the LASA Commission on Compliance with the Central American Peace Accord* (Pittsburgh: Latin American Studies Association, 1988), p. 1.

12. Moreno, "Peace and the Nicaraguan Revolution," p. 405.

13. See, for example, the report of the Latin American Studies Association commission to observe the 1990 Nicaraguan election: *Electoral Democracy: Under International Pressure*, (Pittsburgh: Latin American Studies Association, March 1990).

14. Tim Johnson, "Nicaragua Army Chief Targets Unrest: Tougher Law Enforcement Pledged," *Miami Herald*, July 23, 1992

15. Americas Watch, "Fitful Peace: Human Rights and Reconciliation in Nicaragua Under the Chamorro Government," p. 5.

16. Christopher Marquis, "U.S. Ambivalent on Chamorro Rule," *Miami Herald*, September 2, 1992.

17. Tim Johnson, "Chamorro Dismisses Sandinista Leader: U.S. Urged Shake-up, Official Says," *Miami Herald*, September 7, 1992.

18. Americas Watch, "Fitful Peace," p.7.

19. Foreign Broadcast Information Service, Latin America, September 14, 1990.

20. Tim Johnson, "Sandinistas Strengthen Their Hand in Nicaragua: Chamorro Now Relies on Her Former Foes," *Miami Herald*, January 19, 1993.

21. Darío Moreno, "Nicaragua."

22. Tim Golden, "Salvadoran Accord Aims at Quick End to Long Civil War," *New York Times*, January 2, 1992.

23. Sam Dillon, "Dateline El Salvador."

24. "Joint declaration of Central American Presidents," San Isidro de Coronado, Costa Rica, December 13, 1989.

25. Mark Uhlig, "Top Salvador Rebel Alters His Goals," *New York Times*, March 7, 1991.

26. Ibid.

27. Hemisphere Initiatives, "Endgame: A Progress Report on Implementation of the Salvadoran Peace Accords," pp. 3-4.

28. Shirley Christian, "Salvadorans, Ending their War, Are Cautioned on Peace," *New York Times*, December 16, 1992.

29. Thomas Long, "Salvadoran Officers Retain Power: U.N. Bid for Purges Derailed," *Miami Herald*, January 10, 1993.

30. Christopher Marquis, "New Guatemalan President Faces Formidable Challenges," *Miami Herald*, January 15, 1991.

Bibliography

Books and Articles

Adam, Jan S. *A Foreign Policy in Transition: Moscow's Retreat from Central America and the Caribbean, 1985–1992*. Chapel Hill, N.C.: University of North Carolina Press, 1992.

Aguilar, Gabriel. "La Neutralidad Guatemalteca ante el Conflicto Centroamericano." *Polémica* 2, no. 2 (May–August 1987): 41–50.

———. "Los Dilemas de la Política Exterior de Guatemala." *Centroamérica/ USA*, no. 7 (April–May 1989): 9–11.

Americas Watch. "Creating a Desolation and Calling It Peace." Supplement, Human Rights Report on Guatemala. April 1982.

———. "Fitful Peace: Human Rights and Reconciliation in Nicaragua under the Chamorro Government." New York, July 1991.

———. "Honduras: Without the Will." New York, July 1989.

Ameringer, Charles. "The Thirty Year War Between Figueres and the Somozas." *Caribbean Review* 8, no. 4 (Fall 1979): 4–7, 40–41.

Anderson, Thomas. *Matanza: El Salvador's Communist Revolt of 1932*. Lincoln: University of Nebraska Press, 1971.

———. *Politics in Central America: Guatemala, El Salvador and Honduras*. New York: Praeger, 1988.

———. *The War of the Dispossessed: Honduras and El Salvador*. Lincoln: University of Nebraska Press, 1981.

Araya, Manuel. "La Declaración de Antigua de Guatemala: Economía, Política y la Vaguedad del Consenso." *Centroamérica Internacional* no. 4 (July–August 1990): p. 1.

Arnson, Cynthia J. "Contadora and the U.S. Congress." In *Contadora and the Diplomacy of Peace in Central America*. Vol. 1: *The United States, Central America, and Contadora*, ed. Bruce Bagley, 123–41. Boulder: Westview Press, 1987.

———. *Crossroads: Congress, the Reagan Administration, and Central America*. New York: Pantheon Books, 1989.

Asenjo, Daniel. "Honduras: Condicionamientos, Debilidades y Dilemas en la Política Exterior." In *Las Políticas Exteriores de America Latina y el Caribe: Un*

Balance de Esperanzas, ed. Heraldo Munoz, 253–65. Buenos Aires, Argentina: Grupo Editor Latinoamericano, 1988.

―――. "La Política Exterior de Guatemala: Continuidad en Medio de la Crisis." In *America Latina y el Caribe: Políticas Exteriores para Sobrevivir,* ed. Heraldo Munoz, 325–43. Buenos Aires, Argentina: Grupo Editor Latinoamericano, 1986.

Asenjo, Daniel, and Ricardo Urrutia. "La Política Exterior de El Salvador: Del Alineamiento a la Subordinación." In *America Latina y el Caribe: Políticas Exteriores para Sobrevivir,* ed. Heraldo Munoz, 313–23. Buenos Aires, Argentina: Grupo Editor Latinoamericano, 1986.

Bacevich A., J. Hammulas, R. White, and T. Young. *American Military Policy in Small Wars: The Case of El Salvador.* Cambridge, Mass.: John F. Kennedy School of Government, 1988.

Bagley, Bruce. "Contadora: The Failure of Democracy." *Journal of Interamerican Studies and World Affairs* 28, no. 3 (Fall 1986): 1–32.

―――, ed. *Contadora and the Diplomacy of Peace in Central America.* Vol. 1: *The United States, Central America, and Contadora.* Boulder: Westview Press, 1987.

Baloyra, Enrique. *El Salvador in Transition.* Chapel Hill: University of North Carolina Press, 1982.

―――. "Negotiating War in El Salvador: The Politics of Endgame." *Journal of Interamerican Studies and World Affairs* 28, no. 1 (Spring 1986): 123–48.

Barry, Tom, and Deb Preuch, "The War in El Salvador: A Reassessment." *Monthly Review* 38 (April 1987): 481–86.

Bell, John Patrick. *Crisis in Costa Rica: The 1948 Revolution.* Austin: University of Texas Press, 1971.

Blachman, Morris, William M. LeoGrande, and Kenneth Sharpe. *Confronting Revolution: Security Through Diplomacy in Central America.* New York: Pantheon Books, 1986.

Black, George. *Garrison Guatemala.* New York: Monthly Review Press, 1984.

Bolinger, William. "Pollsters Invade Nicaragua," *Inter-American Public Opinion Report* (January 1990), 11–12.

Booth, John. "Elections and Democracy in Central America: A Framework for Analysis." In *Elections and Democracy in Central America,* ed. John Booth and Mitchell A. Seligson, 7–39. Chapel Hill: University of North Carolina Press, 1989.

―――. *The End and the Beginning: The Nicaraguan Revolution.* Boulder: Westview, 1982.

―――. "War and the Nicaraguan Revolution." *Current History* 85, no. 515 (December 1986): 405–9.

Booth, John, and Mitchell A. Seligson. *Elections and Democracy in Central America.* Chapel Hill: University of North Carolina Press, 1989.

Booth, John, and Thomas W. Walker. *Understanding Central America*. Boulder: Westview, 1989.

Brown, Doug. "Sandinismo and the Problem of Democratic Hegemony." *Latin American Perspectives* 17, no. 2 (Spring 1990): 39–61.

Bulmer-Thomas, Victor. *The Political Economy of Central America Since 1920*. Cambridge: Cambridge University Press, 1987.

Camacho, Daniel, and Manuel Rojas-Bolaños, *La Crisis Centroamericana*. San José, Costa Rica: Editorial Universitaria Centroamericana, 1984.

Carmak, Robert M., ed. *Harvest of Violence: The Mayan Indians and the Guatemalan Crisis*. Norman: University of Oklahoma Press, 1988.

Castañeda, Jorge E. "Don't Corner Mexico!" *Foreign Policy*, no. 60 (Fall 1985): 75–90.

Castillo, Fabio, and Oriel Soto. *Declaración de Zona de Paz Y Cooperación en Centroamérica y el Caribe*. Heredia, Costa Rica: Universidad para la Paz and Universidad Nacional, Escuela de Relaciones Internacionales, 1990.

Chavarría, Ricardo. "The Social and Economic Impact of the War." Lecture delivered at the Latin American Studies Association Research Seminar on Nicaragua. Managua, Nicaragua, June 20, 1988.

Christian, Shirley. *Nicaragua: Revolution in the Family*. New York: Random House, 1985.

Close, David. *Nicaragua: Politics, Economics and Society*. London: Pinter, 1988.

Coleman, Kenneth, and George Herring, eds. *Understanding the Central American Crisis*, Wilmington, Del.: Scholarly Resource Books, 1991.

Cook, Mark. "Nicaragua UNO: One Is Not Enough." *NACLA* 23, no. 5 (February 1990): 4–11.

Cordova, Ricardo. "El Salvador: Un Cambiante Escenario de la Paz." *Polémica* 2, no. 5 (May–August 1988): 21–34.

Crawley, Eduardo. *Dictators Never Die: A Portrait of Nicaragua and the Somoza Dynasty*. New York: St Martin's Press, 1979.

Davis, Shelton. "Introduction: Sowing the Seeds of Violence." In *Harvest of Violence: The Mayan Indians and the Guatemalan Crisis*, ed. Robert M. Carmak, 3–36. Norman: University of Oklahoma Press, 1988.

Dickey, Christopher. *With the Contras: A Reporter in the Wilds of Nicaragua*. New York: Simon & Schuster, 1985.

Dillon, Sam. "Dateline El Salvador: Crisis Renewed." *Foreign Policy*, no. 73 (Winter 1988–89): 153–70.

Doggett, Martha Lyn. "Xabier Gorostiaga: Arias Peace with No Losers." *NA-CLA* 21, no. 4 (July–August 1987): 6–10.

Doyle, Kate, and Peter Duklis, "The Long Twilight Struggle: Low Intensity Warfare and the Salvadoran Military." *Journal of International Affairs* 43 (Winter 1990): 431–60.

Dunkerley, James. *Power in the Isthmus: A Political History of Modern Central America*. London: Verso Press, 1988.

Edelman, Marc, and Joanne Kenen. *The Costa Rican Reader*. New York: Grove Weidenfeld, 1989.

Edmisten, Patricia Taylor. *Nicaragua Divided: La Prensa and the Chamorro Legacy*. Pensacola: University of West Florida Press, 1990.

Eguizabal, Christina. "La Política Exterior de El Salvador en 1987." In *Las Políticas Exteriores de America Latina y el Caribe: Un Balance de Esperanzas*, ed. Heraldo Munoz, 229–38. Buenos Aires, Argentina: Grupo Editor Latino-americano, 1988.

Eschback, Cheryl L. "Explaining U.S. Policy toward Central America and the Caribbean." *Latin American Research Review* 15, no. 2 (1990): 206–16.

Farer, Tom J. "Contadora: The Hidden Agenda." *Foreign Policy*, no. 59 (Summer 1985): 59–72.

———. *The Grand Strategy of the United States in Latin America*. New Brunswick, N.J.: Transaction Books, 1988.

Feinberg, Richard, ed. *Central America: International Dimensions of the Crisis*. New York: Holmes & Meier, 1982.

Fernández, Guido. *El Primer Domingo de Febrero: Crónica Interior de la Elección de Oscar Arias*. San José, Costa Rica: Editorial Costa Rica, 1986.

Furlong, William. "Costa Rica: Caught between Two Worlds." *Journal of Interamerican Studies and World Affairs* 29, no. 2 (Summer 1987): 119–54.

Gammara, Edward, and James Malloy, eds. *Latin American and Caribbean Contemporary Record*. New York: Holmes & Meier, forthcoming.

García, José Z. "El Salvador: Recent Elections in Historical Perspective." In *Elections and Democracy in Central America*, ed. John Booth and Mitchell A. Seligson, 60–92. Chapel Hill: University of North Carolina Press, 1989.

Gilbert, Dennis. *Sandinistas: The Party and the Revolution*. London: Basil Blackwell, 1988.

Gleijeses, Piero. "Guatemala." In *Latin American and Caribbean Contemporary Record*, ed. Abraham Lowenthal, 5: 1985–86, B 299–B 312. New York: Holmes & Meier, 1988.

Gomariz, Enrique. *Balance de Una Esperanza: Esquipulas II un año Después*. San José, Costa Rica: FLASCO, 1988.

———. "Estado Unidos y la Reactivación de Esquipulas II." *Centroamérica/USA* 1, no. 1 (March–April 1988): 8–12.

———. "Primer Aniversario: Deactivación de Esquipulas II." *Centroamérica/ USA* 1, no. 3 (July–August 1988): 16–18.

Gómez, Miguel B., and Mitchell A. Seligson. "Ordinary Elections in Extraordinary Times: The Political Economy of Voting in Costa Rica." Paper delivered at the 14th meeting of the Latin American Studies Association, Boston, October 23–25, 1986.

Gonzalez-Davidson, Fernández. "La Política Exterior de Guatemala en 1987." In *Las Políticas Exteriores de America Latina y el Caribe: Un Balance de Esperanzas*, ed. Heraldo Munoz, 239–51. Buenos Aires, Argentina: Grupo Editor Latinoamericano, 1988.

Gonzalez-Gomez, Mary Lisbeth. "Centroamérica: la paz como desafio." *Centroamérica/USA* 1, no. 1 (March–April 1988): 16–20.

Grieb, Kenneth J. "American Involvement in the Rise of Jorge Ubico." *Caribbean Studies* 10, no. 1 (1970): 5–21.

———. "The United States and the Rise of General Maximiliano Hernández Martínez." *Journal of Latin American Studies* 3, no. 2 (1971): 151–72.

Gutman, Roy. *Banana Diplomacy: The Making of American Policy in Nicaragua 1981–1987*. New York: Simon & Schuster, 1988.

———. "The United States, Nicaragua, and Consensus Decision Making." In *Contadora and the Diplomacy of Peace in Central America. Vol. 1: The United States, Central America, and Contadora*, ed. Bruce Bagley, 142–55. Boulder: Westview Press, 1987.

Haig, Alexander. *Caveat: Realism, Reagan, and Foreign Policy*. New York: Macmillan, 1984.

Handy, Jim. "Resurgent Democracy and the Guatemalan Military." *Journal of Latin American Studies* 18, no. 2 (November 1986): 383–408.

Harris, Richard, and Carlos Vilas, eds. *Nicaragua: A Revolution Under Siege*. London: Zed Books, 1985.

Hatfield, Mark, Jim Leach, and George Miller. *Bankrolling Failure: United States Policy in El Salvador and the Urgent Need for Reform*. Washington, D.C.: Arms Control and Foreign Policy Caucus, December 1987.

Hemisphere Initiatives. "Endgame: A Progress Report on Implementation of the Salvadoran Peace Accord." Cambridge, Mass., December 3, 1992.

———. "Establishing the Ground Rules: A Report on the Nicaraguan Electoral Process." Boston, August 1989.

———. "Nicaraguan Election Update No. 2: Foreign Funding of Internal Opposition," Boston, October 16, 1989.

———. "Nicaragua National Election Survey," Boston, December 11, 1989.

Heubel, Edward J. "Costa Rican Interpretations of Costa Rican Politics." *Latin American Research Review* 15, no. 2 (1990): 217–24.

Hopfensperger, Jean. "Costa Rica's Right-Wing Paramilitary Groups." *Progressive* (September 1986): 24–27.

Hunter, Jane. "The Show Goes On: The Right After Reagan." *NACLA* 22, no. 5 (September–October 1988): 10–15.

Immerman, Richard H. *The CIA in Guatemala: The Foreign Policy of Intervention.* Austin: University of Texas Press, 1982.

Irvin, George, and Stuart Holland, eds. *Central America: The Future of Economic Integration.* Boulder: Westview Press, 1989.

Jonas, Susanne. "Contradictions of Guatemala's 'Political Opening'." *Latin American Perspectives* 15, no. 3 (Summer 1988): 26–46.

———. "Guatemala: Keeping the Lid On." *NACLA* 22, no. 5 (September–October 1988): 7–8.

Karnes, Thomas. *The Failure of Union: Central America 1824–1875.* Chapel Hill: University of North Carolina Press, 1961.

Klepak, H. P. "Obstaculos a la Verificación del Acuerdo de Paz en Centro-américa." *Centroamérica Internacional,* no. 2 (December–January 1990): 1–8.

Kornbluh, Peter. "The Covert War." In *Reagan versus the Sandinistas,* ed. Thomas Walker, 30–31. Boulder: Westview Press, 1987.

———. *Nicaragua: The Price of Intervention.* Washington, D.C.: Institute for Policy Studies, 1987.

Langley, Lester D. *The Banana War: An Inner History of American Empire.* Lexington: University Press of Kentucky, 1983.

LeMoyne, James. "El Salvador's Forgotten War." *Foreign Affairs* 68, no. 3 (Summer 1989): 105–25.

LeoGrande, William. "Roll-back or Containment? The United States, Nicaragua, and the Search for Peace in Central America." *International Security* 11, no. 2 (Fall 1986): 89–120.

Lockey, Joseph B. "Diplomatic Futility." *Hispanic American Historical Review* 10, no. 3 (August 1930): 265–94.

McClintock, Michael. *The American Connection: State Terror and Popular Resistance in Guatemala.* London: Zed Books, 1985.

Martz, John D. *Justo Rufino Barrios and Central American Union.* Gainesville: University of Florida Press, 1963.

Marure, Alejandro. *Efemerides de los Hechos Notables Acaecidos en la República de Centro-America.* Guatemala City, 1837.

Mendez, Maria. "Esquipulas II, Esperanzas en Medio de Contradicciones." *Centroamérica/USA,* no. 2 (May–June 1988): 12–15.

Menjivar, Rafael. "Obstaculo O Ayuda? 8 Anos Centroamericanos de la Administración Reagan." *Polémica* 2, no. 7 (January–April 1989): 13–26.

Meza, Victor. "The Military Willing to Deal." *NACLA* 22, no. 1 (January–February 1988): 14–21.

———. "Honduras: The War Comes Home." *NACLA* 22, no. 1 (January–February 1988): 13–38.

Miles, Sara, and Bob Ostertag. "D'Aubuisson's New ARENA." *NACLA* 23, no. 2 (July 1989): 14–23.

――――. "El Salvador: The Offensive in Perspective." *NACLA* 23, no. 6 (April 1990): 7–9.

――――. "FMLN: New Thinking." *NACLA* 23, no. 3 (September 1989): 15–37.

Molina, Guillermo. "The Politics of Democracy in Honduras." In *Honduras Confronts its Future,* ed. Rosenberg and Shepherd, 23–36. Boulder: Lynne Rienner, 1986.

Moralers, Abelardo. "Ajuste Estructural versus Integración: Los Vericuetos de la Política Regional de Costa Rica." *Polémica* 2, no. 7 (January–April 1989): 27–38.

――――. "Estados Unidos en El Salvador: El Eslabon mas Debil." *Centroamérica/ USA,* no. 7, (April–May 1989): 5–8.

――――. "La Declaración de Antigua de Guatemala: Economia, Política y la Vaguedad del Consenso." *Centroamérica Internacional,* no. 4 (July–August 1990): 1–9.

――――. "Los Acuerdos de Tela." *Centroamérica Internacional,* no. 1 (September–October 1989): 9–11.

Moreno, Darío. "Nicaragua." In *Latin American and Caribbean Contemporary Record,* ed. Edward Gammara and James Malloy. New York: Holmes & Meier, forthcoming.

――――. "Peace and the Nicaraguan Revolution." *Current History* 87, no. 533 (December 1988): 405–9.

――――. *U.S. Policy in Central America: The Endless Debate.* Miami: Florida International Press, 1990.

Moreno, Laudelino. *Historia de las Relaciones Interstatuales de Centroamérica.* Madrid, Spain: Compania Ibero-Americana de Publicaciones, 1928.

Munoz, Heraldo, ed. *America Latina y el Caribe: Políticas Exteriores para Sobrevivir.* Buenos Aires, Argentina: Grupo Editor Latinoamericano, 1986.

――――, ed. *Las Políticas Exterior de America Latina y el Caribe: Un Balance de Esperanzas.* Buenos Aires, Argentina: Grupo Editor Latinoamericano, 1988.

Muslow, Jonathan Evan. *Bird of Life, Bird of Death: A Political Ornithology of Central America.* New York: Dell Books, 1987.

O'Connor, Suzanne E. "Costa Rica in the World Community of Nations, 1919–1939: A Case Study of Latin American Internationalism." Ph.D. diss., Loyola University of Chicago, 1976.

Ojeda, Mario. "Mexican Policy towards Central America in the Context of U.S.-Mexico Relations." In *The Future of Central America: Policy Choices for the U.S. and Mexico,* ed. Richard Fagen and Olga Pellicer, 135–60. Stanford: Stanford University Press, 1983.

Ortega, Marvin. "Notas Sobre Proceso Política y Revolución en Nicaragua." *Polémica* 2, no. 4 (May–August 1988): 41–46.

Pastor, Robert. *Condemned to Repetition: The United States and Nicaragua.* Princeton: Princeton University Press, 1987.

Pastor, Robert, and Jorge G. Castañeda. *Limits to Friendship: The United States and Mexico.* New York: Vintage Books, 1989.

Paz, Ernesto. "The Foreign Policy and National Security of Honduras." In *Honduras Confronts Its Future: Contending Perspectives on Critical Issues,* ed. Mark Rosenberg and Philip L. Shepherd, 181–210. Boulder: Lynne Rienner, 1986.

Paz-Barnica, Eduardo. *La Política Exterior de Honduras 1982–1986.* Madrid, Spain: Editorial Ibero-Americana, 1986.

Peckenham, Nancy, and Annie Street. *Honduras: Portrait of a Captive Nation.* New York: Praeger, 1985.

Perry, Edward. "Central American Union." *Hispanic American Historical Review* 5 (February 1922): 30–51.

Powers, Jonathan. "Guatemala: Stirring of Change." *World Today* 48, no. 2 (February 1986): 31–35.

Purcell, Susan Kaufman. "Demystifying Contadora." *Foreign Affairs* 64, no. 1 (Fall 1985): 74–95.

Rodríguez, Mario. *Central America.* Englewood Cliffs, N.J.: Prentice-Hall, 1965.

———. *A Palmerstonian Diplomat in Central America: Frederick Chatfield, Esq.* Tucson: University of Arizona Press, 1964.

Rojas-Aravena, Francisco. "Costa Rica: Entre la Neutralidad y el Conflicto." In *America Latina y el Caribe: Políticas Exteriores para Sobrevivir,* ed. Heraldo Munoz, 293–312. Buenos Aires, Argentina: Grupo Editor Latinoamericano, 1986.

———. *Costa Rica: Política Exterior y Crisis Centroamericana.* Heredia, Costa Rica: Universidad Nacional, Escuela de Relaciones Internacionales, 1990.

Rojas-Aravena, Francisco, and Luis Guillermo Solis Rivera. *Subditos O Aliados? La Política Exterior de Estados Unidos Y Centroamérica.* San José, Costa Rica: Editorial Porvenir, 1988.

Rosenau, James. "Patterned Chaos in Global Life: Structure and Process in the Two Worlds of World Politics." *International Political Science Review* 9, no. 4 (Winter 1988): 327–64.

———. "A Pre-Theory Revisited: World Politics in an Era of Cascading Interdependence." *International Studies Quarterly* 28 (Summer 1984): 245–305.

———. *Turbulence in World Politics: A Theory of Change and Continuity.* Princeton: Princeton University Press, 1990.

Rosenberg, Mark. "From Transition to Consolidation in Honduras." In *Elections and Democracy in Central America,* ed. John Booth and Mitchell Seligson, 40–59. Chapel Hill: University of North Carolina Press, 1989.

———. "Toward a Redefinition of U.S.-Honduran Relations? Alternatives and Options." Paper presented at the Inter-American Dialogue, September 1988.

Rosenberg, Mark, and Philip L. Shepherd. *Honduras Confronts Its Future: Contending Perspectives on Critical Issues*. Boulder: Lynne Rienner, 1986.

Salazar, Jorge Mario. *Crisis Centroamericana y Política de las Super-Potencias*. San José, Costa Rica: Alma Mater, 1987.

Salisbury, Richard V. "The Anti-Imperialist Career of Alejandro Alvarado Quiros." *Hispanic American Historical Review* 57, no.4 (November 1977): 587–612.

———. "Costa Rican Relations with Central America, 1900–1934." Special Studies Series no. 71, Council on International Studies. Buffalo: State University of New York, August 1975.

———. "Domestic Politics and Foreign Policy: Costa Rica's Stand on Recognition, 1923–1934." *Hispanic American Historical Review* 54, no. 3 (August 1974): 453–78.

———. "Mexico, the United States, and the 1926–1927 Nicaraguan Crisis." *Hispanic American Historical Review* 66, no. 2 (May 1986): 319–39.

Salomon, Leticia. "Honduras: Democracia y Seguridad Nacional." *Polémica* 2, no. 6 (September–December 1988): 31–37.

Sánchez, Néstor. "The Communist Threat." *Foreign Policy*, no. 52 (Fall 1983): 43–50.

Sanders, Sol. *The Costa Rican Laboratory*. New York: Priority Press, 1986.

Sarmiento, Jorge. "Bernard Aronson: La Correcta Elección para América Latina?" *Centroamérica Internacional*, no. 1 (September–October 1989): 5–7.

Sarti, Carlos. "Negociación y Guerra en El Salvador: Una Legitimidad en Disputa." *Centroamérica Internacional*, no. 2 (December–January 1990): 7–11.

Schifter, Jacobo. *Las Alianzas Conflictivas: Las Relaciones de Estado Unidos y Costa Rica desde la Segunda Guerra Mundial y la Guerra Fría*. San José, Costa Rica: Asociación Libro Libre, 1986.

Schlesinger, Stephen, and Stephen Kinzer. *Bitter Fruit: The Untold Story of the American Coup in Guatemala*. New York: Doubleday, Anchor Press, 1983.

Seligson, Mitchell, and William J. Carroll, "The Costa Rican Role in the Sandinista Victory." In *Nicaragua in Revolution,* ed. Thomas Walker, 332–36. New York: Praeger, 1982.

Selser, Gabriela. "Contra Military Offensive." *Barricada Internacional*, November 11, 1989.

Selva, Salomon de la. "On the Proposed Union of Central America." *Hispanic American Historical Review* 3 (November 1920): 566–70.

Serfino, Nina M. "Dateline Managua: Defining Democracy." *Foreign Policy*, no. 70 (Spring 1988): 167–86.

Sergesvary, Louis. *Guatemala: A Complex Scenario*. Center for Strategic and International Studies, Significant Issues Series, 6, no. 3. Washington, D.C.: Georgetown University, 1984.

Shepherd, Philip. "Honduras." In *Confronting Revolution: Security through Diplomacy in Central America*, ed. Morris J. Blachman, William M. LeoGrande, and Kenneth Sharpe, 125–55. New York: Pantheon Books, 1986.

Silverstein, Ken. "El Salvador: The Selling of ARENA." *NACLA* 22, no. 6 (March 1989): 7–8.

Smith, Wayne. "Lies About Nicaragua." *Foreign Policy*, no. 67 (Summer 1987): 87–113.

Smyth, Frank. "Consensus or Crisis? Without Duarte in El Salvador." *Journal of Interamerican Studies and World Affairs* 30, no. 4 (Winter 1988–89): 29–52.

———. "San Diggers and the Strongmen." *Dissent* 36, (Summer 1989): 300–332.

Sojo, Ann. "La Ratio Nacional de Esquipulas II Vista desde Costa Rica." *Polémica* 2, no. 5 (May–August 1988): 35–40.

Sojo, Carlos. "Centroamérica Reflexiones Sobre la Democracia y el Proceso de Pacificación de Esquipulas II." *Polémica* 2, no. 7 (January–April 1989): 39–53.

———. "Impacto de la Política Centroamericana de Arias en las Relaciones con Estados Unidos." *Centroamérica/USA*, no. 2 (May–June 1988): 7–10.

———. "Nicaragua 1989: Una Política Exterior para la Subrevivencia." *Centroamérica/USA*, no. 6 (January–February 1989): 12–15.

Sprout, Margaret J. "Mahan: Evangelist of Sea Power." In *Makers of Modern Strategy*, ed. Edward M. Earle, 415–69. Princeton: Princeton University Press, 1973.

Stansifer, Charles. "Application of the Tobar Doctrine to Central America." *Americas* 23 (1967): 252–72.

Talbott, Strobe. *Endgame: The Inside Story of SALT II*. New York: Harper Books, 1979.

Taylor, Lance. *Report of an Economic Mission to the Government of Nicaragua.* Unpublished confidential report. Boston, April 5, 1989.

Tinoco, Victor Hugo. *Conflicto y Paz: El Proceso Negociador Centroamericano.* Mexico City: Editorial Mestiza and Coordinadora Regional de Investigaciones Economicas y Sociales (CRIES), 1989.

Torres-Rivas, Edelberto, Carlos Sojo, and Abelardo Morales. "Centroamérica y el Tamano de Nuestra Soledad: una vision en 14 proposiciones." *Centroamérica Internacional*, no. 3 (April–May 1990): 1–11.

U.S. Congress, *Report of the Congressional Committee Investigating the Iran-Contra Affair.* New York: Random House, 1988.

Vanden, Harry E., and Thomas W. Walker. "The Reimposition of U.S. Hegemony over Nicaragua." In *Understanding the Central American Crisis*, ed. Kenneth Coleman and George Herring, 153–80. Wilmington, Del.: Scholarly Resource Books, 1991.

Vilas, Carlos. "Crisis, Ajuste y Perspectivas de Reactivación Economica en Nicaragua." *Polémica* 2, no. 9 (September–December 1989): 23–31.

———. *Perfiles de la Revolución Sandinista.* Managua, Nicaragua: Editorial Nueva Nicaragua, 1987.

Villalobos, Joaquín. "A Democratic Revolution for El Salvador." *Foreign Policy,* no. 74 (Spring 1989): 103–22.

———. "Popular Insurrection: Desire or Reality?" *Latin American Perspectives* 16, no. 3 (Summer 1989): 5–47.

Vunderink, Gregg L. "Peasant Participation and Mobilization during an Economic Crisis." Paper delivered at the 15th meeting of the Latin American Studies Association. Miami, December 4–6, 1989.

Walker, Thomas W, ed. *Reagan versus the Sandinistas: The Undeclared War on Nicaragua.* Boulder: Westview Press, 1987.

Weeks, John. *The Economics of Central America.* New York: Holmes & Meier, 1985.

Weigley, Russell J. "A Strategy of Sea Power and Empire: Stephen B. Luce and Alfred Thayer Mahan." In *The American Way of War: A History of United States Military Strategy and Policy,* Russell J. Weigley, ed., 187–92. Bloomington: University of Indiana Press, 1973.

Wickham-Crowley, Timothy. "Understanding Failed Revolution in El Salvador: A Comparative Analysis of Regime Types and Social Structures." *Politics and Society* 17, no. 4 (December 1989): 511–37.

Woodward, Ralph Lee. *Central America: A Nation Divided.* New York: Oxford University Press, 1985.

———. "The Historiography of Modern Central America since 1960." *Hispanic American Historical Review* 67, no. 3 (August 1987): 461–96.

Yopo H, Boris. "Nicaragua 1985: La Política Exterior Come Extratgia de Sobrevivencia." In *America Latina y el Caribe: Políticas Exteriores para Sobrevivir,* ed. Heraldo Munoz, 365–401. Buenos Aires, Argentina: Grupo Editor Latinoamericano, 1986.

Zamora, Rubén, and Shafix Handel. "Proposal of the FMLN/FDR." *Latin American Perspective* 14 (Fall 1987): 481–86.

———. "Nicaragua 1987: La política Exterior en un ano decisivo. In *Las Políticas Exteriores de America Latina y el Caribe: Un Balance de Esperanzas,* ed. Heraldo Munoz, 281–95. Buenos Aires, Argentina: Grupo Editor Latinoamericano, 1988.

Zelaya, Chester, Daniel Camacho, Oscar Aguilar-Bulgarelli, Adolfo Cerdas, and Jacobo Schifter. *Democracia en Costa Rica? Cinco Opiniones Polémicas.* San José, Costa Rica: Editorial Universidad Estatel a Distancia, 1983.

Zubek, Voytek. "Soviet 'New Thinking' and the Central American Crisis." *Journal of Interamerican Studies and World Affairs* 29, no. 3 (Fall 1987): 87–106.

Interviews

Acosta-Bonilla, Manuel. Director of the Legal Affairs Committee, Honduran Bar Association. Tegucigalpa, Honduras, January 17, 1988.

Alegría, Rafael. Project Secretary, National Federation of Farmworkers. Tegucigalpa, Honduras, January 18, 1988.

Arce, Bayardo. Member of Sandinista Directorate. Managua, Nicaragua, November 22, 1989.

Arcos, Chris. U.S. Ambassador to Honduras. Tegucigalpa, Honduras, May 3, 1990.

Azcona-Hoyo, José. President of Honduras. Tegucigalpa, Honduras, January 18, 1988.

Bandana, Alejandro. Secretary-General Minister of Exterior. Managua, Nicaragua, November 24, 1989.

Barrios de Chamorro, Violeta. President of Nicaragua. Managua, Nicaragua, November 23, 1989.

Bengochea, Jaime. COSEP. Managua, Nicaragua, June 23, 1988.

Boardman, John. First political officer, U.S. embassy. Managua, Nicaragua, November 23, 1989.

Bolaños, Nicolás. COSEP. Managua, Nicaragua, June 23, 1988.

Boneo, Horacio. Deputy Chief of the United Nations mission to the Nicaraguan election. Managua, Nicaragua, November 23, 1989.

Chavarría, Ricardo. Vice-Minister INSSBI. Managua, Nicaragua, June 20, 1988.

Del Amico, Mario. Businessman. Tegucigalpa, Honduras, April 28, 1990.

Díaz-Arrivallaga, Efraín. President of the Honduran Christian-Democrats. Tegucigalpa, Honduras, April 30, 1990.

Einaudi, Luigi. U.S. Ambassador to Organization of American States. Washington, D.C., March 18, 1985.

Fiallos, Mariano. President, Supreme Election Council. Managua, Nicaragua, November 22, 1989.

Fortín-Inestrosa, Alfredo. Vice-President of Honduras (1986–90), member National Reconciliation Commission. Tegucigalpa, Honduras, January 18, 1988.

Gamero, Manuel. Director of *Tiempo*. Tegucigalpa, Honduras, January 19, 1988.

Glassman, Jon. Foreign Policy Assistant to the Vice-President. Washington, D.C., April 4, 1990.

Godoy, Virgilio. Vice-President of Nicaragua. Managua, Nicaragua, May 4, 1988, and November 23, 1989.

Guell-Borgan, Jaime. Sub-Secretary of Honduran Foreign Relations. Tegucigalpa, Honduras, May 2 1990.

Gutiérrez, Carlos José. Costa Rican Foreign Minister (1983–86). San José, Costa Rica, November 15, 1990.

Lacayo, Antonio. Minister of the Presidency. Managua, Nicaragua, November 23, 1989.

Madrigal-Nieto, Rodrigo. Costa Rican Foreign Minister (1986–90). San José, Costa Rica, November 14, 1990.

Mejía, Joaquín. Editor of *La Prensa*. Managua, Nicaragua, June 22, 1988.

Menges, Constantine. Adviser to the National Security Council. Washington, D.C., March 15, 1985.

Menjivar-Larin, Rafael. Research Associate, FLASCO. San José, Costa Rica, August 30, 1990.

Meza, Victor. Director Honduran Research Center. Tegucigalpa, Honduras, January 19, 1988.

Molina-Chocano, Guillermo. Director of Centro de Estudios y Promoción del Desarrollo (CEPROD). Tegucigalpa, Honduras, May 4, 1990.

Morales, Abelardo. Research Associate, FLASCO. San José, Costa Rica, August 27, 1990.

O'Kane, Trish. Researcher with CRIES. Managua, Nicaragua, November 25, 1989.

Ossa, Alvaro de la. Research Associate, FLASCO. San José, Costa Rica, August 29, 1990.

Pasos, Myra. Vice-Minister of External Cooperation. Managua, Nicaragua, June 20, 1988.

Ríos, Maynard. Director, School of International Relations, Universidad Nacional. Heredia, Costa Rica, October 10, 1990.

Riveria-Bianchini, Carlos. Vice-Minister of Foreign Affairs. San José, Costa Rica, September 18, 1990.

Smith, David. Central American Desk, U.S. Department of State. Washington, D.C., April 5, 1990.

Urbina-Pinto, Bernal. President of the Free Costa Rican Movement. San José, Costa Rica, September 10, 1990.

Varela, Luis. Costa Rican Ambassador to United Nations (1980–82), San José, Costa Rica, November 15, 1990.

Vargas-Fernández, Alfredo. Costa Rican Foreign Minister (1958–62). Heredia, Costa Rica, August 27, 1990.

Documents

Arias, Oscar. "Address to the United Nations, September 24, 1986." *FBIS*, September 29, 1986.

———. "Inaugural Speech by President Oscar Arias-Sanchez," *FBIS*, May 9. 1986.

———. "Let's Give Peace a Chance." Speech to a Joint Session of Congress. Washington, D.C., September 22, 1987.

"The Caraballeda Message on Central America's Peace, Security, and Democracy." United Nations General Assembly Document A/40/1095. New York: United Nations, 1986.

"Contadora Act on Peace and Cooperation in Central America, June 7, 1986." *International Legal Materials* 25, no.4 (September 1986).

"Contadora Act on Peace and Cooperation in Central America" (revised version). United Nations General Assembly–Security Council Documents A/39/562 and S/16775. New York: United Nations, 1983.

"Contadora Communiqué." *La Estrella de Panama*, January 10, 1983.

"Declaración de Esquipulas." Esquipulas, Guatemala, May 25, 1986.

"Document of Objectives" (adopted by the Ministers of Foreign Affairs of the Central American Countries, September 9, 1983). United Nations Security Council Document S/16041. New York: United Nations, 1983.

"Energy Cooperation Program for Central America and Caribbean Countries Established by Venezuela and Mexico on August 3, 1980." In *Venezuela Oil, Plans and Potential*, ed. Carlson Levine. Washington, D.C.: McGraw Hill, 1983.

"Establishment of Terms of Reference of the United Nations Observer Mission to Verify the Electoral Process in Nicaragua." United Nations Press Kit. New York: United Nations Department of Public Information, 1989.

Inforpress Centroamericana, *Compendio: Proceso de Paz en Centroamérica*, January 5, 1988.

"Joint Declaration of Central American Presidents." Issued at Alajuela, Costa Rica, January 16, 1988.

"Joint Declaration of Central American Presidents." Issued at Antigua, Guatemala, June 17, 1990.

"Joint Declaration of Central American Presidents." Issued at Costa del Sol, El Salvador, February 14, 1989.

"Joint Declaration of Central American Presidents." Issued at Montelimar, Nicaragua. *La Nación*, April 4, 1990.

"Joint Declaration of Central American Presidents." Issued at San Isidro de Coronado, Costa Rica, December 13, 1989.

"Joint Declaration of Central American Presidents." Issued at Tela, Honduras, August 7, 1989. United Nations Press Kit. New York: United Nations Department of Public Information, 1989.

"Joint Franco-Mexican Declaration on El Salvador." United Nations Security Council Document S/14659. New York: United Nations, 1981.

"Letter Dated 21 September 1984 from the Co-ordinator of the Government Junta of National Reconstruction of Nicaragua Addressed to the Presidents of the Member Countries of the Contadora Group." United Nations Security Council Document S/167756. New York: United Nations, 1984.

"Letter from the President of Nicaragua Addressed to the Presidents of the Contadora and Support Group, November 11, 1985." United Nations General Assembly Document A/40/894. New York: United Nations, 1985.

Madrigal-Nieto, Rodrigo. *Memoria Anual: Ministerio de Relaciones Exteriores y Culto, 1986–87.* San José, Costa Rica: Impreso Nacional, May 1, 1987.

———. *Memoria Anual: Ministerio de Relaciones Exteriores y Culto, 1988–89.* San José, Costa Rica: Impreso Nacional, May 1, 1989.

Niehaus, Bernardo. "Address to the School of International Relations on the Foreign Policy of the Calderón Administration." Heredia, Costa Rica, September 20, 1990.

"President Reagan's Letter to the Presidents of the Contadora Four, July 26, 1983." *Department of State Bulletin* 83, (September 1983): 83.

"Procedures for the Establishment of a Firm and Lasting Peace in Central America (Esquipulas II)." United Nations Press Kit. New York: United Nations Department of Public Information, 1987.

"Sapoa Cease-Fire, March 23, 1988." United Nations Press Kit. New York: United Nations Department of Public Information, 1988.

Index

Abrams, Elliot, 70, 87, 88, 99, 103, 137
Agency for International Development (AID), 82, 86
Alajuela (1988), 99–101, 137
Allen, Richard, 52
Alvarez Martínez, Gustavo, 37–39, 41
Americas Watch, 44, 140
Antigua, 127–28
Arbenz, Jacobo, 6, 14, 15, 43
ARENA, 135
Arévalo, Juan, 6
Argentina, 27, 68, 94
Arias, Oscar, 30, 78–79, 80, 83–90, 95, 100, 117, 124, 134, 146; and peace process, 1, 21, 47, 50, 77, 87–88, 90–91, 106, 111; relations with Reagan, 83, 85–87, 97; speech at the UN, 84–85. *See also* Arias Plan; Costa Rica; Esquipulas II
Arias Plan, 1, 21, 22, 33, 42, 87–88, 105, 130, 136–137
Aronson, Bernard, 107, 120, 122
Ayagualo, 34, 144
Azcona, José, 95–96, 100, 114, 116, 137

Baker, Howard, 62, 88, 109, 136
Baker, James, 106, 122
Baloyra, Enrique, 31
Barrios, Justino Rufino, 3
Bermúndez, Enrique, 103
Betancúr, Belisario, 55, 57–59, 65
Bianchi, Francisco, 43
Boland Amendment, 72

Bonilla, Manuel, 4
Boutrous-Ghali, Boutrous, 145
Brazil, 68, 94
Busby, Morris, 39
Bush administration, 109, 114–16, 135; policy in Nicaragua, 29, 106–7, 117, 119, 123, 125–26, 137, 141

Cabrera Estrada, Manuel, 3–4
Calderón, Rafael Angel, 83
Calderón–López, Walter, 103
Calero, Adolfo, 103
Callejas, Rafael, 126
Canada, 115
Cancún Declaration, 59–60
Carabelleda Declaration, 69
Carazo, Rodrigo, 78
Carballo, Bismark, 98
Carías, Tiburcio, 6, 14
Carrera, Rafael, 3
Carter, Hodding, 32
Carter administration, 15–16, 33, 37, 44, 51, 52
Casey, William, 52, 86
Castro, Fidel, 35, 58, 78
Center for Democracy, 119
Central American Common Market, 7–8, 18, 128
Central American Court of Justice, 4
Central American Defense Council (CONDECA), 61
Central American Economic Action Plan (PAECA), 128

Central American Peace Accord. *See* Esquipulas II

Central American Tribunal, 3

Central Intelligence Agency (CIA), 6, 27–28, 61–62, 72, 86, 121–22

Cerezo, Vinicio, 16, 46–47, 75, 77, 146

César, Alfredo, 27, 82, 102, 122, 142

Chalchuapa, Battle of (April 2, 1885), 3

Chamorro, Emiliano, 11–12

Chamorro, Pedro Joaquín, 30

Chamorro, Pedro Joaquín, Jr., 82, 103, 124

Chamorro Barrios, Violeta, 30, 104, 106, 118–27, 140–44

Chamorro-Bryan Treaty (1916), 11

Chapultepec Peace Accord (1992), 143, 145

Chavarría, Ricardo, 26

Chile, 119–20

CIVS. *See* Commission on Verification

Clayton-Bulwer Treaty (1854), 10

CNTC. *See* Confederación Nacional de Trabajones del Campo

Colombia, 49, 55, 56–58, 91, 94, 115

Commission on Verification: under contadora, 65, 70; under Esquipulas II, 91, 93–94, 99, 100, 114, 116

Confederación Nacional de Trabajones del Campo, 96

Consejo Superior de la Empresa Privida (CONSEP), 26–27, 29

Contadora, 21, 49–50, 51, 55–71, 73, 77, 86, 87, 90, 135–36. *See also* Betancúr, Belisario; Colombia; Commission on Verification; Mexico; Panama; Venezuela

Contadora Documents of Objective, 60, 70

Contadora Revised Act for Peace and Cooperation in Central America (1984), 65–67, 69, 94

Contadora Support Group, 68, 69

Contras, 22, 48, 59, 64, 69–70, 89, 109, 126–27, 139, 146; in Costa Rica, 78, 80, 82–86; in Honduras, 36–37, 39–40, 90–91, 113–14, 116; and peace process, 91, 93, 95, 100–103, 110–11; support from the U.S., 21, 25, 27–29, 39–40, 49, 55, 61–62, 72–74, 88, 101, 106–7, 116, 122, 126, 136–37. *See also* Nicaragua; Sandinistas; Sapoa; United States

Coolidge, Calvin, 13

Costa Rica, 6–8, 14, 21, 56, 69, 73, 75, 78–90, 107, 117, 127, 134, 136; conflict with Nicaragua, 68, 79, 82–85; and contadora, 60, 62, 67–68, 70; and peace process, 87–91, 105, 109, 138; support of the contras, 28, 78–79, 85–86, 95. *See also* Arias, Oscar; Arias Plan; Esquipulas II

CREM. *See* Regional Center for Military Training

Cristiani, Alfredo, 34, 114–15, 117–18, 135, 144–45

Cruz, Arturo, 27, 29

Cuba, 7, 15, 24, 27, 35, 49, 51–52, 53, 55, 57, 60, 63, 132

Davila, Miguel, 4

De la Madrid, Miguel, 62–63

Democratic Convergence, 135, 145

Democratic Revolutionary Front (FDR), 34, 52, 54, 57

D'Escota, Miguel, 55, 68, 70

Díaz, Adolfo, 5, 11

Dodd, Christopher, 120

Dominican Republic, 99

Duarte, José Napoleon, 16, 34, 50, 63, 95, 100, 105, 135

Eisenhower administration, 14
El Salvador, 5, 7–9, 14, 16, 41, 44, 47, 50, 63, 69, 73, 76, 79, 83, 117, 127, 131, 134, 136, 146; Christian Democrats in, 23, 31–32, 33; civil war, 24, 31–36, 43, 51, 52–54, 138; and contadora, 59–60, 62, 65–68, 70; death squads in, 32, 80, 133; and peace process, 87, 89–91, 105, 114–15, 129, 137, 139, 143–44. *See also* Cristiani, Alfredo; Duarte, Napoleon; Farabundo Martí National Liberation Front; Soccer war
Enders, Thomas O., 53–54
Espino Negro, Pact of (1927), 13
Esquipulas I (1986), 71, 74–77, 93
Esquipulas II (1987), 1, 21, 36, 32, 47–49, 89–94, 102, 135–36, 138–39, 144; compliance with, 95–96, 101, 109, 129, 133
Estrada, Juan, 11
European Community (EC), 58
European Parliament, 119

Farabundo Martí National Liberation Front (FMLN), 33–36, 40, 42, 48, 51–54, 57, 65, 115, 118, 135, 144–45. *See also* Democratic Revolutionary Front; El Salvador; Villalobos, Joaquín
FDN (Nicaraguan Democratic Force). *See* Contras
FDR. *See* Democratic Revolutionary Front
Federal Republic of Central America (1824–38), 2–3
Fernández, Guido, 88–89
Ferreto, Arnoldo, 80
Figueres, José, 6, 8
Figueres, Mauricio, 8
Fortín, Alfredo, 96

France, 24, 57
Franco-Mexican Statement, 57
FSLN. *See* Sandinistas

García, Alán, 68, 71
García Márquez, Gabriel, 58
General Peace and Limit Treaty (1982), 41
General Treaties of Peace and Amity (1907), 4–6
Gershman, Carl, 119
Godoy, Virgilio, 142
Goldwater, Barry, 62
González, Felipe, 58
Good Neighbor Policy, 132
Gorbachev, Mikhail, 109
Gorman, Paul, 41
Great Britain, 101
Grenada, 60–61
Grupo de Apoya. *See* Contadora Support Group
Guatemala, 3–5, 7, 14–15, 20, 23, 27, 50, 51, 75, 76, 79, 83, 127, 131, 133–34; and contadora, 60, 71; civil war in, 24, 42–47, 53, 138; death squads in, 44, 46, 80, 133; and peace process, 87–90, 129, 137, 139, 146. *See also* Arbenz, Jacobo; Cerezo, Vinicio; Ríos-Mott, Efraín; United Fruit Company
Gutiérrez, Carlos José, 82

Habib, Philip, 87, 95
Haig, Alexander, 52, 53, 55
Hasenfus, Eugene, 86
Helms, Jesse, 141
Hemisphere Initiative, 119
Hernández, Leo, 104
Hernández Martinez, Maximiliano, 5, 6, 13

Honduran Confederation of Workers, 42

Honduras, 4, 5, 7–9, 20, 23, 24, 47, 48, 50, 55, 69, 73, 75, 83, 102, 116, 118, 131, 136; and contadora, 60–62, 65–68, 70–71; death squads in, 40–41, 133; and peace process, 87–90, 93, 96–97, 100, 111, 113–15, 137, 139; support of the contras by, 27–29, 36–42, 90–91, 93, 95–96, 100, 110–11, 113–15, 126. *See also* Azcona, José; Contras; Nicaragua; Soccer war; Suazo Cordova, Roberto

Inter-American Conference at Chapúltepec, Mexico (1948), 6
Inter-American Court of Human Rights, 40
Inter-American Development Bank, 82
International Court of Justice, 111, 114, 118
International Monetary Fund, 82
Iran-Contra, 21, 37, 50, 74, 79, 81, 86, 87, 102, 136
Ireland, 115

Japan, 122, 128, 141–42

Kennedy, Edward, 63, 73
Kissinger Commission, 42

Lacayo-Oyanguren, Antonio, 142–43
La Palma, 34, 144
La Prensa. See Prensa, La
Lasaga, Manuel, 127
Latin American Studies Association, 119
Law for the Maintenance of Order and Public Security, 112
Liberal Party of National Unity, 122

López-Contreras, Carlos, 97, 114
Lucas-García, Romero, 43, 45

Madrigal-Nieto, Rodrigo, 87, 100, 117
Mahan, Alfred Thayer, 10
Manzanillo, 51, 63–64, 136
Mayorga, Francisco, 142
Meese, Edwin, 86
Mejia, Humberto, 46
Menges, Constantine, 51
Mexico, 8, 24, 50, 52, 56–57, 64–65, 94, 146; and contadora, 21, 49, 55, 58, 62, 71; relations with Nicaragua, 4, 12–13, 100; relations with U.S., 57, 62–63, 67, 71
Mitterand, François, 58
Monge, Luis Alberto, 78–84
Montelimar, 127–28

Nandaime, 29, 105, 109, 137, 139
National Endowment for Democracy, 30, 119–21
National Federation of Farmworkers (CNTC), 96
National Security Directive, 17, 27
Negroponte, John, 38
New York Times, 101
Nicaragua, 3–4, 10–13, 16, 20, 25–31, 43, 50–51, 53, 57, 68, 75, 79, 88, 117, 130, 133, 137; civil war in, 9, 27–29, 39, 51, 61, 64, 72–74, 89, 116, 126, 138; conflict with Costa Rica, 78, 82–85; and contadora, 58–59, 61, 64–67, 69; elections of 1990 in, 2, 29–31, 106–7, 110, 112–13, 118–25, 127, 132, 134; peace process in, 89, 91, 96–100, 102–4, 109–11, 113, 118, 136, 139–43; and U.S. trade embargo, 17, 25–26, 108, 119, 125. *See also* Chamorro Barrios, Violeta; Contras; Ortega, Daniel; Reagan

administration; Sandinistas; United Nicaraguan Opposition; United States
Nicaragua Democratic Coordinator, 104
Nicaraguan Democratic Force (FDN). *See* Contras
Nicaraguan Social Christian Party, 122
Nicaraguan Supreme Electoral Council, 30, 103, 112–13
North, Oliver, 72, 86

Obando y Bravo, Miguel, 98–99, 142
Organization of American States (OAS), 8, 40–41, 71, 109, 114, 119, 127
Organization of Eastern Caribbean States, 61
Ortega, Daniel, 25, 26, 35, 63, 66, 67, 69, 73, 87, 98–99, 100–101, 108, 110, 112, 116–17, 123–25, 135, 137, 139
Ortega, Humberto, 54, 125, 140, 142–43

PAECA (El Plan de Acción Económica de Centroamérica). *See* Central American Economic Action Plan
Panama, 10, 40, 94, 119; and contadora, 49, 55, 58
Panama Canal, 10, 56
Pastora, Edén, 27
Pell, Claiborne, 122
Peña, Richard, 89
Peréz, Carlos Andres, 62
Peréz, de Cuéllar, Javier, 97, 111, 115
Peru, 68, 71, 91, 94
Pezzullo, Lawrence, 53–54
Philippines, 119–20
Pitito, Benito, 98
Plan Victoria, 44

Poland, 119–20
Ponce, René Emilio, 145
Powell, Colin, 99, 137
Prensa, La, 29, 54, 98, 104–5, 122, 139
Puentarenas, 127

Quayle, Dan, 126

Radio Católica, 29, 98, 104–5, 145
Ramírez, Sergio, 76
Reagan administration, 16, 21, 44, 49–55, 57, 65, 67, 79, 88, 106; and contadora, 56, 59–63; and Esquipulas, 96–97, 99–100, 135–36; relations with Nicaragua, 29, 36–40, 70; support of contras by, 27, 72–74, 82, 86, 95, 101–3; support of El Salvador by, 33, 52–54
Regional Center for Military Training (CREM), 41
Reichler, Paul, 111
República Mayor (1895–98), 3
Richardson, Elliott, 115
Ríos-Mott, Efraín, 43–46, 133
Río Treaty, 55
Robelo, Alfonso, 27, 82
Rodríguez, Carlos Rafael, 55
Roman Catholic Church, 48, 92, 98–99, 105, 127
Romero, Humberto, 32
Roosevelt administration, 13
Rosenau, James, 131

Sacasa, Juan, 12
San Antonio Sugar Mill, 29, 105
Sánchez, Néstor, 52–53
Sánchez-Salgado, Domingo, 26
Sandinistas (FSLN), 2, 19, 20, 23–24, 25–31, 32, 36, 42, 48, 73, 76, 87, 102–5, 108, 121–25, 127, 131, 134; conflict with United States, 50–51, 53–55,

Sandinistas (FSLN)—*continued*
63–64, 69, 95, 101, 105, 119; and con-
tadora, 56, 59, 60, 62, 66, 68; and
peace process, 91, 107, 109, 111–13,
137, 139; relations with Costa Rica,
79, 82–83, 85.
Sandino, Augusto, 13, 105
San Isidro de Coronado (1989), 117–
118, 135, 144
Sapoa, 51, 102–4
Schuette, Keith, 121
Sepúlveda, Bernardo, 65, 71
Serrano, Jorge Elias, 146
Shelton, Turner, 15
Shultz, George, 63, 65, 70, 95–96
Singlaub, John, 72
Soccer war, 8, 18, 41
Solano-Calderón, Edmundo, 80–81
Solorzano, Carlos, 12
Somoza, Anastasio, 6, 14, 15–16, 56,
109, 124
Soviet Union, 28, 51, 56, 60, 63, 65, 73,
76, 108–9
Spain, 115
Stimson, Henry, 13
Suazo Cordova, Roberto, 16, 38–42
Swan Island, 6

Tambs, Lewis, 81
Tegucigalpa Accord, 67–68
Tela (1989), 112–16, 126
Tesora Beach (1989), 109–12
Tiempo, 40, 96
Tobar, Carlos, 4
Tobar Doctrine, 4–6, 13
Torrijos, Omar, 56
Tower Commission, 81
Treaty of Managua (1960), 7

Ubico, Jorge, 6, 13
Ungo, Guillermo, 52

United Fruit Company, 14, 17
United Nations, 61, 67, 71, 84–85, 97,
110–11, 113, 115–16, 119, 122, 126–
27, 135
United Nations Observer Group
(ONUCA), 110–11, 115, 126–28
United Nations Observer Mission for
the Verification of the Elections of
Nicaragua (ONUVEN), 113, 115
United Nicaraguan Opposition
(UNO), 30, 111–12, 118–25, 142–43,
144–45
United States, 10, 21, 22, 56, 57, 75, 94,
135, 138, 146; and Central American
peace process, 88, 91, 93, 95, 97, 99,
116; and contadora, 58–60, 62, 64–66,
68–69, 73; and contras, 27–29, 95,
116, 126; intervention of, in Central
America, 2, 9–17, 19; relations with
Costa Rica, 13, 81–82, 84–87, 97; relations with El Savador, 13, 31–36,
51–54; relations with Guatemala, 42–
47, 51; relations with Honduras, 36–
42, 90; relations with Nicaragua, 13,
17, 25–31, 47, 50–51, 53–55, 60–64,
69–70, 72–74, 105, 118, 130, 141. *See
also* Bush administration; Carter
administration; Central Intelligence
Agency; Contras; National Endowment for Democracy; Reagan administration; Wright-Reagan Plan
—Congress, 24, 62–63, 65, 66–67, 72–
74, 87–90, 95, 101–2, 107, 119, 121–
22, 125–26, 136
—National Security Council (NSC),
72, 86
—Neutrality Act, 55
Uruguay, 68, 94

Vaky, Viron, 32
Vanden, Harry, 125

Venezuela, 21, 49, 55, 56–57, 62, 94, 115
Verification. *See* Commission on Verification
Villalobos, Joaquín, 35, 144
Vivas, René, 141
Voice of America, 82

Walker, Tom, 125
Washington Peace Conferences: of 1907, 4–5; of 1922–23, 5
Washington Treaties (1907). *See* General Treaties of Peace and Amity

West Germany, 122
White, Robert, 52
Willauer, Whiting, 7
World Bank, 82
World Court. *See* International Court of Justice
Wright, Jim, 88–89, 95, 102, 136
Wright-Reagan Plan, 88–89, 136

Zaldivar, Rafael, 3
Zamora, Rubén, 145
Zelaya Santos, José, 3–4, 11

DATE DUE